THEY CAGE
THE ANIMALS
AT NIGHT

THEY CAGE THE ANIMALS AT NIGHT

Jennings Michael Burch

NAL BOOKS

NEW AMERICAN LIBRARY

NEW YORK AND SCARBOROUGH, ONTARIO

For information address New American Library

Published simultaneously in Canada by The New American Library of Canada Limited

 NAL BOOKS TRADEMARK REG. U.S. PAT. OFF. AND FOREIGN COUNTRIES
REGISTERED TRADEMARK—MARCA REGISTRADA
HECHO EN HARRISONBURG, VA., U.S.A.

SIGNET, SIGNET CLASSIC, MENTOR, PLUME, MERIDIAN and NAL BOOKS
are published *in the United States* by
New American Library,
1633 Broadway,
New York, New York 10019,
in Canada by
The New American Library of Canada Limited,
81 Mack Avenue,
Scarborough, Ontario M1L 1M8

Library of Congress Cataloging in Publication Data

Burch, Jennings Michael.
  They cage the animals at night.

  1. Burch, Jennings Michael. 2. Boys—New York (State)
—Brooklyn—Biography. 3. Children—Institutional care
—New York (State)—Brooklyn—Case studies. 4. Child
psychology—Case studies. I. Title.
HQ775.B829   1984   362.7'32'0924 [B]   84-6809
ISBN 0-453-00469-5

First Printing, August, 1984

1   2   3   4   5   6   7   8   9

PRINTED IN THE UNITED STATES OF AMERICA

To
ALAN ARKIN
and
SCARLET RIVERA

He gave me strength and confidence
She gave me peace and love

Author's Note

This is a true story; only the names of the individuals and institutions have been changed.

PROLOGUE

"Kelly!"

She came away from the rail separating her from the snow leopard. She took my hand.

"Where are your sisters?" I asked as I scanned the area for them.

"Lori took Carolyn to the bathroom."

"Go and get them, will you? We have to leave now."

"Oh, can't we see the seals first?"

"Sure. You fetch your sisters, and I'll meet you by the seal pool."

She scampered off toward the rear of the lion house and the bathrooms. I watched her until she disappeared around the corner of the building.

Kelly is my middle daughter. She's frail and slight, and somewhat shy. She reminds me greatly of myself when I was eight and unprepared. And the moment reminds me of the days when this place, this zoo, was my source of refuge, my home. It may sound strange, but I sought comfort here. I hid from fear and loneliness here. I hid from pain and unkindness here.

I sat on a bench near the seal pool and pressed my hands deep into my pockets. I breathed in the crisp cold air of these last days of autumn, and I remembered. . . .

1

It's unlucky to step on lines and cracks in the sidewalk, but Mom didn't seem to understand this. On the long walk from the subway station, she kept tugging at my arm and telling me to walk straight. It had rained for most of the morning, but now, in the early evening, only a light mist lay heavily in the air. The dark gray smoke from the chimneys along this Brooklyn street didn't have far to travel before blending neatly into the low night sky.

We were on our way to visit with one of Mom's friends. Since it wasn't often I got a chance to be with her all by myself, I didn't mind the wet weather, or her quiet mood, or her tugging at my arm. We walked along at a quick pace. I asked a number of times if we were late, but she didn't answer me. Her usually smooth-skinned forehead was somewhat wrinkled, and her dark eyebrows were bent into a slight frown.

"What's wrong, Mom?"

Her answer was another tug at my arm as I tried to avoid the next line. She released the tight grip she had on my small hand to refer to a piece of paper she had pulled from her pocket.

"Are we there yet?" I asked. I looked up for her answer, but there was none. She studied the paper and then the building numbers.

She regripped my hand and tugged again. The wet ground was beginning to make it way in through the hole in my left shoe. I felt my sock sticking to my toes as I tried wiggling and walking at the same time.

She stopped suddenly and leaned down. She brushed back some hairs sticking up from the top of my head.

"Now, be a good boy."

"I will, Mom." That was my standard answer whether I planned to be good or not.

We climbed a short flight of worn steps bounded by two wrought-iron handrails. We entered the old red brick building through a highly polished wooden door that squeaked as it opened. We were met in the entranceway by a small nun dressed all in white. She nodded to Mom and smiled at me as she greeted us. Her wire-rimmed eyeglasses sat on the very end of her nose. When she spoke, she looked over the top of them.

"And what's your name, little fella?" she asked.

"Jennings," I replied.

"Why, that's a very nice name," she said as she turned to lead us down a very dark and narrow hallway. It was so quiet and still, and the smell of burnt candle wax made me think we were in some sort of a church. Mom often took me or one of my brothers to some new church somewhere.

I held tightly to Mom's warm hand. We reached the end of the hallway and two wooden benches with red felt cushions.

"Be a good boy and wait here," the little nun said over her glasses. "Your mother and I have a few things to discuss."

I nodded my head as Mom and the nun disappeared into an office and closed the door.

I was about to sit on the nice felt cushions when I remembered my pants were still damp from the rain. Instead, I stood on my tiptoes and looked out through the colors of a stained-glass window. I closed one eye and moved from one colored glass to the next.

"Jennings!" I was jolted away from my world of pink cars

and green buildings by the little nun. I turned and regrasped Mom's hand. She looked sad and red-eyed.

"What's wrong, Mom?"

She shook her head and squeezed my hand as we walked back down the hall. We stopped at a door about halfway down, and the nun opened it.

The room was large and blue and filled with noisy children. As we entered, all the children stopped and stared at us. Their silence made me uncomfortable.

Mom leaned down to help me off with my coat, but then hugged me. She kissed my face a number of times. She took one last swipe at my cowlick. I could see the tears on her lower lid as she forced a smile. She frightened me, so I clung to her arm.

"Mom! What's wrong?"

She brought me close to her once again and hugged me. My coat was still only partway off when she straightened up. She gripped my shoulders to hold me off. In a husky sort of voice she said, "I'll be right back."

She turned and slipped through the open door. The nun followed, closing the door behind her.

They left me in the middle of what seemed to be a thousand staring eyes. I felt strange and tingly all over. I couldn't move. I left my coat hanging from one shoulder. The eyes kept staring while my mind raced: What's wrong with Mom? Why did she push me away from her? Where is she? Where am I?

Slowly the children began to resume their play. First some and then all. As they played, I felt more and more as though I could move, but I didn't. When the tension eased, I began to look around the room.

The blue walls were paint-chipped and peeling. Night had now blackened the other side of two very large frosted windows on one side of the room. Above the worn wooden floor hung about half a dozen globe lamps. A high curb ran all the way around the room. I didn't know what it was for until I

4

saw a little girl nearly run down by a speeding tricycle. The curb was for safety. Around the room, at the edge of the curb, there were four large pillars holding up the whole place. And straight across from me there were two doors with signs over them. One said "Boys"; and the other said "Girls."

I made my way around to the corner of the room behind one of the pillars. I sat down. I watched the kids playing and fighting. They all seemed to want to ride the few bicycles and tricycles that were there, but only the bigger kids were on them. There was a large purple tricycle I really liked. I wondered how I might get a turn at riding it. Two boys entered the room and headed straight for the tricycle. They abruptly dumped the boy who was on the bike to the floor, and rode off laughing.

I drew up my legs and folded my arms over them. I laid my head sideways atop my arms and closed my eyes. I was getting sleepy.

"Get up from there!" snapped a gruff-sounding nun. She was towering above me and she was angry. "What are you doing down there?"

I was startled and groggy. I tried to get to my feet, when she pulled me up by my coat collar.

"I'm waiting for my mother."

"Never mind that!" She began dragging me across the floor of the now empty room. I had obviously fallen asleep and all the children had gone home.

"But I'm waiting for my mother!" I garbled out through my tightly grasped coat collar.

In one great sweep she opened the door marked "Boys" and flung me through it. I staggered into a pitch-black darkness.

"Get along!"

"But, Sister . . ."

"Get along!"

She gathered a large chunk of my coat sleeve and arm and lifted part of me off the ground. I was forced through the darkness into a partially lighted room.

The room was long and narrow. On one side, separated by dark doorways, were small pink lights very close to the floor. They lit the bottom part of the room, making the top part seem dark and endless. Along the other wall, running the entire length of the room, was a row of beds, every two separated by barred windows. I was frightened.

She pushed me through one of the dark doorways. She flipped a switch, flooding the room with light. It was a bathroom, made of a million tiny white tiles. Floor, ceiling, walls, and everything. The first thing I thought of was Chicklets.

"Your number is twenty-seven. Don't forget it!" She pointed to the far side of the room and a row of hooks with numbers above them. Most of the hooks had clothes hanging from them, some of them only pajamas. "Do you have a toothbrush?"

Thinking of the one I had at home, I said, "Yes."

"Wash, brush, and change. And don't make a mess!" She left as quickly as she spoke, and I was glad. I was afraid of her.

I lifted the pair of pajamas off hook number twenty-seven. I sat on the long wooden bench under the hooks and looked around. There was a row of sinks on one side of the room and a row of toilets on the other. As I changed into the pajamas, I couldn't stop the tears edging toward my eyes. I went over to one of the sinks and turned on the water. It was cold. I wet my face and looked around for a towel. There was none. I dabbed my wet face with my sleeve.

"What are you doing!" she screamed as she reentered the room. She really startled me.

"I want my mother," I cried.

She slapped my face so hard I felt a million needles of heat rush into my face and cheek.

"She's gone! Now stop that! Where's your toothbrush?"

"It's . . . it's . . ." I was in a race between breathing and speaking. ". . . at home."

From nowhere, she produced a paper-wrapped toothbrush

and shoved it at me. I took it and brought it to my mouth to tear off the paper with my teeth. She slapped me again.

"That's not the way we do things around here!"

I held my stinging face. "I just wanted to take off the—"

"Well, that's not the way we do things around here." She left in a huff, mumbling to herself.

I found some toothpaste on one of the sinks and put some on the paper-wrapped brush. I brushed my teeth. It was yucky, but that's how she wanted it. When I finished brushing I stuck the brush in the back pocket of my hanging brown corduroy pants and went over to the doorway. I peeked out. She was at the far end of the darkened room at a desk with a small lighted lamp. I switched off the bathroom light and approached her. I stood in front of her desk. She ignored me. She got to her feet and brushed past me.

"Come on."

I followed her down the long row of beds. She stopped at bed number twenty-seven and pointed to it. Without another word she returned to her desk.

I gathered up the waist part of the pajamas and with great difficulty climbed up and into the very high white metal bed. There were bars at the top and bottom. I slipped beneath the cold sheets. There was a strong smell of rubber and the blanket was itchy.

I lay faceup trying to see the shapes on the dark ceiling. I could not. I heard an occasional cough and a sniffle. I heard a small voice call out so quietly I almost didn't hear it: "Sister Frances."

I waited for the response, but there was none. A warm tear ran down my cheek and into my ear. Where was I and why was I here? A streetlamp somewhere outside cast eerie shadows across the top of my bedcovers. In the gray light I wondered why Mom hadn't come back for me.

I awoke to the sounds of children's voices. I opened my eyes and looked around. The room looked different from the night before. It was bigger and brighter and it had a ceiling.

Kids were running in all directions. I recognized a lot of them from the playroom. They hadn't gone home after all. There was a chest next to the bed.

I climbed down from the bed. Sister Frances wasn't at her desk. Instead, there was a younger nun. She was prettier, with dark eyebrows and a dimple on each cheek. She was fastening the shirt buttons for one of the little kids. She was smiling.

I entered the bathroom. To my relief, all my things were still there. I hung the pajamas on the hook and stuffed the toothbrush into the top pocket. I didn't feel like brushing again. I dabbed a drop of water on each eye and dried with my shirt sleeve. I was too afraid to ask anyone where they got their towels and facecloths from, and besides, I didn't care. Mom would be here soon and I could go home. I put on my street coat and followed some of the boys out of the bathroom. They were lining up in front of the beds, so I did the same. I noticed I was the only one wearing my street coat. I guessed nobody else was leaving but me.

"Why not put your coat on your hook?" the nun with the dimples asked as she approached me.

"I'm going home," I said.

"Well, we're going to have breakfast first. Why not hang up your coat?"

I left the line and hung up my coat. When I returned, the dimpled nun was gone. I stood by the bed.

Sister Frances entered the room and the line stiffened. She was tall and thin. Her face was shiny and drawn. She spoke not a word, but rather made a clicking sound with a clicker she held down by her side. I remembered having one of those clickers. I got it in a box of Cracker Jacks. With each click the children responded, and I followed. We shuffled down a maze of hallways until we reached a dining room.

It was an enormous room, very much like the lunchroom at school. It had rows and rows of tables, with a dozen or so chairs at each table. As we entered the room, we weaved like a

8

snake around the rows of tables; girls entering from the other side did the same. At the sound of a click, we stopped. On the next, we turned. There in front of me was chair number twenty-seven. I sat. A terrible pain ripped into my left ear. Sister Frances had grapped hold of my ear and lifted me out of the chair. She clicked the others to sit before she let go of me.

"Sit when you're supposed to, and not a moment before!" She pointed to a spot behind the chair. "Now, stand there!"

I stood where she pointed. I stared at the ceiling, trying not to cry. The ceiling in this room looked exactly like the one in the playroom. It had the same globe lamps and the same tiny cracks. I wondered what time Mom might come for me. What was this place, and why were all these kids here? I hoped I wouldn't have to stay too much longer. I didn't like Sister Frances—she hurt me. The kids took forever to eat. The room smelled like waffles or pancakes, I didn't know which, and I wasn't about to look down to find out.

A sharp click brought me back to the room, and the kids to their feet. The next series of clicks took us from the dining room, down a few more hallways to some sort of playroom with a green-and-white-tiled floor. As the line entered the room, the kids broke ranks. They ran for the things they most wanted to play with. I stayed by the door.

One whole wall of the room was made up of glass doors. A few of the panes were cracked, while others were missing altogether. They had been replaced by panels of wood. The doors opened out onto a gray-stone courtyard with a high wire-mesh fence. There were shelves along two of the walls, with all sorts of playthings: games, puzzles, toys, blocks, and balls. A number of tables, with painted checkerboard tops, and chairs were scattered about the room.

I took a seat at the table nearest the door. I ran my fingernail along the edge of one of the painted checkerboards to see if it would move. It didn't. I watched the kids playing and fighting. I felt terribly alone. Maybe Mom was mad at me

9

for something. If I had done something bad, it must have been terrible. I couldn't remember what it was.

"Who are you?" A voice jolted me. There were four boys standing around me. "Who are you?" one of them repeated in a tough manner.

"Twenty-seven," I said without thinking. They roared with laughter before I had a chance to correct myself. "Jennings. My name is Jennings," I said over their laughter.

"What's your first name?" the same boy asked in an equally tough manner.

"That is my first name."

They laughed even louder. The boy who spoke was bigger and older than nearly every kid in the room. He had black curly hair and a few pimples around his chin and near his temples. He announced to everyone in the room that my name was Jenny. I tried correcting him, but I got tongue-tied. They laughed more. The embarrassment made my tears come easily. I clenched my fists and tried to stand, but he grabbed my wrist and flung me back into the chair.

"Look! He's not a boy, he's a girl." He pointed his finger at me. "His name is Jenny and he cries!"

I tried wiping my tears with every dry thing I had, my sleeves, my fingers, the palms of my hands. I insisted I wasn't crying, and wasn't a girl, but nobody heard me. I covered my face with my hands as the laughter and the boys faded away.

"I don't think you're a girl."

I removed my hands and saw a boy about my age sitting across from me.

"I'm *not* a girl. I'm a boy!"

"My name is Mark and my number is nine," he said rather proudly. He was short and chubby and wore a large pair of horn-rimmed glasses. His hair was dark and lay flat on his head, except for a few cowlicks that stuck up from the back. He sort of looked like an owl.

"That's a nice number," I said. "My name is Jennings and I'm twenty-seven."

"Twenty-seven!" he exclaimed with a jolt of his head. "Years old?"

"No." I laughed. "Twenty-seven is my number. I'm only eight and a half years old."

It was the first time I had laughed since I'd arrived.

"Don't pay no attention to those jerks," he said as he flipped his thumb in their direction. "They pick on everybody. All the time!"

I wasn't really listening to what he was saying. I asked, "Where are we?"

"The day room." He looked somewhat surprised at my question.

"No. I mean this whole place."

"Oh! It's the Home of the Angels."

"Oh," I said quietly. My face told him I still didn't know where I was.

"It's a home. Ya know, a home . . . for orphan and foster kids."

"A home?" I was numb. "For orphans?"

He shook his head. "Uh-hum."

"Am I am orphan?"

"I don't know. Are you?"

"I don't know. My mother brought me here. She said she'd be right back . . ."

"Well, then, you're a foster kid," he said matter-of-factly.

"I am? I'm a foster kid?"

"U-hum."

"What's a foster kid?"

"Oh, boy!" He pushed his index finger at his glasses as though they were about to fall off his face. "A foster kid is . . . uh . . . he's a kid who's got parents. But! They don't want him no more."

"My mother wants me!" I snapped.

Mark sat calmly where he was. Slowly he spoke. "Then why are you here?"

I couldn't answer that question. My lower lip began to quiver.

"Oh, boy! Ya know," he said, "it's better to be a foster kid than an orphan."

"Why's that?" I squeaked out. The tears were edging toward my eyelids. I was trying to fight them off.

"Well, a foster kid gets to leave this place."

"Oh, yeah?" I blinked. I quickly wiped a runaway tear. "Will Mom come for me? Will I go home soon?"

"Well . . . I don't know about that, but foster kids sometimes go and live in people's houses."

"People's houses? What people's houses?"

"I don't know, just people. They come and take one kid or another. Just people."

"I don't wanna live in people's houses."

"Oh, boy," he said with a huff.

I guess I got him mad at me, because he stopped talking.

"Are they nice people?" I asked. I wanted him to talk to me again.

"I don't know," he said. "I'm an orphan."

"You mean an orphan don't get to live in people's houses?"

Again he pushed back his glasses. "Most don't. Some do, the little ones. But most don't."

"Did you ever—?"

"No!" He cut me off quickly. "Nobody wants a fat ugly four-eyes."

His response startled me.

"It ain't so bad." He looked around, almost talking to himself. "Once you get to learn all the rules . . . it ain't so bad."

"How long have you been here?"

"I've always been here! Nobody wanted me when I was little, so I've always been here. You want to play checkers?"

I nodded my head. He slipped away to get the playing

12

pieces. I couldn't believe Mom didn't want me anymore. I tried to remember what bad thing I did for Mom to leave me here.

Mark returned. We played two games of checkers. Neither of us spoke very much. I lost both games.

"You don't play very well, do you?"

"I guess I'm just not paying too much attention. I want to go home."

"Now, that's rule number one!" he shot back sternly. "Don't ever think about going home!"

"But I want to."

"I know you want to. We all do. Well, maybe not home, but someplace." He pushed back his glasses. "But you can't go around all day thinking about it. You'll go nuts!" He shook his head as he began setting up the pieces for the next game.

"It's hard not to think about it," I murmured.

"I know. But you'll get used to it. You have to."

We began another game. I tried to obey rule number one, but it was just too hard. I didn't like this place and I wanted to go home.

A click stopped us in mid-move. The next click sent everyone scurrying around the room forming lines. I stood behind Mark to wait for the next click. I hoped it was for lunch. I was starving.

We shuffled our way back through the same maze of hallways to the dining room. As we snaked around the rows of tables, I tried to pick up a hint of what we might be having. Only rolls and butter could be seen. We stopped on a click and turned on the next. I was standing in front of chair number ten. Instantly I was pushed aside by the boy who owned the number. Lost and in trouble again, I closed my eyes and covered my ears as I caught sight of Sister Frances' angry face heading toward me. She grabbed me by the hair and dragged me to chair twenty-seven. She clicked the others to sit. Her free hand was digging straight into my shoulder.

13

All I could do was scrinch up my head and neck and wait. Needless to say, again I did not sit or eat.

Lunch seemed so much longer than breakfast. I paid no attention to the snickers of the other kids. Instead, I studied the kid in chair twenty-six. He had dirty blond hair and large funny ears. I didn't see the front of his face. But I only cared about the back of his head.

Lunch ended with my eyes still glued to the back of twenty-six's head. I thought about Mark saying once you learn the rules, it ain't so bad. If I didn't learn the rules, I was going to starve to death.

The snake slid into a school-type playroom. There were rows of desks toward the front, with play tables and chairs in the rear. There were three large blackboards in the front part of the room, with chalk scribbles all over them. A little old nun, about a hundred years old maybe, sat in one corner of the room half-reading and half-sleeping.

The kids got right into drawing and coloring and painting. I sat with my back against one of the blackboards. The light rain suddenly turned heavy, very heavy. It slapped against the wall of glass doors. A clap of lightning followed by a roll of thunder caused a number of oohs and aahs. I kept my eyes on number twenty-six.

"What are you looking at?" Mark asked as he took a seat next to me.

"It's not a what, it's a who. Twenty-six!"

"I'm sorry I didn't realize you were behind me."

"It's not your fault."

"Well, I shoulda watched." He stuck his hand under his shirt and pulled out a roll.

"It's the best I could do," he said as he handed it to me. "I ate everything else."

I snatched up the roll and ate it. It disappeared in about two bites. It would have gone in one if my mouth had been a little bigger.

"I'll make sure you're in the right spot for dinner."

14

"I'll make sure I'm in the right spot from now on," I said, with my eyes wide and my tongue hanging out. "If I don't . . ." I mimicked my last words by making believe I hung myself.

We were playing tic-tac-toe on the blackboard and laughing about the little nun sleeping in the corner when we were interrupted.

"What are you laughing at, fatso?"

It was the same four boys who had picked on me earlier. The curly-headed pimple-faced kid again did the talking. He was obviously addressing Mark.

"I asked you something, fatso. You deaf or something?"

Mark ignored him and drew another set of lines for our game. I was nervous, but I followed Mark's lead. I placed an X in one of the squares.

"Hey, everybody! We got a deaf dumbo and a little girl over here. They're writing their names in boxes." He managed to get everyone laughing.

Mark seemed to be very natural at ignoring him. I had to work hard at it. They leveled a few more remarks, mostly at Mark but some at me, before they moved off to bother someone else.

"Doesn't he bother you?" I asked.

"Sure he does. But I'm not gonna let him know it. He just wants someone to fight with. That's all. He says lots of things to get you mad. And when you do . . . Wham! He lets you have it. He thinks he's the toughest kid in here."

"Is he?"

"Yeah. I guess so. But one of these days . . ." He made a gesture in the air with his fist. "Butch . . . is gonna get it."

"Is that his name? Butch!"

"Yeah." He placed an O in a box.

"Did you ever notice how all the tough kids are named Butch?" I asked.

He laughed. "I guess they wouldn't be so tough if their names were Felix or Elmer or something."

"Maybe they'd be tougher."

We laughed. We stopped at the same time to look around for Butch. He wasn't there. We laughed harder.

"I got two tough brothers. Well, maybe more mean than tough."

"Are their names Butch?" He laughed.

"No. George and Walter."

"And they're mean? Why do you say they're mean?"

"Ah! They're always picking on Larry and me." I mimicked them, "Do this and do that."

"Who's Larry?"

"Oh! He's another brother."

"Another one! How many you got?"

"Five."

"Five!" He leaned back as though he were about to faint. "I never heard of anybody with five brothers. Do you have any sisters?"

"No. Not no more. I had one, Mary Ann, but she died a little while after she was born."

"Did she just die?"

"Oh, no. She died a long time ago. She would've been six just two weeks ago. October 5. I know her birthday 'cause Mom always cries a lot on her birthday. When's your birthday?"

"Uh . . . ." I surprised him with the question. "I don't got no birthday. At least I don't know when it is."

"How old are you?"

"I don't know. Maybe eight or nine. Something like that. Are all your brothers older than you?" He seemed to want to change the subject away from himself.

"No. I got four older and one younger." I made a face when I said the word "younger."

"What's wrong with him?"

"Oh, nothing. Gene's just a pest, that's all. He's four." I curled the corners of my mouth. "What a pest!"

"Is he in a home too?"

I was stunned by the thought. Tears began to well up in my eyes. "I don't know," I said.

"Oh, boy. I'm sorry I asked. We won't talk about your brothers no more." He went about drawing another set of lines on the board.

"It's all right," I said weakly. I blinked away the thought of Gene being in a place like this.

"Naa. I don't want you to start bawling on me."

"I'm not bawling!" I insisted. "We can talk about my brothers if you want to."

"I like to hear about brothers and things like that."

"Well, George's my oldest brother," I said as I marked an X in the upper-right-hand corner. "He's real good at stickball. He can hit three sewers!"

"What's three sewers?"

"Oh! That's like hitting the ball a whole block."

"Wow!" His eyes widened. "That's far."

"Yeah. He's pretty strong. He'd be a real good brother if he didn't drink and get real mean and argue with Mom."

"He drinks? How old is he?"

"Fifteen."

"Fifteen! And he drinks!"

I nodded my head.

"Don't your father hit him or nothing?"

"I ain't got no father. He died in the war a long time ago."

"Well, what about your mother? Don't she hit him?"

"No. She's afraid of him. We're all afraid of him, except maybe Walter. He's not afraid of him. He fights with him all the time."

"How old is he?"

"Fourteen. He's real smart." I raised my eyebrows. "He's always studying and thinking."

Click!

I froze, but nobody else did.

"What's happening?"

"I gotta go to class," Mark said as he wiped the chalk from his hands on the back of his pants. "All lifers go to class now. I'll see you later."

"Don't I go?"

"No. You're not a lifer, you're a part-timer."

"A part-timer?"

"Yeah. I don't got time to explain it to you now, but I will later." He left to join a line that was leaving the room.

I shot a quick glance around the room. Luckily, twenty-six was still there.

The room was quieter now. Butch was gone and so were his friends. Most of the kids who were left were drawing or coloring, or just sitting and thinking. They were probably all breaking rule number one, but then again, so was I. The rain continued to fall heavily against the glass doors. I wondered where all my brothers were. Could they be in places like this? I was hungry. I found myself really hoping the clicker would sound. I was sure the next one would be for dinner.

Sharp stabs of lightning and the roll of thunder frightened some of the kids. Finally the clicker sounded.

As I and the snake weaved its way around the tables, I smelled the food. I had no idea what it was, but I didn't care. I stopped on the click and turned. I waited years for the one that would let me sit and eat.

Click!

About a foot from me was a large stack of white bread, just standing there. I wanted to grab a piece, but I was afraid. I waited for someone else to grab first. Nobody did. One of the kids took a drink of his milk. I did the same. I never realized how good milk tasted.

I saw a few nuns wearing aprons tied around their necks and waists. They were carrying large bowls of something. One of them reached my table. I watched her serve stew to every kid at the table. By the time she got to me, I had already dreamed of eating everyone's stew. It was great. She scooped up a large ladle of stew and dumped it into my bowl.

It smelled wonderful. I rechecked what everyone else was doing. They were eating. I lifted my spoon and dived in. I ate everything in the bowl and about three pieces of bread. It wasn't until the kid next to me slid his unfinished bowl in front of me that I realized the stew really didn't have much of a taste. I smiled at him and ate his too.

Click!

It was over. I grabbed up a slice of bread and stuffed it into my shirt. The clicks took me and the line from the dining room. We entered the playroom.

Mark and I sat on the curb. We lifted our legs each time a cycle came too close, and placed them back down again in unison.

"What's a part-timer?" I asked. "And why don't they go to school?"

"They got no room for everybody. A part-timer ain't gonna be here all that long. You'll either go home or be lent out to live with somebody." He added quickly, "Don't go bawling on me, now. It don't mean you will be lent out. I was just using that as a for-instance."

"I'm not going to bawl."

"Good! Lifers are here all the time. So we go to school. See?"

"Yeah. I see."

"So tell me about your other two brothers. Larry and the other one. What's his name?"

"Jerome."

"Yeah. Tell me about Larry and Jerome."

"Well, I can't tell you too much about Jerome. I never met him."

"You never met him? You never met your own brother?" He was startled.

"No. He's in a hospital somewhere, dying."

"Dying? Dying of what?"

"A heart condition. My mother said we had to pray for him 'cause he was going to die pretty soon."

"How soon?"

"I don't know. Pretty soon."

"How old is he?"

"He's . . . ah, let me think. . . . He's about ten. He's been in the hospital for as long as I can remember."

"He's a lifer, then, like me."

"Yeah. I guess so. I hadn't ever thought about it like that, but I guess so."

"Is Larry gonna die too?"

"No." I chuckled. "He thinks he is sometimes. He's always being picked on to do this and do that. George and Walter take turns making him do things around the house like cleaning and doing the dishes and stuff like that. Mom works nights for the phone company and sleeps during the day. So George and Walter sort of run things."

"Butch would fit in real good there." He laughed.

"He sure would. Walter calls Larry the 'dumb ox' and George calls him 'four-eyes.' " I shot a glance at Mark as he pushed his glasses back on his face. "I'm sorry. I don't call him 'four—' "

"It's okay. They call everybody with glasses 'four-eyes.' "

"Well, I don't. I don't call him 'dumb ox,' either. I like Larry. He's my favorite brother."

"I think I would like Larry, too. I think I would like to have all your brothers."

"Oh, no you wouldn't!"

"Well, I don't have any brothers. So I wouldn't mind a pesty one, or even a mean one, just so long as I had one."

I hadn't ever thought about it like that. I turned it over in my mind. "No, Mark. You wouldn't like just any kind of brother. You'd like a good one, like Larry, but not just any kind."

We lifted our legs once again as the big purple tricycle zoomed past.

"What does it take to get a ride on that bike?" I asked.

"Guts!" He laughed.

"I saw Butch and his friends throw a kid to the floor last night."

"That's why it takes guts. And they're not his friends!"

"Oh! I thought they were his friends."

"No. There are no friends in here. They just hang around him and laugh when he laughs. They don't want him to pick on them."

"What do you mean there are no friends in here? Aren't we friends?"

He didn't answer me. He sat looking out across the floor at the kids playing and fighting.

"Hey! I'm tired. Want to go to bed?" He stretched and shook as though he had a chill.

"Sure. Okay." I knew he didn't want to answer me. And he knew I knew.

We dashed across the speedway, laughing the whole route. There were only a few kids in the dormitory, and no nuns. We reached Mark's bed first, and he veered off.

"I'll meet you in the bathroom," he said. His arms were outstretched and he made the sound of a plane.

I reached bed number twenty-seven and decided to look through the small cabinet alongside the bed to see what was in it. I found a bar of soap, some toothpaste, a towel and facecloth, and a laundry bag. I took everything but the laundry bag and rejoined Mark in the bathroom.

I changed into the pajamas and hung my things on the hook. I washed and dried my face and put toothpaste on the paper-wrapped brush. I began brushing my teeth.

"What are you doing?" Mark said with laughter in his voice.

"I'm brushing my teeth," I garbled out, the brush still sticking out of my mouth.

"Don't you take the paper off first?"

"I tried to take it off last night, but I got hit for it."

"Really?"

"Really! Sister Frances hit me. She gave me the brush,

21

and when I tried to take the paper off with my teeth, she hit me! She said, 'That's not the way we do things around here!' "

Mark went hysterical with laughter. I thought he liked the way I mimicked Sister Frances' voice, but I was wrong.

"She didn't mean not to take the paper off." He laughed. "She meant not to take it off with your teeth!"

We laughed so hard I thought I was going to burst. My foaming mouth only made us laugh harder. I tried picking some of the soggy paper off my brush and out of my mouth.

Sister Frances passed the bathroom and stuck her head in. "Shut up in here!" she scolded.

Mark and I finished our laughing in silence, or at least as silently as we could. We were just wiping the last of the water off the sinks when I asked, "Mark, what did you mean before when you said there ain't no friends in here?"

I'm sure he didn't like the question, but I had to know the answer.

"Well, it's a rule. Not a home rule like when to sit or when to eat, or like that, but a kids' rule . . ." He paused. "A kids' rule, one you're supposed to learn on your own 'cause nobody likes to talk about it. You know what I mean?"

My face showed him I didn't.

"Oh, boy!" he said. "It's like this. If you got a friend in here and they go away someplace, then you're left by yourself, alone. And if you keep making friends and they keep going away, then over and over again you're alone." He paused. "It hurts."

Mark dashed from the room. He knew he'd said more than he wanted to.

I left the bathroom. I didn't agree with what Mark said. I thought having a friend would make things easier. But then, I wasn't a lifer, and he was. I put my things in the cabinet beside the bed and started to climb up.

"Where are you going?" Mark startled me out of my thoughts.

"To bed. Shouldn't I?"

He shook his head no and waved his hand for me to follow him. We walked to Sister Frances' desk. She was not there. A few kids were already lining up in front of the desk.

"What are we waiting for?"

"Shhhh," came the response from every kid there. I shut up. I couldn't imagine what we were waiting for. Just then a nun entered the dormitory. She was the same nun I saw earlier that morning buttoning the boy's shirt and smiling. She was smiling again. Without knowing her, I liked her.

"Good evening, children," she said warmly.

I was shocked. I didn't think anyone big was ever going to talk nice to us kids.

"Good evening, Sister Clair." The children responded almost in song.

She pulled out a key from a pocket and inserted it into the lock of a cabinet on the wall behind the desk. As she turned the key, all the kids turned it with her. It was the strangest thing. When she opened the cabinet door, I understood. The cabinet was filled with all sorts of stuffed animals. Bears and dogs and monkeys and rabbits and everything. I was so excited.

She removed the animals one at a time. She placed each animal in the arms of the one who most wanted that particular animal. The others' arms remained outstretched and wanting.

"Don't you want one?" she asked. She was looking directly at me.

I nodded my head. I did. I hadn't realized I had wrapped both my arms around my own body as though I were hugging all the animals. I guess because my arms were not outstretched and open, she thought I might not want one. I raised my arms. She smiled broadly and placed a fuzzy brown-and-white dog with black floppy ears in my arms. I cradled the dog to my chest and tucked his big nose under my chin. I walked back to the bed. I made a nice little place for the dog next to my pillow, placed him down gently, and climbed in after him.

"What's your name?" I asked. I paused as though I were giving him time to answer me. "Oh, Doggie. That's a nice name. My name is Jennings." He did not laugh.

I slipped down beneath the covers and pulled Doggie down after me. I cuddled him close to me.

"My mother brought me here. She said she'd be right back. . . . I guess she got busy doing something else. 'Cause she really loves me and wants me. . . . Yeah! That's it! She got very busy. She'll be here soon to take me home, and you can come with me. Would you like that?"

He said he would, and I was happy.

"I'm going to ask Mom to take Mark home, too. With all my brothers around, she won't even notice an extra kid."

"Jennnings."

I was startled by a voice. I poked my head from beneath the covers to see Sister Clair standing above me.

"Hello," I said, and grinned. "I was just saying hello to Doggie. I'm sorry if I made too much noise."

"No, no. You weren't making any noise. I just came by to say hello. May I sit down?" She smiled.

"Yes, Sister." I pushed back on my elbows to lift myself up a little.

"I'm as new here as you are," she said. "I started here the day before you came."

"Do you know where my mother is?"

"Your mother went away to rest. She wasn't feeling very well. You know, it's hard for her to raise all you boys all by herself and hold down a job at the same time. And it's hard for her to face Jerome being sick. Do you know about Jerome?"

I nodded my head.

"Well, you have to be a strong soldier until your mother is better. All right?"

"All right," I said as I started to cry.

24

Sister Clair put both her arms around me and held me.

I must have fallen asleep, because the next thing I saw was the morning sun. I wanted to show Doggie.

"Hey, Doggie," I whispered. I lifted the cover to retrieve him but he wasn't there.

"Hey, Doggie. Where are you?" I felt around the tightly tucked edges of the bed, but still, no Doggie. I stretched my neck out as far over the side of the bed as possible without falling to the floor. No Doggie. I'd lost him.

I pulled myself back up and slid deep beneath the covers. As quietly as I could, I cried.

A sharp rap to my ankles and a shout, "Last one up's a rotten egg!" brought my head from beneath the covers.

"Come on, Jennings!" Mark shouted from the bathroom doorway, then disappeared inside.

I climbed down from the bed, took my things from the cabinet, glanced once more under the bed, then followed Mark.

He was at his hook when I reached mine.

"Hi, sleepyhead," he said.

"Hi."

"What's the matter with you?"

"Nothing."

"Nothing! When you look like that?"

I looked around to see that nobody was within earshot of me. "I lost Doggie." My lip quivered.

"Oh, boy." He chuckled.

"It's not funny. I lost him. I looked everywhere."

"You didn't lose him. They took him."

"They took him? Who took him?"

"The nuns did." He turned and took his shirt from the hook.

"Why?"

"Why?" he said impatiently without looking at me. "They just do, that's all. After we go to sleep." He looked at me. A slight moistness covered his eyes, and he swallowed. "They come around and collect them."

"But why?"

"It's the rules!" he snapped. "They cage the animals at night! It's the rules."

2

After breakfast, Sister Frances told everyone who wanted to go out in the courtyard to get their coats.

The sun was bright but not warm. I walked to the far side of the yard and sat down. I was very careful not to have stepped on any lines, and there were lots of them. The yard was made up of hundreds of squares. Great for box ball or hit the stick. Three sides of the yard were bordered by the high wire-mesh fence. Each section of the fence was separated by a pole. I sat between two of the poles. The fence gave way a little as I leaned back on it. I looked for Mark.

He hadn't come into the yard. I wondered why not. I watched the boys on one side of the yard and the girls on the other. The boys played ball or Johnny-ride-the-pony, while the girls skipped rope. I was amazed to see how many girls in this world had ropes. All of them.

"Hi! What's your name?"

I looked up to see a little girl looking down at me. She had fluffy blond hair that was pulled into two bunches, then tied with blue ribbons. Her cheeks were freckled. Her eyes were blue and sparkly.

"Hi."

"What's your name?" she asked again.

"Jennings," I said weakly. I wasn't at all used to talking to girls.

"Jennings! What's your first name?"

"That is my first name."

"My name is Stacy. Stacy Ann Perry. Can I sit down?"

Before I could even thing of an answer, she was sitting. "Uh . . . yeah. Sure."

"How old are you?"

"Uh . . . eight and a half."

"Me too! Well, almost eight and a half. Are you a part-timer or a lifer?"

"Uh . . . part-timer."

"Yeah, me too. My mother is having a baby. Probably a girl. I asked her to have a girl. I'd love to have a sister. Do you have any sisters?"

I couldn't believe how fast she could talk. "Uh . . . no. I got brothers."

"Brothers. That's nice. How many brothers do you have?"

"Five."

"Five. That's nice. I don't have . . . Five! That's a lot of brothers. Are they all in here?"

"Uh . . . no. They're . . . I don't know where they are."

"Oh. Do you like it here?"

"No. No, I don't."

"No. I don't either. My mother says if I behave myself, she'll buy me a doll when I get home."

I looked around the yard from time to time to see if any of the boys saw me with a girl. They hadn't. I still didn't see Mark anywhere. She talked so fast and about so many different things, it was hard to keep up with her. I smiled every so often and grunted a little; that seemed to satisfy her. Finally I spotted Mark.

"I think my friend wants me," I said. I got to my feet.

"Oh. All right." She seemed disappointed.

"I'll see you later." I smiled weakly and backed away.

"All right!" She brightened up. "I'll see you later."

Mark was playing box ball with a milky-white skinny kid

with sandy brown hair and two giant front teeth. He looked like a beaver.

"Can I play the winner?" I asked.

"Naa. I don't want to play any more after this," Mark said as he missed his point. He retrieved the ball and served. "Why not find someone else to play with?"

His remark was sharp and it hurt.

"Okay," I said. I backed away. I thought he might say something else, but he didn't. He just kept on playing his game. I wandered back over to the fence. Stacy wasn't anywhere to be seen, so I sat down.

I watched Mark and the kid playing. I didn't know why Mark didn't want to play with me. Maybe he was mad at me from this morning. When he explained to me about Doggie.

I watched silently from my stone seat with the wire-mesh back. I thought back to Our Lady of Mercy's schoolyard. There was something different going on here. The sound was different. The kids in the schoolyard were noisier. These kids weren't noisy enough to be playing. They're not playing! They're waiting, they're not playing at all. Every kid in this yard was waiting for something. I was waiting for Mom. Other kids were waiting to be lent out. Others, like Mark, were waiting for the next click. I hated this place.

The click snapped the yard to attention. I laughed a little to myself, because he hadn't had long to wait. The second click sent everyone scurrying about the yard forming lines. I hesitated for a moment, but only a moment. The memory of the pain to my shoulder and ears made me get to my feet. I located twenty-six's funny ears and followed them.

I ate some of the stew and drank some milk. I looked around the room, as I had done before. But this time I saw the kids. For the first time, I really saw them. They were eating in silence; their faces were drawn and blank. They weren't frowning, but neither were they smiling. They weren't anything at all. I moved my glass into a spot where I could look at my own face in the reflection. I was one of them.

I found Mark sitting by himself just outside the classroom door.

"Want to play tic-tac-toe?" I asked.

"Naaa."

"Want to play box ball?"

"Naa."

"Want to—"

"Look, Jennings. I ain't mad at you or nothing. I just don't wanna play with you today."

We sat in silence.

"Don't you see, if we keep playing with each other all the time . . ." He broke off to kick some make-believe object from one foot to the other. "We're gonna become friends. And you know that's—"

"Yeah. Against the rules." I finished his words and got to my feet. As I made my way across the yard to the fence, I looked back. Mark was still kicking his make-believe object. He was interrupted.

"Hey, dumbo! What are you doing?" Butch snarled at him.

I turned away and kept walking.

I reached the fence and leaned into it. To my surprise it had a lot of give to it. I sprang off the fence. It was like a great vertical trampoline. I leaned into it and sprang off again. It was fun. I did it again.

"What are you doing?" Stacy asked as she approached.

"Bouncing."

"That looks like fun. Can I bounce too?"

Of course, I didn't have to answer her. In a flash she was standing alongside of me, bouncing.

"You have beautiful red hair and freckles," she said.

"Oh, gosh!" The heat rose instantly into my face and neck. I was sure I was close to the color of my hair.

I quickly shot a glance in the direction of the boys. The last thing I wanted was for any of them to overhear her or see us playing together. I was safe; they hadn't noticed. We bounced a few more times before I heard the giggles from the girls' side of the yard. I turned my head, and not ten feet from us were about a dozen girls. If at all possible, I got redder.

One or two of the girls selected a spot in another section in the fence and began to bounce. It wasn't long before all the girls began selecting spots and bouncing on and off the big fence.

Suddenly I became aware of the laughter from the direction of the boys. I was afraid to look, but I did. To my surprise, they weren't laughing at me. They were bouncing on and off the wire fence. The whole yard of kids was now bouncing.

"Stop that! Stop that!" screamed a nun as she came running from the building. "Stop that!"

The whole yard was in an uproar of laughter. As the nun approached, the kids began bouncing off the fence and running in all directions. The laughter continued as the nun chased us into the building.

I sat on the curb of the playroom. I watched Butch ride the big purple bike and wondered how long he'd be in this place. I was hoping he'd go home or something so I could ride the bike. I spotted Stacy enter from the far side of the room. I crawled away from the curb and around to the back of one of the pillars. The last thing I wanted was for her to get talking to me again.

"Hello. What are you doing back here? Are you playing a game or something?" Stacy looked around to see who I might be playing with.

"No," I said. "I was just thinking."

"About what?" she asked as she plopped down next to me.

"Oh, gosh."

"There, you said it again. Why do you say, 'Oh, gosh'?"

"Uh . . . I like to say, 'Oh, gosh.' "

"Why?"

"Oh, gosh!"

"I think you're embarrassed. Are you embarrassed?"

I felt the redness approaching. "I'm not embarrassed," I fibbed. "I'm just not used to talking to girls. That's all."

"Is it different than talking to boys?"

"Oh, gosh!" I got to my feet. "I'm tired now. I'm going to go to bed." I began to back away from her toward the curb. "I'll see ya."

"All right," she said quietly.

I dashed across the raceway and opened the door marked "Boys." I looked back. She was still on the floor where I left her. There was disappointment on her face, almost a sadness. I saw in her what I felt in me when Mark told me he didn't want to play with me. I closed the door. I took a deep breath and began to make my way around the room back to Stacy. I thought if I went the long way, I might gather some courage on the way. I reached her.

"You came back!"

I didn't explain why, and she didn't ask me. I let her do the talking. She was good at that. She told me she lived in Elmhurst, Queens. She said her real father left her mother when she was a little baby.

"Mom's new husband talked her into putting me in this place. I don't think he likes me very much."

I was half-listening and half-watching out for anyone who might be watching me. Suddenly she leaned over and kissed me. She jumped to her feet, dashed across the floor, and slipped through the door marked "Girls." I sat on the floor with my hand covering my cheek. The redness I expected to overcome me never came. I got to my feet. Slowly I retraced my steps the long way around the room.

The dormitory was dark and empty. I took the things from the chest alongside bed twenty-seven and entered the bathroom. I felt as though I were in slow motion. I couldn't understand what was wrong with me. I changed, washed only one half of my face, and then floated out of the bathroom.

The dormitory was now lighted, and some of the kids were coming in. The line began forming at Sister Clair's desk, and

I joined it. I waited with the others as the line grew longer. Mark joined the line. I looked in his direction, but he was looking down at the floor. Sister Clair was late, and the line was getting long. Some of the bigger kids started coming into the room.

"Look at the babies waiting for their dollies," Butch shouted.

His remark caused some of the kids to leave the line and their fuzzy friends. I didn't; Mark didn't.

"Hey, fatso! I didn't know you had enough room in your bed for a dolly," Butch taunted someone behind me. It wasn't hard for me to guess who it was.

I turned my head. Mark ignored Butch as usual, but Butch wasn't about to give up.

"What's the matter, four-eyes? Can't you hear me talking to you?"

Mark again looked down at the floor. Some of the kids began laughing, while others left the line. I stayed.

"Hey, fatso! What are you looking down there for? Can't you find your feet?"

The room filled with mean laughter. I wanted to punch Butch in the nose, but I remembered what Mark had told me: "Just ignore him and he'll go away." I kept my eyes on Mark. He was hurting and I knew it. He wanted his little animal as much as I wanted mine. He stayed and took Butch's insults.

"Maybe, dumbo, if you got a really skinny dolly . . ."

Butch didn't have to finish his remark. He had won. In a roar of laughter, Mark left the line. I watched him make his way toward his bed, his head hung low.

"Where are you going, four-eyes? The dollies are over here in this direction," Butch continued, to the laughter of all the others.

I leapt from my place onto Butch's back, knocking him to the floor. My advantage of surprise lasted but a few seconds. I threw as many punches as I could before he grabbed my arm. In one motion he flipped me over his head and landed on my chest. He was the strongest kid in here. As my body slammed against the floor, he punched me in the eye. I saw stars. He was about to take a second shot when Sister Frances grabbed his arm and yanked him to his feet. She slapped her hand flush against his ear and dragged him to his bed. I was just getting to my feet when she returned for me. The blow to my ear was deafening. The next moment, I crashed into the top bars of bed twenty-seven.

I untwisted my body, worked my way down under the blanket, and pulled it up over my head. I hurt. My eye and my ear were killing me. I lay beneath the covers for a long time. I wondered if I had made a mistake. I was in pain, Butch was going to kill me tomorrow, and worst of all, I didn't get Doggie. But then again, friend or no friend, rule or no rule, I couldn't let Mark be hurt like that and not do anything about it.

Some time passed before I poked my head from beneath the covers. The room was quiet and dark. The gray light from the streetlamp made its way through the barred window across my bedcover. The ceiling was gone and I was alone.

Suddenly there was a tug at my sleeve. I pulled my arm from the tug but recognized the hair sticking straight up from the top of Mark's head.

"What are you doing here?"

"Stop talking down there!" Sister Frances shouted from her desk.

I whispered, "What are you doing here?"

Mark's head turned almost a full circle, checking for safety. He whispered, "I want to thank you . . . for sticking up for me."

"Ah! It's nothing. That's what friennns . . ." I gulped down the last words. "It's nothing."

"No. You're right. That's what friends are for!"

"But we're not friends," I said.

"Says you!" He spoke louder, then slapped his hand over

his mouth. "Says you," he whispered. "Maybe it's not the smartest thing to do. You know . . . have a friend in here. But I'd like to try it."

A tear began to sting my eye. I wiped it away.

"Let's shake on it." He extended his hand to me.

I brought my hand around to meet his, but it wasn't there. He had replaced his hand with Doggie. I grabbed him up and hugged him.

"How'd you get him?"

"Well . . . I got him instead of Brownie. He's my bear."

"But, Mark!"

"But, nothing! Brownie'll understand." He paused. "That's what friends are for." He slipped down beneath the bed and was gone.

I held Doggie close to my face. One minute I had had no friends, and the next minute I had two.

For the next few days I wore my black eye proudly. Butch didn't kill me after all. In fact, he didn't say a single word to me. He still picked on as many kids as he could, but he seemed to leave Mark and me alone.

Stacy wanted to kiss my eye when she saw it. "To make it better," she said. But I didn't want her to. First, I couldn't let her keep on kissing me, and second, I didn't want it to get better. I kind of liked having a black eye.

I was in the playroom with Mark when I saw a kid get off the big purple bike.

"I'm going to take a ride," I said.

"Oh, boy!" Mark quickly looked around the room for Butch.

I didn't tell Mark, but I had already done that. I climbed aboard the bike. It was beautiful. It rode smoothly and quickly. On the second turn around the floor, Butch came into the room. He spotted me on the bike and started toward me. My heart pounded. He reached the edge of the curb, then sat down. My relief forced me to smile. He smiled back.

In the weeks that followed, Butch, Fuzzy, and Bryan—

they were two of the boys who hung around with him—spent more and more time with Mark and me. We played games together, like punchball and tag. And when it rained we stayed inside and played Steal the Old Man's Pack and Slap Jack. Butch stopped picking on almost all the kids, but kept on telling everyone how tough he was. We let him talk.

Butch, Fuzzy, Mark, and I were in the dayroom one afternoon, playing Go Fish when the first snow started to fall.

"Look, it's snowing!" somebody yelled out.

We were all excited. Mark told us about a snowman he had built one year. Fuzzy had to top him, and told us he built a bigger one. Butch said he made the biggest one, and that was the end of that. I told them about sliding down Teibout Avenue on a crushed-up cardboard box I got from the A&P. They listened intently. They were all lifers and had never slid down any kind of a hill. We watched the silence of the falling snow.

"Jennings!" Sister Frances called out.

My goose bumps faded by the time I reached her. She took me from the room and brought me to the same front hall I'd been in about a thousand years earlier, when my mother had left me here. Maybe she'd come back?

"Is my mother here?"

Sister Frances didn't answer. My excitement grew. She opened the door next to the benches with the red cushions. Mom wasn't there.

In the far corner of the office behind a desk was a nun I had never seen before. Alongside her desk sat a man and a lady. The man had a pudgy little face, a mustache, and wore glasses. He was bald on top of his head but had curly brown hair on the sides. He wore a dark overcoat and a gray suit. He was holding his hat in his hands. Well, he wasn't exactly holding it, he was more like crushing it. He was twirling it all around his fingers. The lady had brownish-gray hair and wore a giant black hat tilted to one side. There were large flowers all over it. It looked awful. Her face was pasty, with gobs of red stuff plopped on each cheek. She wore a dark green coat and a blue dress with large white polka dots all over it.

"Jennings," the nun at the desk said. "This is Mr. and Mrs. Carpenter. They're going to take you home with them."

"Why?"

"Because they like you. They want you to live with them for a while." She smiled.

"But . . . but . . . they don't know me. How could they like me? I want to stay with Mark."

"You're going!" She stood up. She wasn't smiling anymore.

"How will my mother know where I am?"

"I'll tell her!" she snapped. She nodded to Sister Frances, then turned to me. "Get your things!"

Sister Frances took me into the dormitory and left me. She told me to hurry up and to meet her in the hall. I fought back the tears as I took all the things out of the cabinet alongside bed number twenty-seven. I stuffed them into the laundry bag. As I approached the doorway to the hall, I stopped. If I go out there, I won't get a chance to say good-bye to Mark or Stacy or anyone. I left through the rear door.

I burst into the dayroom. Mark was still by the glass doors watching the snow. Mark's head turned as the door slammed into the wall. He saw me and knew. He turned back toward the snow.

"I'm leaving," I mumbled.

"Yeah."

I extended my hand to his shoulder. He didn't look up at me, but he took my hand. He shook it.

"Are you going home?" he asked, as though he were talking to the glass doors and the snow.

"No. I'm being lent out." My lip quivered, as did my voice.

Mark didn't say anything, he just sat there watching the gently falling snow.

"Will you say good-bye to Stacy and the others for me?"

He nodded his head. I stood there wanting to say more, but

I couldn't. I slowly backed my way to the door and slipped out. Mark never looked back.

Sister Frances took me to the front hall and the Carpenters. They led the way down the now snow-covered steps, and I followed.

"Wait!" I shouted. I turned back toward Sister Frances. "Sister, I want Doggie! Can I have Doggie?"

"No! He doesn't belong to you." She started in the door.

"Oh, yes! He does! He does!" I grabbed her around the waist. "Oh, please, Sister, let me take him!" I cried.

"No! He belongs to all the children."

"No, Sister, he doesn't! He belongs to me. Nobody else wants him but me. Oh, please."

"No!" She pushed me away and slammed the door.

Doggie was gone. I felt the worst pain I had ever known. It wouldn't go away. The tears did not come to my eyes. I hurt too much.

Mr. Carpenter put me in the backseat of the car and we drove off. They may or may not have spoken to me; I could hear nothing. My friend Doggie was gone, and I never even got a chance to say good-bye to him for keeps.

3

The windshield wipers squeaked and thumped, hissed and clicked. The strange collection of sounds lulled me into a sort of half-stare and half-sleep.

"Here we are," Mr. Carpenter said.

I sat up as the car pulled to the curb. I tried looking through the fogged-up window, but I couldn't see anything. I took a swipe at the window.

"Keep your dirty hands off the glass!" Mrs. Carpenter snarled.

"Oh, leave him alone. He isn't hurting anything. Come on, Jenkins, let's go."

The street was quiet. Everything in sight was covered by a pretty white blanket of snow. Even the garbage cans in front of all the houses along the street had little white hats on them. Mr. Carpenter opened a black metal gate and passed through it. Mrs. Carpenter followed him, and I followed her. We walked around to the back of the house, climbed the stairs, and went in through the kitchen.

The room was warm and quiet. There was a small lamp lit over a large kitchen table. The room was sparkling clean.

Mrs. Carpenter gave me some paper and a pencil and told me to sit at the small table.

"My table" was a small wooden table with a chair to match. It was across the room from the large table with the lamp above it. She switched on the ceiling light and started fixing a pot of coffee. The clock above the stove said 5:45 P.M.

"Can I help you?" I asked.

"No!" She was abrupt. "You'll break something, and then where will my profits go?"

I didn't understand the profits part, but I did understand the "no."

When she finished she turned off the ceiling light and left the room. I could hear whispers through the closed door. I was sure they were talking about me.

The room grew darker as the daylight faded. What I thought was a little light from the lamp above the big table wasn't any light at all. It only lit the area of the table. The walls with sink, stove, and icebox were in the dark shadows. So was I.

Mrs. Carpenter came back into the kitchen and turned on the ceiling light. She began to prepare dinner. Mr. Carpenter came in and sat at the big table. He unwrinkled a newspaper and started to read.

"There's a Bogart film at the King's Park," he told her. *"Treasure of the Sierra Madre."*

"You know I can't go anywhere with this damn kid around."

"Well, who the hell asked you to take him?" He dropped his paper to the table.

"You know we need the money," she said. Then she added sarcastically, "You certainly don't earn enough. And I can't work . . . sickly as I am."

He grunted, then continued to read his paper. She served him a sandwich.

"Isn't he going to eat?" he asked.

I perked up. I was hungry. I wouldn't mind one of those sandwiches.

"No. He told me he ate plenty before he left the home."

She lied, but I didn't know why. I didn't like this lady, I didn't like her at all.

After Mr. and Mrs. Carpenter left the kitchen, I drew a

picture of Doggie. I put a hat and a scarf on him. I made all the dots for the snowflakes, and then drew some trees around him. It was the first time Doggie was ever away from his cage and out of the home. I kissed him.

Light flooded the room. Mrs. Carpenter came in and yanked me from the chair. She dragged me through the dining room and a foyer, then pushed me into a bedroom.

The room was small and bare. There was a bed with a brown blanket and no pillow, a chest like the one at the home, and a chair by the window. The window had no bars. I sat on the bed as Mrs. Carpenter switched off the light. I said good night to a closing door.

I lay alone in the dark of the small room. It was the first time in my life I was ever alone in a bedroom. I was frightened. Not afraid of the dark or anything like that, just afraid. When I was at home with Mom and my brothers, Larry, Gene, and I slept in one bed, while George and Walter slept in another. We all slept in the same room. I remember how we used to lie in the dark and play alphabet games. Someone would pick a topic like cars or something, and we would all try to name things in that topic with the letters of the alphabet. Gene never played. He always fell asleep right away. I never got much past C or D myself, but it was fun. I sure wish my brothers were here now to play with me.

"A. Let's see, now . . . uh. Austin-Healy. B. Uh . . . uh . . . Buick! C . . ."

In the morning, I dressed and left the bedroom for the kitchen. I passed a staircase in the hall, then stopped. With Mrs. Carpenter in the kitchen, I thought, this might be a good time to explore. I climbed the stairs.

"Where are you going?" she screamed.

She was standing just above me on the stairs. She wasn't in the kitchen at all. I turned in mid-step and scurried down the stairs. I ran through the dining room into the kitchen. I sat at the table, my heart pounding. She came in. I cowered in the chair, covering my ears. She brushed past me, heading for her work counter. She didn't hit me.

She switched on a radio next to her. A man with a very deep voice said, "Duz does everything."

She changed stations.

Another man with an even deeper voice said, "The Guiding Light." A whole bunch of high-pitched voices began singing a jingle as Mrs. Carpenter began speaking to me from over her shoulder.

"You better get used to the rules around here, or I'll beat the daylights out of you."

I tried listening to her and the singers.

"The bedroom is for sleeping. The rest of the house is off limits to you. You're to sit at that table, and that table only. If you don't, you'll get it. Understand?"

I nodded my head, but she didn't see me.

"Do you understand?" she screeched.

I jolted to attention in the chair. "Yes," I said.

"Yes, *ma'am!*" she added.

"Yes, ma'am," I repeated.

"And . . . if you break anything around here, God help you." She mumbled, "I make little enough money off you as it is."

She turned from the counter and rushed at me. I ducked my head below my hands. She plopped a bowl down in front of me.

"Eat!" she commanded. She went back to her counter.

It was a grayish blob of icy stuff. I think it was oatmeal, but I really couldn't be sure. It was thick and gluey, and it smelled funny. I tasted it.

"Eck! I don't like this stuff!"

Again she rushed at me and I ducked. She snatched up the bowl.

As I waited for her to bring me something else, I looked around for my picture of Doggie.

"Did you see my picture anywhere? Ma'am."

42

"I threw it out! I don't want a whole lot of junk cluttering up my kitchen."

I felt badly. It hurt me to think of Doggie in the garbage. I decided if I ever drew something I wanted, I'd never leave it lying around.

Mrs. Carpenter finished her work at the counter, switched off the radio, and left the room. She didn't fix me anything else. I guess I wasn't surprised. Hungry, maybe, but not surprised.

I sat looking up at the wall next to the table. There was a lot more on the wall than I realized. There were tiny dots and little lines. There were bumps and cracks.

At about one o'clock I stuck my head out the door and called, "Mrs. Carpenter, ma'am."

"What do you want?"

She startled me. She was sitting not five feet from the door.

"Uh . . . I'm hungry. I was wondering . . ."

"We eat breakfast and dinner around here and that's all," she snarled. "I can't afford to be feeding you anytime you feel like eating. Besides, you're not worth it, you dirty little bastard. Now, get back to your table."

I pulled my head into the kitchen. I returned to the table and buried my head in my arms. I didn't want her to hear me crying.

The day gave way to night, and the room darkened. I sat looking at the thin strip of light working its way in under the door from the dining room.

I was falling off to sleep when Mrs. Carpenter came in. I covered my eyes to readjust to the room light. She went to work at her counter.

She was making hamburgers for dinner. I was starving. When they started to cook, they smelled and sounded wonderful. I couldn't imagine how she could ruin them, but I decided I'd better wait until I tasted them.

Mr. Carpenter came in at 7:15. He sat at the big table and

unfolded his paper. He read a few things to her, but she didn't seem interested. He didn't speak to me at all.

"I sure would like to get a television set," he said.

"A what?"

"A television set."

"How could we afford one of those?" she asked.

"They're really improving them, you know. Look how many programs are on the air now." He held up part of the paper for her to look. She didn't.

"What's wrong with radio?" she asked.

"Nothing. I like radio. But I thought a television would be nice. *Texaco Star Theatre. The Life of Riley. Toast of—*"

"Frank! Forget about television sets and eat."

She served each of them a hamburger. She placed the same bowl of gray gook I had rejected that morning in front of me. I was disappointed. I decided to try it again. I tasted it. It was cold and sticky and awful. I could barely get the mouthful down before gagging. I pushed it away.

Mr. Carpenter finished his hamburger and left. I covered my head with my arms until she finished cleaning up. She took the bowl from the table but said nothing. When I was sure she wasn't going to hit me, I uncovered my head. She turned off the ceiling light and left the room.

I sat at the little table and wondered if I'd ever eat again. I started to think about the first days at the Home of the Angels, when I didn't eat for a long time. I wished I had some of that stew now. Even a piece of bread or a roll would be great. I wished I was back at the home with Mark and Doggie. I drew another picture of Doggie. This time he was standing in the middle of all these trees, with a great pile of hamburgers next to him. After I kissed him I folded him up and stuck him in my pocket.

The next morning, I sat at the little table in front of the same bowl of sticky stuff. I didn't bother to smell it or taste it or anything. I just pushed it to the edge of the table and closed my eyes. The next little tap sent it crashing to the floor. Mrs. Carpenter went into a rage. She grabbed me by the hair and yanked me from the chair. She punched me in the side of the head and threw me to the floor. I drew in my arms and legs to make myself a smaller target, but it didn't help. She smashed me across the back with a stick or something. On the second hit, she caught me across the back of my legs. I crawled under the big table. Her third shot hit the table legs and the chairs.

"Come out!" she screamed.

I wouldn't move. She again hit the sides of the table legs with her stick. I crawled in deeper. She mumbled to herself while she cleaned up the pieces of the broken bowl. She slammed things around and took one more shot at the table legs before she gave up and left the room.

I lay piled up on the floor. I began to feel the pain in my back and legs. I thought I might die under this table and maybe it would be soon. I was hurting and hungry. I reached down into my pocket and pulled out Doggie's picture. I kissed him and pressed him close to my face. "I don't think Mom's ever going to come for us," I told him. "I don't think we're ever going to leave this place." I closed my eyes. "Doggie, I'm going to stay under here forever." I clenched Doggie tightly in my hand. The floor was hard and cold. Each time I thought I heard her coming, I held my breath. The table and chair legs were like the bars of a cage around me. This time they weren't keeping me in, they were keeping her out.

The hours passed slowly. The morning sun turned to afternoon shadows, then the shadows to night. I lay on the floor watching the thin strip of light under the kitchen door.

I was awakened by Mrs. Carpenter moving around the kitchen. I could see only her legs and her feet. I knew she was fixing dinner; I could smell it.

"Where's Jenkins?" Mr. Carpenter asked as he entered the room. He didn't wipe his feet very well. The edges of his shoes were still wet from the snow.

"He's under the table."

"Under the table? What's he doing under there?" He poked his head under to see me.

"He's playing or something. What the hell do I know about these damn kids? Half of them are crazy," she said.

"Hey, son. What are you doing down there?"

I crawled in deeper. I stuffed Doggie in my pocket for fear they might take him and throw him in the garbage again.

"What's the matter, Jenkins?"

"Nothing."

"Come on out of there." He offered me his hand.

He had always been nice to me. He wasn't very friendly or anything like that, but he'd never hurt me. I gave him my hand and crawled out. As I stood up, he touched my back and I winced.

"Did you hit him?" he asked sternly.

"No," she lied.

He lifted my shirt and saw the welt mark. "You hit him, dammit!"

"I did not. He fell."

"That's it, Edna. Hit him one more time and he goes back. You hear me? Money or no money, he goes back. I'm not going to have you beating up all these kids. You listening to me, Edna?"

"He fell! Goddammit! I didn't hit him," she screamed.

He held my shoulders and looked me in the eye. "Now, don't be afraid, Jenkins. Did she hit you?"

I didn't have to answer him. My tears came easily.

"I'm warning you, Edna . . ."

She slammed things around the counter. "He breaks my good bowl and that's okay. Don't punish him. Oh, no! Just mollycoddle the son of a bitch."

Mr. Carpenter sat me at the little table. He sat at his usual place and picked up his newspaper. I stared at the spots on the wall and planned my escape. I had to get out of here before he left for work in the morning. She served the dinner.

I didn't bother to look at what they were having. It didn't matter.

"Aren't you going to feed him?" he asked.

"After he breaks my good china? Not on your life."

Mr. Carpenter was now his usual self; he said nothing.

With dinner now over and the Carpenters gone from the room, I sat and watched the thin strip of light. I was ready. I went over to the back door and tugged. It was locked. I opened one of the two bolts. The other one I couldn't reach without a chair. As quietly as I could, I got a chair from the big table. I pushed as hard as I could, but the bolt wouldn't open. I searched around the kitchen for something I might use to hit it. In one of the bottom cabinets I found two things. The hammer I needed for the bolt, and a box of Jell-O powder.

I tore open the box and tasted it. "Wow! That's sour!" I said quietly. I took another taste. I was so hungry, it didn't matter how sour it was, I was going to eat it. My eyes were almost closed completely from the sourness of the Jell-O. I ate the whole box before I could get my eyes open again. I crushed up the empty box and stuck it in my pocket. I returned to the door. I tapped lightly at the bolt on the door, but nothing happened. I knew I would have to give it one good whack. "What if I can't get the chair out of the way before she gets in here?" I thought out loud. "Ah, what difference does it make, she's going to kill me anyway." I closed my eyes and swung as hard as I could. I missed. The hammer went crashing through one of the panes of glass in the door. Mrs. Carpenter was there in a flash. Before I could even think about getting down from the chair, the room was ablaze with light and she was on me. She punched me in the stomach and knocked me to the floor. She began kicking me.

"What the hell is going on here?" Mr. Carpenter screamed as he rushed into the room.

"I'm going to kill him!" she screeched.

I believed her. Her eyes were red with fire. She leaned

down and clenched my shirt with her hand. She lifted me straight off the floor a few feet, then dropped me. He grabbed her arm and swung her around. I thought he was going to hit her, but he didn't. He just held her off.

"That's it, Edna! Tomorrow he goes back!"

4

Sister Frances grabbed my ear and led me from the office. "Now see what you've done?" she scolded. "Those nice people won't take any more kids, thanks to you. It's hard enough to find places to house you kids without . . . Ah, what's the use?"

She pushed me through the dayroom door and left me. I once again stood in the middle of what seemed to be a thousand staring eyes. This time I smiled.

"Jennings!" Mark shouted. He was just coming in from the yard and he was covered with snow.

As I made my way through the kids, one or two of them patted me on the back. In a strange sort of way, I was home.

"Well, that didn't take long," Mark said.

"Long enough. I'm starving. When do we eat?"

"Soon. Pretty soon. Either you're getting like me or they didn't feed you."

"They didn't feed me." I sat down at one of the checkerboard tables. I held my aching stomach.

Some of the kids gathered around to hear the tale of the Carpenters.

"Mrs. Carpenter is crazy!" I said. "She cursed all the time, yelled and screamed at me, and made me sit at this little tiny table. The whole time I was there."

Some of the kids made faces, others just stared at me.

"It was awful," I said. "She gave me this gluey stuff that smelled like dirty feet. I couldn't eat it. Then she beat me up." I lifted my shirt to show them my welt marks.

After a time, the group of kids drifted off. I stayed talking to Mark.

"Oh, wait!" I said. "I got something to show you." I took out the picture of Doggie. "What do you think?"

He looked long and hard at the picture. "Don't show this to Doggie."

We laughed.

"Jennings!" someone called out.

I looked up and saw Stacy in the doorway. Her two hands were touching her lips, like the way you hold your hands in church. Tears were in her eyes. I stood up when she reached me. I took her outstretched hand and she kissed my cheek.

"Oh, gosh," I said. I slid back down into my seat. My face grew very red.

She sat down. "I didn't think I'd ever see you again," she said.

"I didn't think so either."

"Some of the kids in the yard told me a boy had just returned from an awful home. I didn't know they were talking about you. I'm sorry they treated you so badly."

"Oh, gosh."

Click!

I shot straight out of my chair, then panicked. I couldn't find twenty-six's funny ears. The second click sounded and the kids lined up. I stayed where I was and covered my ears as a nun I hadn't seen before approached me.

"Well?" she said.

"I don't know where I'm supposed to be, Sister. I just got here." My heart pounded. I didn't want to be punished just now, I was too hungry for that.

"Come along," she said. She took my hand.

She placed me at Mark's table. My new number was twelve, just three places away from Mark. We managed to smile at each other. I watched the sisters serving meatloaf. My mouth watered and my stomach ached. I gobbled down everything in minutes, including some bread and butter. I began to feel sick. My head started spinning and my stomach ached even more.

"Sister! I'm going to be sick!" I called out.

Sister Frances was there in a flash to race me from the room. I just barely made it to a sink in the kitchen before it all came up. Sister Frances held my head and my shoulders.

"Get the nurse," she told someone.

She sat me down on a chair. When the nurse came in, she felt my forehead and asked me how I felt and what was wrong.

"I don't know, ma'am."

"Well, what did you eat this morning?"

"Nothing."

"And last night?"

"Nothing. Oh, wait! I did eat a box of Jell-O powder."

"Jell-O powder! No wonder you're sick."

"Why did you eat Jell-O powder?" Sister Frances asked.

"I was hungry, Sister. I had to eat something."

"Didn't they feed you?"

The tears came to my eyes. I shook my head no.

"Not at all?" the nurse asked.

Again I shook my head no.

Sister Frances sat me down at a table in the kitchen. She ordered one of the kitchen sisters to bring me some soup. "No bread," she said, "just the soup."

She brushed back the hair on my head and left. For a moment she seemed different. A little like Sister Clair.

I finished the soup. Sister Frances came back and took me through the now empty dining room to the outside hall. We entered the stern nun's office, and she sat me down.

"Now, Jennings, I want you to tell Sister Margaret and me about your stay with the Carpenters."

At first I hesitated because I was nervous, but then I told

them everything. They listened in silence. I said I was sorry for breaking the bowl and the window. I thought they would be angry with me, but they weren't. I told them about the curse words Mrs. Carpenter used all the time. I wouldn't say the words, but I did use the first letter of each of them. I showed them my welt marks, and then I showed them my picture of Doggie.

"What are these things beside him?" Sister Margaret asked.

"Hamburgers."

She laughed.

Sister Frances took me to the dayroom.

I sat near the glass doors and watched some of the part-timers playing in the yard. Stacy was helping with a snowman. Mark and the other lifers were at school.

At bedtime Sister Frances handed me Doggie. I hugged him. He felt so soft and good. I carried him to bed number twelve and made a place for him. I showed him his picture. He thought it was a good likeness. I waved to Mark and he waved back. I slid beneath the covers and brought Doggie close to me.

"I love you, Doggie," I whispered.

I closed my eyes to sleep. I was very tired.

After breakfast the next morning, we were clicked into the playroom. Some of the kids got their coats and went into the yard. Mark and I as well as some other kids stayed in. It was too cold.

Click!

We sat at attention. Sister Frances called Stacy. Mark and I looked at one another as Stacy cautiously approached Sister Frances. They left the playroom.

"What do you think?" I asked.

Mark shrugged his shoulders. "Maybe she's being lent out."

"Oh, gosh." I shuddered.

"But . . . maybe she's going home," he added.

"Yeah!" I smiled. "Maybe she's going home." The sudden happy thought faded. It was replaced by a feeling I hadn't felt before.

"Now you know what I mean," Mark said dryly. He pushed his glasses back on his nose.

"What?"

"About the kids' rule 'No friends,' " he said. "It's hard to explain the feeling, you just feel it."

"I feel it," I mumbled.

Stacy burst into the room. "I'm going home!" she screeched.

The room fell into silence. Some of the girls gathered around her. After she spoke to them, she came over to Mark and me.

"I'll think about you," she said. Her eyes sparkled. She looked beautiful.

"I'll think about you, too," I said.

"If you ever get to Elmhurst . . ." She broke off.

I nodded my head.

She leaned over and kissed my cheek. " 'Bye," she said.

" 'Bye."

" 'Bye, Mark."

" 'Bye, Stacy."

She slipped out the playroom door. I looked for a long moment at the closed door. My hand was covering my cheek and the kiss.

" 'Bye," I said to no onc.

"Come on," Mark said. He tugged at my arm. "It's better to forget about her as soon as possible." He spoke like a wise old man who had experienced these things so many times before that you just had to listen to him. He nodded his head. "It's better."

It took me quite a few days to forget about Stacy. Well, not exactly forget about her, but at least be able to get through the day without thinking about her too much or longing that much more for home.

One morning Mark woke me. "Get up!" he said. He was excited about something.

"What's up?"

"I gotta show you something." He ran off into the bathroom.

I got out of bed and followed him. I was still very sleepy. I walked with my eyes a little open and a little closed.

"Well?"

"You'll see." He grinned. "You'll see."

He looked around and then reached into his laundry bag. He pulled out his bear, Brownie.

"He escaped!"

"Shhhh." He put his finger to his lips.

"He escaped," I whispered.

"Last night," he said quietly. "He somehow got stuck under my pillow. They didn't collect him."

"Wow! That's terrific!"

"Shhh."

"That's terrific," I whispered.

I spent the rest of the day planning Doggie's escape. Night finally came. I anxiously waited on line for Doggie. Sister Clair came in.

"Sister Clair!" I shouted. I slapped my hand over my mouth. I was so surprised to see her, I had forgotten the rule of silence.

"That's all right, Jennings," she said. She put out her hand for me to come to her.

I ran from my place in line. I reached her and threw my arms around her waist. She leaned down and kissed the top of my head.

"Where have you been?" I asked.

"I was on retreat."

"What's retreat?"

"That's where sisters go to pray."

"Oh. That don't sound like much fun."

"Well, it's fun for me." She smiled.

She turned and unlocked the cabinet. She opened it and handed out the animals. She handed me Doggie.

I tucked him under my arm. As I passed Mark's bed, I

winked, and he winked back. I placed Doggie down on the bed and climbed in after him. We slid beneath the covers.

"I got a plan," I said.

He was anxious to know what it was, so I told him. He was as excited about it as I was. In case things didn't go very well, I gave him an extra kiss and a hug. I tucked him under my pillow and I lay back. Sister Clair came over to me.

"And how have you been?" she asked.

"All right, Sister."

"I heard you had a bad experience."

"I did?"

"At the Carpenters'."

"Oh, yeah. It was awful." I made a face.

"Sister Margaret isn't going to send any more children there. Listen, Jennings." She brushed the hair off my forehead. "I want to say good-bye to you."

"Good-bye!" I sat up. "Where're you going?"

"I've been reassigned. I'm going to teach at a girls' school in Queens."

"In Queens? Oh, gosh!" I fell back on my pillow.

"Now, don't be sad," she said. "You promised to be a good soldier for me."

"Oh, gosh. But I'll miss you, Sister."

"I know. I'll miss you, too," she said. "I'll pray every day for you. All right?"

"Well . . . it's not as good as seeing you."

"No." She laughed. "It's not as good as seeing me. But it's the best I can do."

"Oh, all right. If it's the best you can do." I sat back up and put my arms around her. I hugged her.

She hugged me back and then placed me back down on the pillow. She brought the blanket up to my chin.

"Where's Doggie?"

"Doggie?"

"Yes, Doggie. Remember the brown-and-white fuzzy thing you sleep with every night?"

"Oh, that Doggie!"

"Yes, that one." She laughed. "Where is he?"

"Oh, he's around."

"Around where?"

I lifted my pillow and took him out.

"What's he doing under there?"

"He was just sleeping."

She smiled. "You know, Jennings, if Doggie were under your pillow when I collect them later, I might miss him."

"Really?"

"Really! Maybe you ought to keep him tucked under your chin where he belongs," she said. She put him alongside me under the blanket.

"Sister, why do you do that?"

"Do what?"

"Cage the animals at night?"

"Well . . ." She looked up and out through the barred window before answering me. "We don't want to, Jennings, but we have to. You see, the animals that are given to us we have to take care of. If we didn't cage them up in one place, we might lose them, they might get hurt or damaged. It's not the best thing, but it's the only way we have to take care of them."

"But if somebody loved one of them," I asked, "wouldn't it be a good idea to let them have one? To keep, I mean?"

"Yes, it would be. But not everyone would love them and take care of them as you would. I wish I could give them all away tomorrow." She looked at me. There were tears in her eyes. "But I can't. My heart would break if I saw just one of those animals lying by the wayside uncared for, unloved. No, Jennings. It's better if we keep them together." She kissed my forehad and left.

I hugged Doggie and thought about what Sister Clair had said. I knew I couldn't take Doggie now. I knew he'd understand. "Doggie," I whispered, "if I ever do take you, I promise I'll take good care of you and love you."

I awoke to the sound of a thud. I popped my head out from the covers to see what had made the noise. The sun was just starting to come up over the building across the courtyard, so I knew it was too early to get up. The thud was the boy in the next bed. He had fallen out. He was just getting to his feet and rubbing his head when I thought of Doggie. He was gone! I looked at the other sleeping kids; their animals were gone too. I pulled the cover back over me and snuggled to my pillow. Suddenly I sat up and lifted my pillow. There was Doggie, looking up at me. A note was attached to him. I took it off and read it:

Dear Jennings,

When I said praying for you was the best I could do, I was wrong. Let Doggie out once in a while for air. Most of all, be good to him. Our kind of animals need lots of love.

Forever in my prayers,

Sister Clair

I hugged Doggie and put him under my pillow.

Each morning Mark and I put our friends in our laundry bags. At night we took them to bed. We shared a secret that somehow made us a little different from the other kids. It made us a little closer.

The weather was getting very cold. Most of the kids stayed in the dayroom. Sister Frances told us it was Wednesday, the twenty-first of December, and Christ's birthday was just four days away. She gave us some paper and paste and scissors to make some cutouts for the blackboard. Mark was making a snowflake, while I was making an angel. I was telling Mark how Christmas was on the outside.

"Whatcha doing?" Butch asked.

"Making cutouts," I said.

"That's kid stuff."

"Yeah, we know," Mark said, "we're kids."

"Whatcha wanna go and make that junk for?"

"It's not junk! It's angels and snowflakes, for Christmas."

"It's junk!"

"You sound like Scrooge," I said.

"Who?"

"Ebenezer Scrooge. You know, Scrooge, from the story."

"No. Who's he?"

"He's the guy who hated Christmas. Didn't you ever hear of him?"

Butch shook his head no. So did Mark.

"Well, last year a sister from my school told us a story. . . . Let's see. I can't think of the name of it. . . . Uh. 'A Christmas Carol,' " I remembered. "It was all about this guy who hated Christmas."

"Will you tell us the story?" Mark asked.

"Yeah! Will ya?" Butch sat down.

"Sure. Sure, I will."

I told the story the best I could. As I talked, more and more kids began to gather around. Some of those who knew the story helped me in the parts I got stuck on. But the story went along very well. Soon every kid in the room was sitting on the floor or in chairs or on the tables, listening to the story. Their wide eyes bulged at the parts of the different ghosts. When the story was finished, everyone drifted off. Mark and I returned to our cutouts. Butch joined us.

We talked about Christmas at the home. They told me the nuns sing a lot and put the baby Jesus in his manger.

"Do we get a Christmas tree?" I asked.

"No. No tree. The sisters don't like trees, I guess," Mark said.

"Do we get presents?"

Both Mark and Butch shook their heads no.

"Well, that's okay," I said. "I didn't always get a present on the outside either. My mom didn't always have enough money for presents."

"I never got a present," Mark said.

58

"Never?"

Mark shook his head. "Some lifers got presents. When they were little, if they were out during Christmas, they got some. Did you ever get a present, Butch?"

"Yeah. I got one a long time ago, when I was real little."

"What was it?"

"Oh. It wasn't anything special."

"What?"

"It was a . . . uh . . . a panda bear."

"Oh, yeah!" Mark said. "Where is it? What happened to it?"

"Oh, it's gone. The lady who gived it to me took it back. She said she'd save it for me if'n I ever went back."

"Jennings," a nun called me from the doorway.

A cold chill ran all over me. I looked at both Butch and Mark.

"Jennings Burch!" she called again.

Oh, gosh, not another Carpenters'. I put down my angel and got to my feet. I approached the nun. She took me from the room.

"Am I being lent out?" I asked.

"I don't know, son. I was only told to fetch you."

"Oh, gosh. I don't want to go away again. I want to stay here." I felt the stinging in my nose.

She opened the office door and there was Mom.

"Mom!" I cried.

I ran into her open arms. She kissed and hugged me. I cried uncontrollably.

"Shhhh, dear. I'm here now, I'm here now."

I couldn't talk. I tried, but I couldn't. I leaned into her and cried. She smelled like Mom. It was really Mom.

"Where were you?" I yelled at her through my tears. I clenched my fist and hit her.

"Don't hit your mother!" Sister Margaret snapped.

I fell back into Mom and cried harder. "I'm sorry, I'm sorry."

"Shhhh, Jennings. Don't cry anymore." She hugged me and kissed my forehead. "Come on, now. Stop crying," she said.

After a few minutes, to calm myself I asked, "Mom, can we take Mark home with us?"

"Mark? Who's Mark?"

"Don't be foolish, Jennings," Sister Margaret said. "Go now, and get your things."

"Mark is my friend. He lives here. Can we take him home, can we?"

"What will his mother say?"

"He don't got no mother. He's a lifer. An orphan. Can we take him?"

"Jennings, I'm sorry. I just can't take—"

"Certainly she can't!" Sister Margaret stood up. She was mad. "Now, that's enough of that! Go and get your things!" She pointed toward the door. "Now!"

"But—"

"No buts. Now!"

"Oh, gosh!" I whined. I left the office.

I went into the dormitory and packed up all my things, including Doggie. I left through the rear door for the dayroom.

Mark and Butch were still at the table working on their cutouts. I approached them.

Butch looked up and saw me first. "Are you going?" he asked.

"Yes!" I said.

"Home?" Mark asked.

I nodded my head yes.

Butch crumpled up the cutout he was making and pushed himself away from the table. " 'Bye," he said quietly. He walked over to the glass doors and pushed them open.

" 'Bye," I whispered.

I turned over the angel I was making. I wrote on the back of it. "To my friend, Mark. From Jennings and Doggie." He stopped working on his snowflake and took it. As he looked down at it, a single tear splashed off the back of his hand.

"Thank you," he said.

"I'll miss you, Mark."

I offered him my hand and he took it. He never took his eyes off his present. He just reached across his body toward his shoulder and met my hand. He shook my hand and then pushed his glasses back on his nose.

I walked over to the dayroom door and opened it.

"Wait!" he cried out. "Don't leave me! Please don't leave me!" He rushed at me and grabbed my arm.

I threw my arms around him.

He cried into my shoulder. "Don't leave me. Please don't leave me."

He shook so hard I could hardly hold him. The hundred-year-old nun came over to us and took Mark from me. He buried his face against her and cried. I slipped through the dayroom door for home.

5

I crossed my legs on the shiny wicker-covered subway seat and leaned heavily into Mom's arm. I held Doggie under my chin and thought of Mark. He couldn't know it hurt as much to leave someone there as it did to be left.

"Mom?" I shouted over the clatter of the train noises.

"Yes?"

"Why did you leave me there? Why didn't you come back for me?"

"I couldn't, dear. I was sick."

"Did you throw up and everything?"

"No," she said, "it wasn't that kind of sickness."

"What kind was it?"

"Well, it was a different kind."

"Sister Clair said you were at a rest home, resting. Were you tired, Mom?"

"Yes, dear, I was. I was very tired."

"Were you tired of me?"

"No." She hugged me. "I wasn't tired of you. I was tired of trying to do too many things at once. Can you understand that?"

"Uh-hum. Sister Clair said you were worried about Jerome and things like that."

Mom didn't say anything. She just kept looking out the side window into the blackness of the tunnel.

"Mom?"

"Yes, dear?"

"You're not tired anymore, are you?"

"No, dear, I'm not tired anymore. I promise I won't leave you again."

"You promise?"

"Yes, dear, I promise."

I leaned into her. "Hey, Mom?"

"Yes?"

"Did everybody stay at a home like me?"

"No. Only you and Larry were in homes."

"What about Walter and George?"

"They stayed with a nice family through the church."

"They stayed in a church?"

"No." She laughed. "The church made arrangements for them to stay with a nice family. They'll be home tomorrow."

"And Larry? Will he be home tomorrow, too?"

"He's home already. He's minding Gene."

"Oh, great! I really miss him."

We changed trains at Fourteenth Street. Mom bought me a Little Lulu comic book and a Sky Bar. I loved Sky Bars— they're like having a box of those fancy chocolates all in one little row. Each section tastes better than the last.

I read my comic book to Doggie and shared my Sky Bar with him. Mom read a magazine.

I found myself drifting off, thinking about Mark. I wondered if he had ever read a comic book. There were none at the home. I wondered if he ever rode in a subway or an automobile. I guess he never had a Sky Bar either.

"Is Jerome ever going to come home and go to the movies with me?"

"I don't know, dear. I hope so."

"When you visit him next time, can I go?"

"No, I'm afraid not. They don't allow children under twelve to visit hospitals."

"Why not?"

"Well, I think they're afraid you might get germs and get sick."

"And if you're over twelve, you can't get germs?"

"Not as easily as you can when you're under twelve. Let's not talk about it anymore," she said. "Let's just keep on praying for him. All right?"

"All right," I said.

We came up from the subway at 188th Street and the Grand Concourse. My first glimpse of the only world I had ever known until three very long months ago was the Loew's Paradise Theater. *The Great Lover*, with Bob Hope and Rhonda Fleming, was on the marquee.

We began our two-block walk down 188th Street for home. I couldn't believe how small everything had gotten. The cobblestone road seemed so much narrower now than I had remembered.

We passed Krum's Candy, a big ice-cream parlor and candy store. All the kids from the neighborhood would go there for a two-cent plain. If you were there with your mother or father and they bought ice cream, they'd give you the two-cent plain for nothing. That was a good deal. We passed Lutz's shoe-repair shop at the corner. We crossed Valentine Avenue to my block.

The street was unusually quiet. The street was normally filled with lots of people, lots of kids. Maybe it was the cold weather?

Mom pushed open the heavy black iron door with the glass panel. The hallway of number 267 smelled like pine soap. Mr. Zabo, the super, mopped the hallways every day with pine soap. It smelled good. We climbed the three flights of stairs to apartment thirty-two. I was home.

"Larry!" Mom shouted.

She was angry. The front hall was filled with towels and toilet paper and everything that was supposed to be in the bathroom. Gene was sitting in the middle of it, smiling. Gene was a scrawny little kid who hardly ever talked. His hair was blondish and looked a lot like shredded wheat. He was four years old and slept almost all the time.

"Larry!" Mom shouted again. "Where are you?"

"I'm coming," he shouted back. He came running into the hall and slipped on a misplaced bar of soap. He crashed to the floor and bumped his head. His glasses flew off his face. Gene started to laugh, but Larry started to cry.

"It serves you right," Mom said. "God punished you for not taking better care of your brother."

He got to his feet, rubbing his head. He picked up his glasses and put them on. Larry was very much like me, except he was older, eleven, taller and stronger. He had as many freckles as I did, and his hair was as red as mine. I think without his glasses we looked pretty much like twins.

"Jennings!" he shouted as he got his first good look at me. Larry couldn't see anything without his glasses on.

"Hi. How've you been?" I asked.

We clasped hands. He sniffled back his tears and rubbed his head again.

"Hey! I got something to show you," he said.

"Not until you clean up this mess," Mom said.

"Oh, Ma! Do I have to?"

"Yes!"

"Come on, I'll help you," I said.

Larry and I cleaned up the mess while Mom took Gene into her bedroom for a nap.

"So where were you?" I asked.

"I first stayed at a home. Ugh! It was awful. Scary." He made a face. "Then I stayed with Mrs. Keys. She gave me a present. She was nice."

"What did you get?"

"I can't tell you. That's what I got to show you."

We got the last of the bathroom things back into the bathroom. We crossed through the living room into the back bedroom. All the rooms in our apartment, except the back bedroom, were off the front hall—the kitchen, living room, bathroom, and Mom's bedroom.

"Whatcha got?" I asked.

"A bugle." He held it up.

It was all tarnished and dented. He tried to blow a few notes, but all he got were fat cheeks and some squeaks.

"I gotta practice," he said.

I showed him Doggie and told him about the Home of the Angels. I told him about the Carpenters and about Mark.

"You mean he ain't never going to leave the home? Never, ever?"

I shook my head no.

"Wow! That's awful."

Larry told me about his stay with Mrs. Keys. He told me he could eat anything he wanted, anytime he wanted.

"And milk, too," he added. "As much as I wanted." He slipped into thinking about something, probably food. "I kinda would have liked to stay there," he said.

"And not come back?"

"Yeah. I kinda would have liked that."

"But wouldn't you miss not being here anymore?"

"No. I don't like George or Walter, and they don't like me. They're always pushing me around and calling me names. And Mom don't like me, either."

"She does so."

"Says you."

He lay across the bed, staring up at the ceiling. He sounded very unhappy. I looked over toward the window. I could see across the alleyway to another building. Some of the lights were lit. I thought about the barred windows at the Home of the Angels. I thought about Mark and about Larry. Both of them were unhappy and both of them were wishing they were someplace else.

I awoke to shouts coming from the kitchen.

"What's up?" Larry asked. He squinted his eyes and felt around the floor for his glasses.

"I think George and Walter are home."

"Oh, darn." He moaned.

George and Walter were fighting with Mom. They were angry about living someplace else while Mom was resting.

George and Walter looked very much alike. Both of them were tall and both of them had black hair. George had a lot of pimples on his face, and he was skinnier. Walter had dark-rimmed glasses and smooth skin.

"How could I leave you home by yourselves?" Mom asked them.

"Easy! Just do it. Leave us here, that's all," Walter snarled.

"And what would you eat? How would you take care of yourselves?"

"We don't eat all that much now to worry about it," George said.

"And I take care of myself anyway," Walter added.

"You? Take care of yourself?" George laughed at Walter. "You couldn't take care of garbage without Mom around to help you."

"I could so," Walter growled back. "I do more around here than you do."

"Says you."

"Now, stop it!" Mom yelled. "I don't understand you kids. I try to do the best I can. I put you where you can continue with your school . . . this is what I get for it."

"Well, your best isn't all that good," Walter said.

"Look who's talking. You sure get everything you want," George said. He got to his feet. "I'm going out."

"Yeah, run out! You always do!" Walter yelled at George as he left the kitchen.

George pushed past me. "Hi," he mumbled.

"Hi."

The door slammed. Mom started to cry.

"Now look what you did!" I snapped at Walter. "You made Mom cry."

"I didn't do anything. George did. For Christ's sake, you can't say anything around here without . . ." He broke off and stormed out of the kitchen.

"Don't cry, Mom," I said.

"I'm not crying." She wiped her tears on a handkerchief she pulled from her pocket. "I'm not crying." She got up and lit the stove under the coffeepot. "I have to go to St. Vincent's this morning," she sighed. "I have to see if we can get a food basket for Christmas."

"Can I go?" Larry asked as he came into the kitchen.

"No. I want you to stay here and mind Gene. I'll take Jennings with me. He'll help me carry whatever we get."

"Oh, darn! Why do I always have to mind Gene? Why can't Walter or George do it?"

"Walter has to study and George's not here."

"Oh, darn!" He pouted. He stomped out of the kitchen.

"Lift your feet!" she called after the clomping sound going down the hallway.

Mom and I returned from St. Vincent's about one in the afternoon. We got a turkey and a basket of vegetables, but no toys. We came into the apartment. Larry was standing in the living room with his arms outstretched. He was crying. As soon as Larry spotted Mom, he ran to her.

"What's going on?" she asked.

"Nothing," Walter said. "He wouldn't clean the kitchen, so I punished him."

"I'll do the punishing around here," she said. "Not you!"

"I was only trying to teach the dumb ox how to do what he's told. That's all."

"Well, I'll teach him anything he needs to know. And stop calling him a dumb ox!"

She gave Larry a hug. "Now, go and clean up the kitchen," she said.

"Do I have to?" he whined.

"Yes. Don't you want to help your mother?"

"Oh, darn! Why do I always have to do everything around here?" He stomped off into the kitchen.

I followed him with the basket of vegetables. "I'll help you," I said.

"Did we get any toys?"

"No. They didn't have any left."

"Oh, darn. We never get any toys. I wish I was . . ." He broke off.

"Where's George?" Mom asked as she came into the kitchen with the turkey.

"Where do you think?" Walter answered sarcastically.

"He's out," Larry said. "Him and Walter were fighting again."

"About what?"

"Nothing! They always fight about nothing."

Mom took Gene into her bedroom for a nap. Larry went into the back bedroom to read a comic book. I went into the living room to where Walter was studying.

"Walter?" I whispered. I knew better than to talk loud when he was studying.

"What?"

"Uh . . . do you think Mom would let me sing at midnight Mass?"

"Why not?"

I was surprised at his answer. I thought for sure he would yell at me for bothering him. "Uh . . . that's great," I said.

"But it's not up to her. It's up to Sister Liviticus."

"Oh. Do you think Sister Liviticus will let me?"

"If you wait about half an hour, I'll go to the convent with you and we'll find out," he said. "I want to sing too."

"All right," I said. "I'll wait downstairs for you." I left.

Walter and I were the only two of the family in the choir. George used to be, but now that he's in high school he doesn't have time. Larry never liked the choir. He was an altar boy once, but they fired him. He was carrying everything for the altar one day when he tripped. And Gene of course is too little.

"So, how you been?" George interrupted my thoughts. He sat down beside me on the front step. He lit a cigarette.

George smoked Luckies. Even though he was only fifteen, Mom said he was the man of the house and could smoke if he wanted to.

"Mom is looking for you," I told him.

"Mom's always looking for me. Whatcha doing here? It's cold out."

"I'm waiting for Walter."

"Okay. I'll see you." He got up.

"No. Don't go," I said. "He won't be here for a while."

He sat back down. "Were you with a family or in a home?" he asked.

"In a home."

"How was it?"

"It was okay. Once you learn the rules, it ain't so bad."

"What rules?"

"Oh, like don't talk to nobody after the clicker sounds, and remember your number. Things like that."

"That's tough, kid."

"Hey, George! How come you and Walter fight all the time?"

"He's a mama's boy and I don't like it. She backs him up all the time. Right or wrong, she backs him up. It ain't fair."

"Isn't it because he's smart?"

"Smart ain't got nothing to do with it. I'm just as smart as him, and so are you. But we don't get the books and stuff he gets. Whatever he needs for school, he gets!" He got to his feet. "He'll get a book before you eat, kid!" He walked off.

I watched him walk down 188th Street and turn onto Tiebout Avenue. He sounded as unhappy as Larry did.

Walter came out of the building and we walked up the street together.

"I just saw George," I said.

"So?"

"How come you and him don't get along?"

"He's a bum, like the old man."

"What old man?"

"Never mind. Just take my word for it, he's a bum."

"But . . . I like him . . . sometimes."

"Well, I don't! All the time!"

We stopped talking. He looked like he was gonna get mad, so I let it go. I had to skip along to keep up with him. He was so much taller, I had to take a whole lot of steps to just one of his.

Sister Liviticus gave us permission to sing. She told us to be at practice in the morning. I was excited. I loved singing in the choir, especially at midnight Mass.

On Christmas Eve, George and Larry went out to try to find us a Christmas tree. We got our tree after the Christmas-tree man was sure he wasn't going to sell any more. Then he would throw them away. If you caught the one he threw, it was yours. Mom always sent George or Larry for the tree because they were the strongest. Whenever they went together, we would get a really good one.

Sister Liviticus wanted everyone at church early to go through the moves once more, before Mass. After the practice, we all waited for Mass to begin. I saw Mom near the front. She waved to me and I waved back. The altar was beautiful. All the candles were lit and there were lots of red flowers with red bows on them. There was a Nativity set up on one side of the altar, but the manger was empty. They didn't bring the baby Jesus to his manger until midnight.

Finally the Mass started. We filed out in our black-and-white outfits with stiff collars. We all wore giant red bows and carried lighted candles. It looked beautiful. As I marched in the procession, I thought about Mark. I wished he could be here. Sister Justine, the principal, brought up the baby Jesus and laid him in the manger. The choir sang like angels, and chills ran all over me.

When we got up to the choir loft, I looked down to the manger and the baby Jesus, and I whispered, "Merry Christmas, Mark."

Snow started falling as we walked up the long hill toward home. We walked with a crowd of our neighbors. Everyone was excited about the snow and about how beautiful the Mass was.

We got home to find George and Larry had gotten us a really big tree. It almost looked like one you might buy if you had the money. We decorated the tree together. Mom and Gene did the bottom part. Larry and I did the middle. George and Walter did the top. They argued about who was going to put the star on top, and of course, Walter won.

Mom didn't have very much money for presents, so she bought Gene a string of four ducks, and a Monopoly game for the rest of us. Nobody but Gene liked the ducks. All we heard, until he broke them, was quack, quack, quack. It nearly drove everyone crazy.

Christmas gave way to New Year's and to school. I was anxious to get back to see my friends. Most of all, I wanted to see Sister Ann Charles, my teacher.

Our second-grade classroom was in total disorder. Spitballs and airplanes were flying everywhere. Many of the kids were showing off some of the things they had gotten for Christmas. It was good to be back.

Sister Ann Charles came into the room and went straight to her desk. A warm feeling came over me at the sight of her. The last of the paper planes landed and the kids took their seats.

Sister Ann Charles was tall and thin. Her face was smooth and soft. She had dark eyebrows that bent over the top of her wide eyes, making them seem larger than they actually were. She had dimples like Sister Clair's. She looked a little like her.

We said our morning prayers and the Pledge of Allegiance. We no sooner ended when Sister Ann Charles called my name.

"Jennings."

A cold chill froze me. The sound of the clicker ran through my mind and I couldn't move.

"Jennings? What's the matter?"

I couldn't speak. The calling of my name brought back all the memories of the home in one great wave. She got to her feet quickly and came over to me. She saw both the fear in my face and the tears in my eyes. She hugged me. I pressed my face into her and cried.

"Shhh," she whispered. "Don't be frightened."

I cried hard as she held me. Nobody in the room laughed. They sat silently in their seats. Perhaps I frightened them.

"You're not in an institution anymore," she said. "You're home now, with your friends. We care about you."

"I'm sorry, Sister."

"Don't be sorry. We understand." She gave me her handkerchief.

I wiped my eyes and blew my nose. I handed it back to her.

"No, you keep that," she said.

She went back to her desk and picked up an envelope. She brought it to me. "Give this to your mother for me, will you?"

"Yes, Sister."

"Are you all right now?" she asked.

"Yes, Sister."

I tucked the envelope into my pocket. As the day moved on, I realized I had missed a lot of school, and they had learned bunches of new things. There wasn't anything I understood. Before the home, I just went to school and it was fun. I got one hundred on almost every test I took, and I didn't think anything about it. Now it was different. I listened to the questions that were asked and didn't know any of the answers. I was lost.

That evening I found out what the note said. I had missed

too much of the school year and would be left back. Larry got the same kind of note from his teacher.

"Now everyone's gonna call me a dumb ox," he cried.

"No, they won't," Mom said.

I was a little afraid of the same thing, but I didn't say it. I was sorry I wouldn't be going into the third grade with all my friends, but I wasn't sorry I would be staying with Sister Ann Charles. I'd see my friends after school and at lunchtime.

For the rest of the term I was made a monitor. I didn't take part in any of the exams or other schoolwork. I erased the blackboards and slapped the erasers. I handed out books and helped Sister. It was fun being her helper, even though some of the kids were calling me teacher's pet.

Winter turned into spring, and with it April, and my ninth birthday. Mom bought me a coloring book and a box of forty-eight crayons. I loved coloring, and so did Larry. I shared my coloring book with him.

On the last day of class we said good-bye to some of the kids who would be going away for summer vacations with their families. Sister Ann Charles spoke to us.

"Children, as most of you might already know from your parents, or from the radio, there is a war going on in Korea. War is a very bad thing. People get hurt and die. Innocent civilians as well as soldiers. We have to pray for all of them."

"Yes, Sister," we said in unison.

"So often when war happens," she said, "many children lose their families and their homes. These children have no place to go and no one to care for them."

As she spoke about the children, I thought back to the Home of the Angels and Mark. I knew what she was talking about. I wanted to tell Sister you didn't need a war to find children like that, there were a whole bunch of them somewhere in Brooklyn.

"Now, children," she was saying as my mind returned to the room, "as you all know, I am a Maryknoll Sister. I have been trained to help and care for children in all parts of the world, especially where there are no sisters, or where there is trouble. In a few days I am leaving for South Korea to try to help with the little children who need me.''

I couldn't believe my ears. I stared at Sister Ann Charles. Some of the kids began to cry. I was in shock. She looked directly at me as she spoke. I think she knew my heart was breaking, but there wasn't anything she could do about it.

"Would you pray for me and all those homeless children?'' she asked. She never took her eyes from me.

I could barely see her through the blur in my eyes. I was losing Sister Ann Charles.

I hugged her good-bye, as did all the other kids. She held me for a long time.

"Jennings,'' she whispered, "please don't be too angry with me. I'll always love you and pray for you.''

The pain I felt the day I left Doggie at the home and had to go alone to the Carpenters' returned to my throat. I pressed it as hard as I could, but it stayed. I believed I was crying on the inside. I believed the tears were running down my throat.

On Friday, June 23, 1950, I looked back from the doorway of the second-grade classroom at my friend and never saw her again.

George passed all his exams at Cardinal Hayes High School and would be a sophomore next year. Walter graduated with honors and won a scholarship to St. Regis High School. Larry and I were left back.

Now that Sister Ann Charles was gone, I hated the idea of not going on with the others to the third grade. I felt stupid and alone. Larry and I palled around together almost all the time. We never spoke about it, but we both felt the same way, dumb.

Every day Larry and I went up to St. James Park to play. We stayed until we heard the church bells at six. Then we started for home. Mom wanted us in about six for supper, and the bells were our alarm clock.

One particular day Larry and I came in from the park to find a nun in our kitchen.

"What's she doing here?" he asked.

I shrugged my shoulders.

"Hello," she said. "Who are you?"

"Uh . . . I'm Larry and that's Jennings. Who are you?"

"I'm Sister Mercedes. I'm here to take care of your mother."

"Mom! What's wrong with Mom?" Larry asked.

"Quiet now or you'll wake her."

"What's wrong with Mom?" I whispered.

"She's ill, very ill."

"Oh, boy!" Larry said. "Here we go again." He stomped off down the hall.

"What's wrong with her?" I asked again.

"I don't know, but for one thing, she doesn't eat enough. She gives all the food to you kids. She goes for days without eating. That's no good."

I was dumbfounded. I didn't know Mom didn't eat. It's true I hardly ever saw her eat, but I thought she ate at work or someplace. "Are you sure?" I asked.

"I'm sure!" she snapped.

"Uh . . . do you think she'll, uh . . . have to go someplace to rest?"

"I don't know. The doctor will be here soon. Now, get along with you and wash up for dinner. And don't make a mess!"

"Oh, gosh!" I followed Larry into the back bedroom.

He had all his things scattered all over the bed, his bottle-cap collection, his baseball cards, most of his comics, and his bugle.

"What are you doing?"

"I'm packing! I'm not going to be surprised like I was last time. I'm gonna be ready."

"Ready? Ready for what?"

"You know. You know as well as I do."

I did know. But I didn't want to think about it.

76

"But Mom promised!" I said.

"Yeah, well . . . she promised me a bike for every birthday I can remember. I never got one."

"Oh, gosh!" I said. I fell back on the bed in the only empty spot Larry left for falling back on. I pulled Doggie from the side of the bed and hugged him.

Two days later Larry left. George and Walter had already gone to stay with one of Mom's brothers. They didn't want any of the little kids who would cause them any trouble, so they didn't want Gene or Larry or me. Gene went to a neighbor's.

I watched Larry leave with a strange lady. He cried as he tucked his bugle under his arm. He pushed his glasses back on his nose the way Mark used to do. We said good-bye.

A short time later a man came for me. He had gray hair and a leathery sort of face. He was wearing a brown sweater and a hat. He took my laundry bag and put it into the backseat of his car. He put Doggie and me in the front. We drove off.

I sat quietly. As much as I missed Mark and wanted to see him again, I was mixed up about my feelings of going away again. I wondered if Mark got any taller or fatter. I wondered if Butch was still the toughest kid there. I asked the man how Mark was, but he didn't know. He said he was only a driver and didn't know any of the kids.

We pulled up in front of a large white house with a green screened-in porch.

"Here we are," he said.

"But . . . but . . . this isn't the Home of the Angels?"

"No," he said, "this is St. Teresa's."

My heart sank. A thousand thoughts ran through my mind. I hadn't ever thought I might be going to some other home.

I cradled Doggie in my arms and got out of the car. A numbness came over me as I climbed the rickety front steps of this strange new place. I was frightened.

6

The driver left Doggie and me on the porch side of the screen door. I watched him leave. I regripped my laundry bag and slung it over my shoulder. I pushed open the heavy front door.

The room smelled musty and old. I stood in the middle of the dark front hall and listened to the door creak as it closed behind me. There were no other sounds. There were three doors off the hall, and a twisting staircase. Halfway up the carpeted stairs was a small round window that let in a long stream of sunlight. It ended at my feet. I was afraid to move any farther. I heard a squeak from the stairs. Someone was coming down.

"Jennings Burch?" a cold and distant voice asked as the figure reached the window and stopped.

I couldn't speak.

"Are you Jennings Burch?" she asked. There was annoyance in her voice as she started down the last section of steps.

"Yes, ma'am."

"Yes, Sister!" she snapped. "Follow me."

She brushed past me and pushed open one of the three doors. I followed her.

"What do you have there?" she asked from over her shoulder.

"Well, I got a laundry bag with some things—"

"I don't mean the bag."

"Oh! This is Doggie. He's my friend." I held him up to her back.

"What do you intend to do with it?"

"Uh . . . nothing. He's just my friend. That's all."

She quickened her pace through the maze of hallways. I quickened mine. She stopped and opened the door to a dormitory. We went in.

The room looked familiar. There were two rows of metal beds, one on each side of the room. A small chest separated each of them. At the far end was a bathroom. The light wasn't on, but I could see the tiles in the dark shadows. The windows were large and barred.

She led me to bed number seventeen and pointed to the cabinet alongside of it. "Put that thing in there and leave it there!" she ordered. "Under no circumstances are you to sleep with it. Do you understand me?"

I fought back the tears as I placed my little friend in this wooden chamber.

"Do you understand?" she shouted.

I jumped. I nodded my head to show I understood.

She slapped me hard across the face. "When I speak, I expect to be answered."

"Yes, Sister," I cried.

"Yes, what?"

"I understand," I said. I held my stinging face and wiped my eyes and nose on my sleeve.

Sister Frances, at the Home of the Angels, was nice compared to this sister. She was tall and thin. Her face was bright red, with a vein that ran up from her temple to her forehead. I was sure the headpiece surrounding her face was the cause of her redness. She talked with her teeth clenched tightly together. She frightened me.

She led me from the dormitory to a playroom, pushed me through the door, and closed it behind me. The room was empty. I sat near the door on one of the many small wooden chairs scattered all around the room. The feeling of wanting to cry was overwhelming, but I fought it off. I swallowed hard and forced my eyes wide open.

The room was large and bright. There were two patched-up screen doors that could open out onto a grassless yard. Every so often a swirl of wind would lift a small puff of dust off the yard and carry it away.

There were four long tables, two on each side of the room. The shelves along each wall were filled with games and playthings. The floor was wooden and well worn. I heard a strange sound coming from the hallway. It was low at first, but then it grew louder. I couldn't figure out what it was. It kept getting louder and louder. It pulsated like a heartbeat. Suddenly I knew what it was. It was the thunderous steps of all the kids marching down the hallway. The door opened and the kids began to file in. The uniform line turned to chaos. Most of them ran for the screen doors, throwing them open. They dashed out into the grassless yard, raising whole clouds of dust. A few kids took games from the shelves to play with on the tables. I stayed where I was. I hadn't been noticed and I was glad. I stayed in the safety of the chair for the entire afternoon. I tried to figure out who might be number sixteen. Naturally, I picked the kid with the biggest and the funniest-looking ears.

The sun began to dip down below some of the trees on the far side of the play yard.

"All right, children, dinnertime!" a nun called out. She slapped her hands together.

I couldn't believe my ears: she actually sounded nice. This one was a fat roly-poly nun with bright red cheeks and a sweet smile.

As the kids started forming lines, I approached her.

"Sister?" I spoke with caution.

"Yes," she said. She smiled.

"Uh . . . I'm new here, Sister. I don't know where I'm supposed to be."

"Well, we'll take care of that. What's your number?"

"Seventeen."

"Stevie! You're number sixteen, aren't you?" she asked one of the boys on line.

"Yes, Sister Ann Catherine."

"There, son. Stand behind Stevie," she told me. "And, Stevie!" She recalled the boy. "Would you see that this boy is okay?"

"Yes, Sister."

"What's your name?" she asked.

"Jennings."

"What's your first name?"

"That is my first name, Sister."

"All right, Jennings, enjoy your dinner."

Gosh! She sure sounded nice. I stood behind Stevie. He didn't have big funny ears. In fact, his ears were kind of normal. He was about a half foot taller than me, and skinny. He had dirty-blond hair that stuck straight up, sort of like a brush. Sister Ann Catherine clapped her hands together for the second time, and the line started moving. It crossed my mind to tell her about the little clicker, but then I thought better of it. I really hated that little clicker.

The dining-room tables were laid out in long rows. There were about a dozen kids at each table, boys on one side of the room and girls on the other.

I played with a boiled frankfurter and some stiff waxlike beans. By the looks on the faces of the other kids and the unfinished food in front of them, it was obvious that everyone shared a dislike for the tasteless supper. My eyes met those of the boy across from me. He had red hair that stuck up like a rooster and two large front teeth. He smiled. I smiled back. He quickly lost his smile and looked in both directions for the whereabouts of the nuns. When he realized he was safe, he smiled again. His actions told me the rules were the same, here, no smiling in the dining room.

We were marched back to the playroom by the nun with

the cold eyes and the popping veins. I took a seat at one of the tables near the doorway and watched. None of the kids went into the yard this time. I think maybe the door was locked. I kept my eyes on Stevie. I wasn't sure what the next move would be, and I didn't want to get into any trouble. I figured watching him and doing whatever he did would be the safest thing.

"Look!" one of the kids yelled out. "A firefly!"

Many of the kids went over to the screen doors to look out. I stretched my neck up to try to see over them. I'd never seen a fly on fire before and was anxious to see one. I got up and slowly made my way around the side of the room toward the screen doors. I reached the group of kids with their hands cupped around their eyes and their faces pressed against the door. I tried to see over them.

"Fireflies!" the boy with the roosterlike hair said to me. He was waiting for a spot so he could see them too.

"I never saw a fly on fire," I said.

"They're not on fire," he laughed. "They just light up. That's all."

"Didn't ya ever see a firefly?" Stevie asked. He was standing behind me.

"No," I answered.

"Hey, move over!" He pushed some of the kids away from the door. "Look!" he said. He pointed to the spot he had just cleared for me.

I stepped up to the screen door and pressed my face against it. I cupped my hands around my eyes to adjust to the darkness. Suddenly I saw them. First a slight glow and then they went dark.

"Wow!" I said. "How do they do that?"

"They got bulbs in their tails," someone said.

"No dey don't, stupid," Stevie said. "Dey got some stuff on dere tails dat glows in the dark. Like dose statues, ya know."

"Oh, yeah. Those plastic statues. I know. Wow!" I said. I was held captive by the blinking lights.

"What's ya name?" Stevie asked.

"Jennings," I said into the screen door.

"What's ya first name?"

"That is my first name."

"Dat's a funny name," he said. By the way he said it, I'm sure he didn't mean to hurt my feelings. "My name is Stevie."

I came away from the door and shook his hand. "Yeah, I know. I heard Sister Ann Catherine call you Stevie."

"Are ya a lifer?" he asked.

"No, a part-timer."

"Yeah, me too. Are ya tired?"

"Yes."

"Come on. I'll take ya to the dorm."

I followed Stevie. When we reached the dormitory, he went to his cabinet and I went to mine. I reached in for my laundry bag to get my pajamas, but I found Doggie's nose instead. I crouched on the floor to talk to him.

"Hi, Doggie," I whispered.

I gave him time to answer.

"I'm sorry you have to be locked up in here." I kissed him and held his fur to my cheek.

"Don't let Sister Barbara catch ya wit him," Stevie said. He was standing behind me.

"Sister Barbara? Is she the one . . . ?"

He twisted up the corners of his mouth and nodded his head yes. I didn't even have to finish what I was saying; he knew whatever I was going to say was right.

"She's mean," he said. "Real mean." He left for the bathroom, and I followed.

The room looked very much like the one at the Home of the Angels. It had the same kind of numbered hooks and the same uncovered toilet bowls.

We washed and brushed. I was at my hook changing when Stevie pulled off his shirt. His back was scarred and torn.

Some of the cuts were new; they were still oozing blood. I cringed.

"What happened?"

"Nuttin," he said. He continued to change in silence.

I didn't ask again.

The lights were out and the room was quiet. Only a single lamp burned at the far end of the room at the night nun's desk. No one was there. I tried to adjust my eyes to the darkness of this new place, but I couldn't. I looked toward the window but saw nothing. The night sky was so dark, and there were no streetlamps outside. I heard someone cough and someone else sniffle. If I couldn't see, I thought, I'd listen. I heard someone crying.

I heard a sound I had never heard before. It was coming from outside. It was sort of like a whistle, a broken-up whistle. It must be some wild animal. I was frightened.

I sat up and looked around. There was still nothing but the single lamp burning, and no nun. I slipped from my bed to the floor. I opened my cabinet. It squeaked. I scrinched up my face and shut my eyes as I fully opened the door. I removed Doggie, reclosed the door, and got back into bed.

"Hi, Doggie," I whispered. "If I hid you at the Home of the Angels, I can hide you here." I kissed him.

I hugged him once or twice before sliding him under my pillow. I lay back and felt his nose. I wasn't frightened anymore.

Breakfast at St. Teresa's was an adventure. Each kid was served a metal cup of hot cocoa. It was much too hot to drink, so you had to let it cool. When it did, a thick film covered the top. The idea was to get the film off without spilling the cocoa on the white tablecloth. I watched some of the others, to see how they'd do it. They didn't. They just let it sit there and didn't bother to drink it at all. Stevie poked my arm.

"Watch!" he said with his eyes. I watched.

He took the spoon from his prunes and licked it off. Then

he held the spoon over the top of the cocoa. He gently lowered it. When he reached the bottom of the cup, he pulled it straight out. The spoon had the film wrapped all around it. He drank the cocoa. I smiled. I slapped my mouth and looked around. I was safe—nobody had seen me smile. I followed Stevie's silent instructions, and did the same with my spoon. It worked.

After breakfast the lifers went to class. The rest of us were marched into the playroom, where the screen doors were open. I walked across the grassless yard to a spot near a tree. I sat down. The yard was very wide and long. It was bounded on two sides by very tall trees and on the others by the building and a small creek. I sat by the tree watching the other kids run around. The boy with the rooster hair approached me.

"Hi, Jenix."

"Hi. It's Jennings," I said.

"Oh. Jennings. My name's Bobby, but everyone calls me Rooster." He laughed. "I guess I look like a rooster. Do you wanna play tag?"

"Okay."

I no sooner spoke than he hit me across the head.

"You're it," he shouted, and disappeared into a cloud of dust.

I sprang to my feet. I wasn't too sure who was playing, but it wasn't all that hard to figure out. Anyone who ran as I approached was playing. I chased after quite a few kids but couldn't catch anyone. Then I remembered what I used to do when I played with my brothers and couldn't catch any of them. I fell down. I didn't move. The laughter that first erupted quieted. A few of the boys approached me. I stayed still.

"Are you all right?" one of them asked.

I didn't answer. I lay motionless, my face toward the ground.

"Hey, kid, are you hurt?" another asked as he drew closer to me.

When he was within reach, I shot out my hand and struck his foot. "You're it!" I shouted, and sprang to my feet.

The whole yard broke into laughter. All but the boy I tagged, of course.

We played tag for quite some time. I didn't get tagged again, and I was glad. I knew the possum trick wouldn't work twice. The game began to peter out. Some of the kids drifted off to do other things. I sat by the tree. Stevie sat next to me.

"As soon as we catch our breat," he said, "we'll go 'n wash up. If we go into lunch like dis . . ." He raised his eyebrows. "Sister Barbara will kill us."

Our faces, hands, and arms were filthy. We had dark rings around out necks. We reached the sinks.

"Whatever ya do in this bat'room—" he started to say.

"Don't make a mess!" we said together, and then laughed.

"You been in many of dese homes?" he asked.

"Just one other. Home of the Angels in Brooklyn."

"I never been to dat one. Dis is my fifth. It ain't so bad as some others I been in."

"Are the rules any different here?" I asked.

"Naa. Dey're all the same. Keep ya mout' shut and don't pee in bed."

"I ain't done that in years."

"What are ya in for?" he asked.

"My mother's sick."

"Is she gonna die?"

"Uh . . . I don't think so. I hope not."

"Well, my mudder's dead. She died a long time ago, and my fadder, he's a drunken bum. He's da one who gived me dis." He whirled around and revealed his back to me. "He gets real drunk and beats me up. Da neighbors call da cops and dey take him away. Dey bring me to dese places. It ain't fair," he mumbled. "I gets da worst of it. I hate him."

86

"How long do you stay here?"

"Until they let him out. Den he comes 'n gets me. He promises he ain't gonna do it no more 'n den, wham! I'm right back in one of dese places. It ain't fair."

We finished washing and were wiping down the sinks when Stevie started talking to himself.

"One of dese days, he ain't gonna hit me no more. One of dese days, I'm gonna . . ." He didn't finish his words, but he nearly rubbed the porcelain off the sink, he rubbed so hard. He threw his towel from where he was standing and it landed on his hook.

"Pretty good!" I said. I threw my towel. It landed on the floor in front of me.

"How old are ya?" he asked.

"I'm nine."

"Well, I'm ten. I'm da toughest kid in here. If'n ya gots any trouble . . . see me!" He stuck his thumb in his chest to emphasize his last word.

Stevie was the Butch of St. Teresa's, but it didn't bother me. I liked him. He was angry and bitter about his father, but he was also sad and alone and hurt. I don't mean because he's in this place, we're all sad and alone being here, I mean because it's inside him. When we leave here, we won't be sad and alone no more. But, I think Stevie will be. What bothered me the most was the thought that Mom might die. I hadn't thought about it until Stevie said it. It scared me.

After lunch, Rooster, Stevie, and I went down by the creek to catch some frogs.

"Are there any alligators in here?" Rooster asked.

"A few," Stevie said. "But not too many. Mostly snakes."

"Snakes!" I jumped back from the edge of the creek.

"Dey're just little ones. Dey don't eat much."

"Oh, gosh," I said. "This place is crawling with wild animals. Just last night I heard one."

"Oh, yeah?" Rooster said. "What kind of animal?"

"I don't know, but he was a big one."

"What did he sound like?" Stevie asked.

"Well, let's see . . . it was like a whistle, but it was all broken up. Sorta like this." I made the sound as best I could.

Stevie started to laugh. So did Rooster.

"What's so funny?"

"Dat wasn't a wild animal," Stevie laughed. "Dat was a cricket!"

"A cricket? Like Jiminy Cricket?"

"Yeah. But dese ones ain't got no clothes on," Stevie said.

"Oh."

Stevie, Rooster, and I palled around together. Nobody spoke about friends, but that was okay with me. I remember how it felt when I left Mark. I didn't want to feel that way anymore. It hurt. Stevie taught Rooster and me how to climb trees without scraping our knees, and how to make a frog jump.

At night I took Doggie from the cabinet to bed with me. For the first few minutes, we would talk about the day and about how I felt. I loved Doggie so much. I needed him. One morning Doggie wasn't under my pillow, but in my arms. I quickly sat up and looked around. Sister Barbara wasn't there. I was safe. I jumped down from the bed and stuck him in the cabinet. I was about to leave for the bathroom to get dressed when Sister Ann Catherine danced past me, singing. She always danced and sang in the mornings. I listened to her song.

"Well, if I had a Doggie cute as him, I wouldn't sleep with him under my pillow. La dee da de da de dillo." She laughed.

She knew I had Doggie and she wasn't mad at me. That made me happy, but I had to be more careful. If Sister Barbara ever found him, she'd kill me. Worse than that, she might take him away from me.

I was in the yard sitting by the tree with Rooster after breakfast. We were waiting for Stevie.

"I'll go and find him," Rooster said.

"Okay."

Rooster walked off. He dragged his feet every step of the way just to raise as much dust as he could. We all did that when we crossed the yard; it was fun. As the dust began to settle, I saw Stevie coming from the house.

"Did you see Rooster?" I shouted.

He didn't answer me. He reached me and dropped down.

"Did you see Rooster? He went to look for you."

Again he didn't answer me.

"What's wrong?"

"Nuttin," he sighed. "Wanna run away?"

"Run away? Where?"

"I don't know. Anywhere."

"What's the matter, Stevie?"

"Dey told me my fadda was comin' for me today," he mumbled. "I ain't goin' wit him no more." He toyed with the ground between his feet. "I ain't gonna get hit no more." He got to his feet. "I'll see ya," he said as he started to walk away.

"Wait!" I scrambled to my feet. "Where you going?"

I caught up to him. There were tears on his cheeks.

"Stevie, where you going?"

"I'm leavin'. I'm goin' where no one will find me. Where no one can hurt me no more. I'll see ya."

"But . . . but . . . didn't you ask me to go with you?"

"Ah. I was jist talkin'. I gotta go by myself." He stopped in his tracks and I almost ran into him. "Hey, Jennings . . ." He paused to look at me. "I'll see ya." His eyes told me good-bye more than his words did. He turned and walked away alone.

I watched him walk into the trees. I stood watching the trees for a long time. The tops of them swayed gently in the morning breeze. Stevie was gone. I sat down where I was and stared at the trees.

It didn't matter whether you said the word "friend" or not. If you felt "friend," it was all the same. It hurt.

Rooster came back. He told me he couldn't find Stevie. I didn't tell him what had happened. I didn't tell him Stevie was gone. I told him I didn't feel very well and didn't feel much like playing. He left to play with someone else.

At lunch and dinner I stared at Stevie's empty chair. I wondered where he was and if he was afraid. I would be afraid, very afraid. I went right to bed after dinner. I took Doggie under the covers with me and hugged him. I didn't have to tell him Stevie was gone, he just sort of knew. I kissed him a few times and tucked him under my pillow. I fell asleep.

I was awakened in the middle of the night by someone lifting my pillow and removing Doggie. I opened my eyes, but it was too dark to see anything. Suddenly Doggie was placed into my arms and the hair on my forehead was brushed back. Somebody kissed me. I blinked my eyes into focus as the dark figure walked down the row of beds. It was Sister Ann Catherine.

In the days that followed, Rooster and I played together, but it wasn't the same. We both missed Stevie, but neither of us said anything. It was better that way. Sister Ann Catherine continued to give me Doggie in the middle of the night, and the kiss.

One morning Sister Barbara brought a new boy over to chair number sixteen and slammed him into it. His eyes were red. The dried tears on his cheeks were smeared and streaky. I guess he'd tried wiping them away with his dirty hands but couldn't. He sat perfectly still; he didn't move. I knew how he felt and wanted to say something to him, but I couldn't. Even if I could, what would I say? Everything is going to be all right? I didn't know if everything was going to be all right. I didn't know anything. Sister Barbara poured him hot cocoa. Before he realized it was in a metal cup, he lifted it to drink and burned his hand. He dropped the cup on the table, spilled the cocoa across the white tablecloth. I jumped to my feet.

"Sister! I spilled my cocoa!" I yelled. I moved my cup in front of the new boy.

Sister Barbara came at me like a wild animal. She slapped me hard across the ear and knocked me into the table. She grabbed my hair and pulled me over the chair. I fell to the floor. She grabbed the back of my shirt collar and dragged me toward the front of the room. As she dragged me across the uneven wooden floor, great and small splinters began ripping into all parts of my body. I screamed and cried, but the pain kept coming. She reached the front of the room and dropped me. She kicked me in the side, knocking my breath away. She opened a closet door and in one sweeping motion lifted me from the floor and dropped me in. She slammed the door.

In the dark black silence of the dining-room closet, I lay in one great heap of pain. I stayed as motionless as possible for what seemed forever. My face was pressed hard against the wooden floor. I felt moistness all over me. It could be sweat or blood, I wasn't sure. I began to feel around at my hurt body. Each time I touched a jagged piece of floor sticking from my body, I winced in pain. My pants were soaking wet, but not from blood. I had wet my pants. The pee began to burn some of the cuts on my legs. I tried to find some comfortable position, but I couldn't. No matter what I did, something else hurt. I closed my eyes and made believe I was hugging Doggie. His fur was soft and warm. He felt so good to be near. He was my friend and I loved him. I fell asleep.

I was awakened when someone tried to move me. The sharp pain shot across my side as a piece of wooden floor was pushed into me. I screamed.

"Shhhh, baby. Poor baby. You'll be all right," Sister Ann Catherine whispered.

She and a nurse lifted me onto a blanket or something. They carried me from the room.

I was taken to a room and placed down onto a soft bed, but it didn't matter. The splinters still worked their way deeper into me, and I cried. The nurse gave me a needle while Sister Ann Catherine sat alongside me and gently held my hand. The nurse began to cut away my clothes with scissors. Sleep closed over me like the dark closet.

I awoke the next morning. I was alone. The sun peered in through the window. I turned a little in the bed to relieve a pain in my shoulder, and there alongside me was Doggie.

"Oh, Doggie," I cried. I held him close against my face. "She hurt me, Doggie. She hurt me so much."

"Good morning, Jennings, how do you feel?" Sister Ann Catherine asked as she pushed open the door.

"I don't know, Sister." I wiped my eyes.

She sat down. "Someone is here to say hello to you. Do you feel up to it?"

"Yes, Sister."

"Peter," she called out.

The door pushed open and in came the boy who had spilled the cocoa. He came over to the bed and just stood there. His lip quivered as he tried to speak. He started to cry. Sister Ann Catherine pulled him down toward her and hugged him.

"He wanted to thank you for taking the blame, but he's upset right now."

"It's okay," I said. I reached over and took his dangling hand. "Hi, Peter."

"Hi," he said as he straightened up and wiped away his tears. "Thank you."

"Do you play checkers?" I asked.

He nodded his head yes.

"Good. Maybe we can play sometime."

"Well, not now. Jennings has to rest," Sister said. She took Peter to the door and let him out.

" 'Bye," he said as he left.

" 'Bye."

Sister Ann Catherine put medicine on some of the cuts and

rebandaged some of the others. She brought me some oatmeal and fed it to me. She gave Doggie a taste, and I laughed.

She came every day to fix the bandages and to read to me. Peter and Rooster came to play checkers and cards with me. No one at all mentioned Sister Barbara's name to me. I hated her.

I stayed in the little hospital for six days. On the morning of the seventh day the nurse laid some clothes on the bed and told me to put them on. I did. The pants and shirt were both light brown. They were kind of nice. A lot better than my old stuff. I sat at the edge of the bed.

"You can go now, Jennings," she said.

"Go? Go where?"

"Back. Back to the dining room to have breakfast. You're all right now, you know."

I was frightened. I didn't want to go back. I didn't ever want to see Sister Barbara again.

"Can't I stay here?"

"No, dear. This room is for sick people. Go and have a nice breakfast. All right?"

"All right," I said.

I gathered up Doggie under my arm and left. I went down the hall to the playroom. I pushed open the screen door and stepped out into the bright morning sunshine. I thought about Stevie. I knew what he felt the day he was supposed to go back to his father. The fear that grew inside of him, the one that reminded him of pain. I knew if he were afraid of running away, the fear of staying was greater. I headed for the same trees he headed for the day he decided not to go back.

Doggie and I walked for hours. We had no idea where we were, but we kept walking. We wanted to get away from there.

"Are you hungry, Doggie?"

He said he was.

"Yeah, me, too. Maybe we should've stayed for breakfast?"

93

He didn't think so.

We passed a park with some swings and a slide.

"Hey, Doggie! Wanna go on the slide?"

He did.

We played in the park for quite some time. The sun began to dip down below a row of buildings that bordered the park. We were tired and hungry. We decided to stay in the park, to find some nice spot in the bushes where we could rest.

"There's a good bunch of bushes. What do you think?" I asked.

Doggie thought they were fine. So we slipped into the bushes. I lay down with Doggie and closed my eyes. I thought if we slept, we might not be so hungry.

I was awakened by beeping horns. I stuck my head out of the bushes and saw a whole lot of cars and some buses. It was morning. I dusted off Doggie's fur and tucked him under my arm. We left the bushes and made our way toward the exit of the park.

"We gotta get a plan, Doggie. We gotta find out where we are, and most of all, we gotta get some food."

He agreed.

We passed a row of stores and some people. I saw a lady standing by the curb waiting for a bus or something. I decided to ask her where I was.

"Excuse me." I smiled. "Can you tell me where I am? Please."

"Are you lost, little boy?"

"Uh . . . you could say that."

"Where's your mother?"

"Uh . . . she's resting someplace."

"Resting! Resting where?"

"I'm not exactly sure. That's why I was asking you where I am. You see?"

"Not exactly. But you're in Yonkers."

"Yonkers!" I tapped my upper lip while I thought of what next to ask the nice lady. "Uh . . . is Yonkers in Brooklyn?"

"No," she laughed. "You're a long way from Brooklyn. Do you live in Brooklyn?"

"No, not exactly. I live in the Bronx."

"Oh, well, you're not that far from the Bronx. Where in the Bronx do you live?"

"188th Street."

"188th Street! How did you get all the way up here?"

"Well, it's a long story. Could you tell me which way is 188th Street?"

She pointed down the street in the direction of 188th Street.

"Thank you, ma'am," I said.

"But, sonny! Can I help you get there? Shouldn't I call your mother or somebody?"

"No thank you." I smiled again. "She sure was a nice lady, wasn't she, Doggie?"

He said she was.

We walked in the direction the lady had pointed out. We passed a lot more stores; one of them was a bakery.

"Wow! That smells good, doesn't it, Doggie?"

He thought it smelled great.

"I'll bet if we go around to the back, we'll find something to eat."

He agreed.

We went around to the back of the bakery and found a whole bunch of brown paper bags. I went through them. Most of it was just old bags of flour and empty cans.

"Oh, look!" I pulled up some potato peels and some bread. "What do you think?"

He thought it was food. He was starving.

"Yeah, me too."

I gave Doggie a taste of the bread. Then I ate the whole piece. We ate some of the potato peels and some more bread. The bread was much better than the potato peels.

We left the alleyway and continued in the direction the

lady had pointed. As we walked, we looked at the stores for another good one. We were still very hungry.

"Hey, kid!" a man's voice called from behind me.

I turned and saw a policeman just getting out his car.

"Come here, son."

I cautiously approached him. I was scared. I tightened my grip on Doggie. "Yes, sir?"

"What's your name son?"

"Uh . . . Stevie."

"Stevie what?"

"Uh . . . uh . . ." I gulped. I didn't know Stevie's last name.

"Well, never mind, son. Come along." He extended his hand to me.

I took his hand. He opened the front door of the police car and led me in. Doggie and I sat in the car while he went around to the other side and got in. I started to cry.

"Don't cry, son. I'm only going to give you a ride to the police station, so we can find out who you are and take you home. All right?"

I couldn't speak. I was too frightened. I held Doggie very close to my chin and stretched my neck. I wanted to look out the window, but I couldn't see over the dashboard.

"A lady told me you were lost," he said.

Oh, gosh! I thought. She wasn't such a nice lady after all.

"Well, we'll be there in a minute, and we'll get you home."

I knew that wasn't true, but I knew he didn't know that.

We pulled up in front of the police station. It was a scary-looking place. The building was all brown stone, and ugly. There were two large globe lamps, one on each side of the front door. The policeman held my hand as he led me from the car into the building. He pushed open the front door. The room was big. There was a great wooden desk behind a black handrail; it ran the entire length of the room. There were at least a dozen policemen going and coming through different doors around the room. Someone was typing somewhere, but I couldn't see who it was. I could only hear them. The walls were cracked and dirty.

"Hey, Sarge! Bob captured Dillinger," one of the police-men said.

I looked around to see who this Dillinger person was, but I didn't see anybody.

The policeman continued to hold my hand until we were in front of the giant desk.

"I think I got a runaway, Sarge," he said to the policeman behind the desk.

He leaned over the desk and looked down at me. He was the only policeman in the room not wearing a hat. His hair was gray and parted in the middle. He put on a pair of glasses only to look at me. As soon as he saw me, he took them off.

"Hi, son! What's your name?"

"Stevie, Sarge. His name is Stevie," the policeman said.

"No, it's not. Now, what's your name, son?"

Somehow this policeman named Sarge knew my name wasn't Stevie.

"Well, son?"

I was so frightened I couldn't answer him. I hugged Dog-gie a little closer and blinked back my tears. Sarge left the desk and came around to the front. He crouched down.

"Are you hungry?" he asked.

I shook my head no.

He scratched Doggie's head. "I'll bet your dog is hungry. Are you hungry, little fella?" he asked Doggie.

I moved Doggie's head up and down.

"I thought so. We'll take care of that in a jiffy." He stood up and shouted out some orders to a few of the policemen who were standing around. He sent one of them to get Doggie a hamburger. He crouched back down. "Now, son. While we're waiting for the dog's hamburger, suppose you tell me his name."

"Doggie."

"Oh, Doggie. Now, why didn't I think of that? And what's your name?" he asked me.

"Jennings."

"Now, that's better. And where do you live, Jennings?"

"Uh . . ." I hesitated. I didn't want to go back to St. Teresa's. "The Home of the Angels."

"Home of the Angels? Hmmm." He scratched his chin.

"In Brooklyn," I added.

"In Brooklyn?" he said. "Well!" He placed a hand under each of my arms and lifted me and Doggie in one sweep onto the top of his high desk.

I winced in pain as he pressed some of my splinter cuts.

"Are you all right?"

I nodded my head that I was.

"Let's see," he said as he lifted my shirt. "Oh! My god! How did you get these?"

"Uh . . . splinters."

"Splinters!" He lifted the front of my shirt. Two other policemen standing near him leaned over to look. "Okay. How'd you get them?" He sounded angry.

I didn't answer him. I was afraid to.

"All right, never mind," he said. He went around to the other side of his desk.

The policeman who went for the hamburger came in. "One hamburger comin' up!" he said.

Sarge took the package from him. He unwrapped the hamburger and gave Doggie a bite. "I think this is much too big for this little fella. Can you help him eat it?" he asked.

I nodded my head yes.

He handed me the hamburger and a container of milk. I was starving. I gobbled down some of the hamburger and drank the milk. Sarge spoke quietly to one of the policemen and made a telephone call.

"I know you're from St. Teresa's, son," he said. "It's written on your shirt."

I pulled up my shirt collar to see, but I couldn't see anything.

"It's in the back."

I remembered the nurse had given me new clothes. I didn't know she put the home's name on them.

"I know they hurt you there, son, and I know that's why you ran away. But you'll have to go back."

My eyes filled with tears as I muched on the hamburger.

Sarge came around to the front of me. "Now, son, I'm going to promise you something. I'm going to promise you nobody's going to hurt you ever again. Will you believe me?"

He had been so kind to me, I believed him. I nodded my head yes.

"Good!" He wrote something on a piece of paper and stuck it in my shirt pocket. "That's my name, Sergeant Pierce Meagher, and my phone number. If anybody—anybody! —tries to hurt you again, I want you to call me. Will you do that?"

"Yes, sir," I said. "Oh! Sir?"

"Yes."

"I thought your name was Sarge."

"Well, everyone calls me Sarge. You can call me Sarge too, if you'd like." He smiled. "Now, finish your hamburger. I'm going to take you back myself. I got a few words for those people."

We drove away in Sarge's car.

"Now, how did you get the splinters?"

I hesitated.

"Don't be afraid," he said. "I just want to make sure I yell at the right person. I'll find out anyway."

"Sister Barbara," I mumbled. "She dragged me across the dining-room floor."

"All right," he said. He patted my leg with his hand.

We entered the front gate of St. Teresa's. My heart pounded. He flipped a switch on his dashboard.

"What's that?" I asked.

"That's my dome light. It makes us look a little more scary." He winked.

The police car drove up the dusty road to the front of the house and stopped. As I got out of the car, I hid Doggie behind my back.

"What's the matter?" he asked.

"Sister Barbara doesn't like Doggie."

"Oh, she doesn't! Well, we'll see about that!" He pushed open the screen door.

We went into the dark hallway.

"Wait here," he said. He pushed open a door marked "Office" and went in.

As I stood by the front door watching the red light from the police car flash across my face, I heard yelling coming from the office. A few minutes later Sarge came out with Sister Barbara. I couldn't tell who was more red, him or her.

His face softened as he crouched down near me. "Now, Jennings," he said, "it's okay for you to keep Doggie." He looked up with anger in his eyes at Sister Barbara.

"Isn't that right, Sister!" he snapped.

She didn't answer.

He looked back at me and again softened. "And if anybody hurts you here . . . you call me. All right?"

"All right." I mumbled.

"Good!" He hugged me very carefully, then straightened up. "So long, son," he said, and left.

Sister Barbara didn't say a word. She just pointed to the door she wanted me to go through and returned to her office.

In the weeks that followed, Sister Barbara never bothered me. She didn't speak to me or order me around. I was allowed to sleep with Doggie. I kept Sergeant Pierce Meagher's phone number with me all the time.

Rooster, Peter, and I played together most of the time. When we didn't, I sat by the tree with Doggie and looked over the tops of the tall trees and thought about Stevie and

Mark and Mom and home. I always kind of hoped that Stevie would come back so that I could tell him about Sarge. I was sure that Sarge would help him.

One afternoon I was by the tree when I saw a car coming up the driveway. I wondered who it might be. A new kid, maybe, or an old one coming back. Either way, it was their beginning. I didn't envy them.

The car stopped. Mom got out of the car. I leapt to my feet and ran as fast as I could to her. I reached her and fell into her open arms and cried. She hadn't died after all.

7

I knelt on the backseat of the taxicab and looked out the rear window. The dust from the driveway swirled up in great clouds behind the car as we drove toward the front gate. I could still see Sister Ann Catherine and Rooster waving good-bye to me, even though the dust hid them from time to time.

"Did you have a good time?" Mom asked.

I looked at her. I couldn't believe she was seriously asking me that question.

"You broke your promise, Mom."

"I didn't mean to. I couldn't help it."

"Why do you keep getting sick?"

Her eyes filled with tears. "I don't try to get sick . . ." She couldn't talk any more than that without crying.

"I'm sorry, Mom. I just missed you, that's all. I was afraid you was gonna die."

"Oh, no, no. I'm not going to die." She hugged me. "I'm not going to die."

I held on to Mom the whole way to the bus station. We didn't speak. I didn't want her to cry anymore. When we reached the station, Mom turned to me and said, "I have a surprise for you."

"Oh! What is it?"

"I can't tell you. If I do, it won't be a surprise anymore."

Maybe it's a bike, I thought. Naa. Mom could never afford a bike. Gosh, I was curious.

The bus let us off at Fordham Road and the Grand Concourse. I held on to Mom's hand as we walked down Fordham Road. As we turned the corner at Teibout and 188th Street, I remembered the surprise. I dashed up the stairs and ran into the apartment. There was nothing in the front hall. I ran down the hall and into the living room. George was sitting on the couch with a strange boy I didn't recognize. There was nothing in the living room. I went into the back bedroom. Nothing there, either. I walked back into the living room. Mom smiled.

"Well?" she said.

"Well, what?" I scratched my head. "I don't see no surprise."

"You don't?" She laughed. "That's Jerome!" she said as she pointed to the strange boy sitting alongside George.

"Jerome!"

He was very pale. His hair was brown and curly. He had a round face and a wide forehead. His cheeks and nose were lightly freckled. His ears stuck straight out from the sides of his head. They were holding up a giant pair of horn-rimmed glasses.

I was speechless. My disappointment at not finding something like a bike faded into curiosity.

"Aren't you going to say hello?" Mom asked.

"Oh, yeah," I said. "Hi."

"Hi," Jerome said, and smiled.

"Uh . . . my name is Jennings." I extended my hand to him. "That's my first name."

He laughed. "Yeah, I know, we have the same last name."

"Oh, yeah." I laughed.

"How old are you?" he asked.

"I'm nine and a half."

"Jerome was eleven last week," Mom said. "We're going to have a party for him on Saturday."

"A party!" Jerome shrieked. "I never had a party!"

"Well, you're going to have one now," she said.

"I didn't get a party for my birthday," Walter said as he came into the living room.

"Well, you're not sick," she said.

"You gotta be sick to get a party around here," George mumbled. He got up from the couch and headed down the hall.

"Where're you going?" Mom asked.

"Out!" he snapped as the door slammed.

"He'll be back soon," she said.

"Don't bet on it," Walter snarled. He sat at his usual spot to study.

"Where's Larry?" I asked.

"He's at the store."

"And Gene?"

"Sleeping."

"I should've known. Gene sleeps all the time," I told Jerome.

"Well, he's just a kid," he said. "Do you play chess?"

"Chess?"

"Yeah, chess. Do you play?"

I shook my head no. "I play checkers. Wanna play checkers?"

"Okay."

I got the checkerboard and the pieces. Mom began to fix supper. Jerome told her he wanted meatloaf, so that's what we were having.

"It must be icky living in a hospital," I said.

"No, I don't think so," he said. "It's all right."

"Oh, I thought you'd hate it. I hated the homes I was in."

"Well, that's because you didn't live there, you only stayed there."

I scratched my head. I didn't understand that, and he knew I didn't.

"You see," he said, "I lived in the hospital. It's the only place I ever lived. I might hate living here."

"Really?"

"Could be. I only know Mom. I met George and Walter once or twice, but I don't know them. I don't know you, either."

"But we're brothers, aren't we?"

"What does that mean?"

"Uh . . . it means . . . uh . . . I don't know, what does it mean?"

He laughed. "It means more than just having the same last name, doesn't it?"

"Uh . . ."

He laughed again. "Now I got you thinking."

"Hi, Jennings!" Larry shouted as he came into the living room.

"Hi," I said as I jumped up to greet him. "How you been?"

"Okay. I lost my bugle."

"Where?"

"I don't know. Somewhere. Did you stay at a home?"

"Yeah." I raised my eyebrows to show I didn't like it.

"Me too."

"Larry!" Mom called from the kitchen. "Will you run to the grocer's for me?"

"Oh, darn. Do I have to?" he whined as he left the room.

Jerome and I played another game of checkers. He told me what it was like in the hospital. It sounded a lot like the homes, only they let you talk more. He showed me some of the model airplanes and boats he'd made. They were terrific. I showed him Doggie.

"Aren't you a little big to have a stuffed dog?" he asked.

"Too big? No, I'm not too big. Doggie's my friend. We were at the homes together. He was the only one I could talk to." I hugged him.

"Well, then, I guess you're not too big. I guess you're just right."

"Supper's ready!" Mom called out. I got up to go, but Jerome didn't.

"Aren't you coming?"

"I can't. I'm not allowed to walk around."

"Never?"

He shook his head no. "Not until the doctor says I can."

"You mean you gotta sit there forever?"

"No," he laughed. "I'll get settled somewhere. Mom said she'd figure it out later."

She did. We borrowed a cot from Mrs. Clark, the lady next door, and set it up in the living room. We had to move things around a bit, but we did it. Mom took a small table from her bedroom and put it alongside his cot. We started a game of three-handed Slap Jack on his new table.

"Larry," Mom called. "You and Jennings better get yourselves to bed. You have school tomorrow."

"Oh, darn. I don't wanna go to school," Larry whined.

"Why not?" Jerome asked.

"Everyone is going to make fun of us," I said.

"Why?"

" 'Cause we were left back. We missed too much school last term."

"Why should anyone make fun of you?"

Larry laughed a sarcastic laugh. "Are you kidding? They'll call us dumb ox and stuff like that."

"I don't know," Jerome said. "I wish I could go to regular school. I wouldn't care what they called me."

"Didn't you ever go to regular school?"

He shook his head no.

"Ain't you gonna go to school now?" Larry asked.

He again shook his head no.

"How you gonna learn anything?"

"I'll have to have a tutor."

"What's a tutor?"

106

"A teacher who comes in and teaches me right here."

"In bed?" Larry asked.

Jerome nodded yes.

"Boy! Gene sure would like that."

We all laughed.

Larry was right about school. After the first day, I was miserable. I went straight home. Larry was already there. He was lying across our bed, crying. I didn't have to ask him how things went. I sat on the edge of Jerome's bed.

"How was it?" he asked.

"Awful. I'm the oldest kid in the class, and the biggest. I stick out like a big toe."

"Why didn't you sit in the back?"

"I did. That's how I know I'm the biggest."

"Did anybody call you names?"

I nodded my head yes.

"They really picked on Larry," Jerome said. "He doesn't ever want to go back."

"I know how he feels. I don't want to go back either."

"I like Larry," Jerome said.

"Yeah. So do I. He's my favorite brother."

"That's not hard to understand."

"What do you mean?"

"Well, you and Larry are very much alike. You play together. You went through the same things. You know, the homes. You were both left back. You feel the same things. George and Walter are in high school. They don't know what you two are going through. And Gene is just a baby. That's why it's not hard to understand you liking each other the best."

Jerome reminded me an awful lot of Mark. There seemed to be a little wise man inside of each of them. He even looked a little like Mark.

In the days that followed, I played with Jerome every day after school. Larry started to play hooky and hang out with some kids who went to a different school. They, too, were playing hooky. Even though I knew about Larry not going to school, I didn't tell anybody.

On Saturday afternoon Mom sent me and George to Hanscom's Bakery for Jerome's cake.

"How's school?" he asked.

"Lousy."

"Why? What's the matter?"

"Ah. I don't like school no more. None of the kids I used to play with play with me anymore."

"That's tough, kid. I'm sorry to hear that."

"Larry don't like school no more, either."

"I know. I saw him a couple of times in the street when he shoulda been in school."

"Uh . . . really?" I said. I was trying to look surprised.

"I ain't gonna tell Mom."

"Oh, good. The kids really pick on him a lot."

"Yeah, I figured that."

We got Jerome's cake and started for home. I was glad George wasn't mad about Larry playing hooky. I was glad he wasn't going to tell Mom. Sometimes George can be pretty nice. Sometimes he shows he really does know what Larry and I are going through.

"Do you think someday Jerome will get better?" I asked. "You know, so he don't have to stay in bed all the time?"

"I don't know. He's pretty sick. Mom said they only sent him home to die."

We walked the rest of the way in silence. I had heard that for as far back as I could remember, but it hadn't meant all that much to me. I guess it was because I hadn't ever met him. Now that I had, I liked him. I didn't want him to die. I wanted him to teach me how to build model airplanes and to play chess. I wanted us to have more than just the same last name.

Jerome's party was fun. Mom bought him two model-airplane kits, and Gene a coloring book. She always had to buy Gene a present when she bought someone else anything.

108

He'd cry if she didn't. George and Walter got Jerome some paints to go with his models. And Larry and I, after carrying packages at the A&P, got him a Captain Video secret decoder ring. I think we liked it more than he did. Jerome didn't know all that much about Captain Video.

After the party, Larry and I cleaned up the kitchen and went to bed. Gene was already asleep. Mom and George and Walter stayed up to have some coffee.

"Want to play an alphabet game?" Larry asked.

"Naaa. I'm kind of tired," I said. I hugged Doggie to my cheek.

"Do you think Jerome's gonna die?" Larry asked.

"Uh . . . I hope not."

"I hope not too."

"You know, George knows about you playing hooky."

"What!" he said. He sat up.

"Yeah. He told me today, he knew."

"Oh, darn. Now I'm in trouble."

"He said he wasn't going to tell Mom."

"Yeah, sure! The first chance he gets, he'll tell her."

"He said he wouldn't."

"And you believed him? Oh, darn!" He fell back.

I drifted off, hugging Doggie and thinking about Jerome.

After church on Sunday, Jerome gave me a chess lesson. It sure was a hard game. I kept jumping his pieces.

"You'll get the hang of it one of these days," he laughed.

"I doubt it."

"You will. Hey! Do you like baseball?"

"Oh, yeah. I love baseball. Phil Rizzuto is my favorite player. They call him the Scooter," I said.

"Mine is Yogi Berra. The Yanks are going to play Philadelphia in the Series, I'll bet."

"Oh, the Yankees'll win."

"A lot of people in Philadelphia would argue with you there."

"Don't you think they'll win?"

"Sure I do. I'm just kidding you. I think the Series will go at least six games."

"Hey! I got pictures of Phil Rizzuto and Yogi Berra. In my baseball-card collection. Wanna see them?"

I got my collection and we looked at all the players. I gave him my Yogi Berra card to hang on his wall over his bed.

"Where's Larry?" Mom asked as she came into the living room. George and Walter were with her.

"Uh . . . I think he's downstairs," I said. I wondered if George had told Mom about Larry playing hooky.

"Get him," she said.

I dashed down to the front of the building and found Larry with a boy who lived in the next building.

"Mom wants you," I told him.

"Oh, darn."

On the way upstairs, I told Larry what I suspected, just so he could be ready in case I was right.

"What should I say?" he asked.

"I don't know. Tell her you got amnedia."

"What?"

"Amnedia. You know, when you can't remember anything. Tell her you forgot where the school was."

"You're nuts!"

We went into the apartment. Everyone was sitting in the living room waiting for us.

"Sit down, boys," she said. "We have something to talk about."

"I got amnedia," Larry said.

"You got what?" Walter asked.

"Amnedia. I can't remember anything."

"You mean amnesia."

"Yeah. That's what I mean. Ya see, I couldn't even remember how to say it."

"Well, we'll talk about your amnesia later." Mom laughed. "Right now we have something to tell you. George is quitting school."

"What!" Larry and I said.

"Yes. George is going to quit school to take a job. With Jerome home now, we need a bigger apartment. I can't afford one on my own, so George decided to help out."

"I don't mind staying in the living room," Jerome said.

"It's more than that," George said. He lit a cigarette. "I want a room of my own. Walter needs a better place to study . . ."

I couldn't believe my ears. George was going to quit school so that Walter could have a place to study?

". . . and the most important point of all is Larry and Jennings."

We perked up.

"Being sent to those homes has destroyed their schooling here. They're unhappy and they have no friends. I think the best thing is for me to get a job so that we can move out of here. Does anyone have any objections?"

Nobody spoke.

"Good! As soon as I can get a job and we can locate a new place, we'll go."

Larry and I jumped to our feet and cheered. Everyone was happy. Mom was going to have help. Larry and I were going to go to some new school and make new friends. Walter was going to have a better place to study, and Jerome wouldn't have to sleep in the living room.

"Oh, one more thing." George broke into everyone's excitement. "I want you, Jennings, and you, Larry, to do the best you can with school until we move."

It took a few months for George to get a job and save enough for the move. He worked at a machinery company somewhere in Brooklyn as a draftsman's trainee. Walter, so he wouldn't be outdone, took a part-time job after school. Larry and I took the abuse and went to school every day. It was easier for us, knowing it wouldn't be forever. Mom changed jobs and was now working for a real-estate company.

111

She found a house to rent on Coolidge Avenue in Kew Gardens, Queens.

Larry and I were in charge of packing. I divided my time between packing and playing with Jerome. He finally taught me enough chess to play him. He beat me. Larry and I packed everything in the house and repacked everything Gene unpacked. We packed up Jerome's things last.

I was putting his models in a box while Larry was taking the things off his wall.

"I didn't know you liked Phil Rizzuto," Larry said to Jerome.

"I put that up for Jennings," he said, "when Rizzuto won the MVP in the American League."

I looked up, and sure enough, there was the Scooter's picture. "Thanks," I said.

"Don't mention it. If Berra wins next year, I'll expect you to put his picture up."

"You got a deal."

We shook hands. He quickly pulled his hand away and grabbed his chest.

"What's the matter?"

"I don't know." He gasped.

"Mom!" I cried out. "Jerome's sick!"

Mom and George rushed into the living room.

"What's the matter?" she screamed.

"I don't know, he just grabbed his chest."

Jerome fell forward on the bed. He turned as white as snow. George ran from the room to call the police. Mom lifted Jerome and held him in her arms. She cried and rocked his limp body. George returned from the phone. He pushed Larry, Gene, and me into the back bedroom and closed the door.

Five or ten minutes later we heard many voices coming from the living room. Larry was trying to see through one of the cracks in the door. I was trying to see through another. Gene was playing with Doggie.

112

I saw some men lift Jerome onto a stretcher. I pushed open the door.

"Jerome!" I cried.

He turned his head in my direction and smiled. His eyes were closing. One of the men put a green thing over his pale face. I was close enough to touch his hand. He closed his fingers around my hand. He tried to squeeze, but couldn't. He didn't have any strength. He opened his eyes and blinked. He mumbled something through the mask, but I couldn't understand him.

"We have to take him now, son," one of the men said.

I leaned down and kissed his fingers. They wheeled him away.

" 'Bye," I said in a whisper.

Is that all I would ever know of Jerome? Would he die now, like everyone always told me he would? I hurt so much inside. The pain told me we had more than just the same last name.

8

We moved into the new house the week of Thanksgiving. Mom and George were having such a hard time keeping up with all the new bills in this more expensive place, there wasn't any money for Thanksgiving. Thanksgiving passed unnoticed.

The new house was small, white with green trim, and set back from the quiet tree-lined street. We were wedged in between two larger houses. It made our house look a little like a doll's house. There was a cherry tree in the front yard next to a wishing well, and hedges all along the front.

It was really very different living here. It was quiet. There were no neighbors to speak of, no friends, and no people around. The toughest part of living here was the lack of money. There was hardly any food around, and I was hungry all the time. There was no money for books or school supplies. That made a real difference in this new school we went to. Everyone seemed to be from wealthy families. They had everything they needed, and more. They looked at me as though I were a rag picker, and even called me that sometimes.

St. Benedict's in Richmond Hill was in the next town, about three miles away. Needless to say, there was no money for bus fare, so Larry and I walked.

"I hate this school as much as I hated Our Lady of Mercy," Larry said. "Maybe more."

"The school's okay. It's the kids I don't like."

"Yeah, well, I mean the kids. They're all rich and they sure let you know about it. I feel like a beggar in these clothes."

We walked in silence. I was feeling pretty much the same as he was. I had socks with holes in them, and baggy pants. I had so many knots in my shoelaces I couldn't untie my shoes even if I wanted to.

I sat in the back of the room to hide the holes in my socks and the knots in my shoelaces. Some of the kids made fun of my name or my clothes, but most of them just ignored me. I liked that better.

I was at St. Benedict's about a week when Miss Keller called me up to the blackboard. Miss Keller was a lay teacher—that meant she wasn't a nun. She was very short and dumpy. She twitched her left eye almost constantly. Anytime she turned her back, all the kids would twitch their faces and blow air into their cheeks to look very fat. Everyone was continually giggling throughout the day. She gave me a problem that involved adding fractions. I had never been taught fractions, so I didn't have the slightest idea even where to start.

"Excuse me, Miss Keller," I said.

"What is it now, Burch?"

"I don't know anything at all about fractions."

That got a great round of laughter from the kids.

Miss Keller paid no attention to me or what I had said. She addressed the class. "Now, boys. I want you to see what a really stupid kid looks like."

Everyone laughed.

"This is what's going to happen to you if you don't study and don't pay attention in class."

"But, Miss Kel—"

"Look, Burch!" she snapped. "You're going to stand at that board until you solve that problem. I don't care how long you have to stand there. Now, boys, let's turn to page one-twenty-seven," she told the class.

I stood at the board looking at the problem. I tried shutting out the giggles and remarks like "Dummy" coming from behind me, but I couldn't.

"Look at Burch's Catholic socks," somebody said. "They're holy!"

I wanted to disappear.

"Quiet down, boys," Miss Keller said.

There wasn't any way I was going to solve this problem, I thought. I'll just stand here until school is over. Tonight I'll talk to Mom. Maybe she can figure out a way for me to learn fractions.

While Larry and I did the dishes, I told him what had happened.

"Don't ask me about no fractions," he said. "I had them and still don't understand them. They're hard."

"When I'm finished here, I'm gonna ask Mom to take me out of school."

"Are you nuts? She ain't gonna take you outta school. She'll say 'Do the best you can.' " He did a poor job of mimicking her voice.

"Well, it don't hurt none to ask."

We finished up the dishes and left the kitchen. Mom was in her bedroom reading a magazine. Larry followed me in.

"I gotta talk to you about this new school," I said.

"Don't tell me you don't like it, because I don't want to hear that. I had a hard time getting you into that school in the middle of the term."

"I don't like it."

"Well, that's too bad."

"Oh, Mom!" I pouted. "I don't understand anything they're doing."

"Well, you'll just have to do the best you can."

"I told you," Larry quipped.

116

"Oh, gosh!" I huffed. I stamped my feet as I left the room, to show my disappointment.

"Lift your feet," she called out.

"I told you so." Larry sneered as we went into our bedroom.

I plopped down on the bed. "Yeah. You told me."

"Now you want me to tell you how to solve the problem?"

"I thought you didn't know anything about fractions."

"I don't. But that ain't the problem I'm gonna help you solve."

"I don't understand you."

"I'm gonna help you solve the problem of school, period!"

"How?"

"Play hooky!"

"How do you get away with it? Don't the school check?"

"Sure they do, at least in the beginning they did. I just waited around for the mail and took out any letters that came from school."

"What did the letters say?"

"I don't know. I never read them. I just threw them away."

"Where do you go every day?"

"I sneak under the turnstile in the subway and go to Manhattan."

"Alone?"

"There ain't nothin' to it."

"I don't know," I said. "Maybe I'll ask Walter to help me."

"Are you kiddin'? Walter wouldn't help you. He wouldn't help anybody but Walter."

I hugged Doggie and tried to fall asleep. I was kind of scared of playing hooky. I didn't think I would be able to go into Manhattan all by myself. If I went with Larry and I got lost, oh my gosh! Naaa. I'll try to work out something else.

The next day, Miss Keller didn't even let me go to my desk. She grabbed a handful of my ear and pushed me toward my spot at the board. I stood there for the entire day, even through lunch. I wasn't going to eat anyway, but she didn't know that. At day's end I left the board and the unsolved problem. I left the school. Some of the kids from the class were waiting out front to taunt me. They called me all the same old names like "Dummy" and "Stupid." I walked away as quickly as I could. One of them threw a rock at me and hit me in the back. I wouldn't flinch or turn back. There were too many of them.

I waited up for Walter. I sat at the kitchen table and wrote the problem on a piece of paper for him. He was extra late, and I was getting tired.

"What are you still doing up?" he asked as he came in through the kitchen door.

"I was waiting for you. I got a problem."

"What kind of a problem?"

"Fractions," I said as I handed him the paper.

"What do you want me to do with this?"

"Well, I thought you might help me solve it."

"What about your teacher, why don't you ask her to help you? That's what she's there for."

"I told her I never learned fractions, but she just called me stupid and made fun of me."

"So if I give you the answer to this problem and she gives you another one tomorrow, what then? Do you want me to go to school for you?"

"Ah, never mind," I said. "I just thought you'd help me." I took the paper and left the kitchen.

I lay back on the bed without taking my clothes off. A tear ran down the side of my face as I picked up Doggie and hugged him.

"I sure wish you knew fractions. You'd help me."

I fell off to sleep.

The next morning I didn't bother to go to my seat and get my ears pulled. I went straight to the board and stood there.

I ran my fingers along the edge of the chalk rail as I had done every day for the past two days. I was really getting bored.

118

"What the hell is going on here!" a voice rang out.

I turned and saw Walter standing in the doorway. Miss Keller, as well as everyone else in the class, was startled, including me.

"Who the hell do you think you are, lady?" he screamed. "That's my brother you got standing there!"

Miss Keller sat at her desk with her mouth wide open. She was speechless.

"Listen, you stupid bitch. If you can't teach him anything, tell him. We'll find someone who can."

I wanted to run from the board and hug him.

"Where the hell did you get your teaching credentials from? I'll tell you where you got them—you didn't! Come on, Jennings." He held out his hand for me to come to him.

"I'll put you into a real school," he said. "One where the teachers teach and don't take out their frustrations on the children."

He slammed the door as we left the room. I was never so happy to see Walter in all my life.

"Thank you," I said. I hugged his arm.

"Don't mention it," he said. He was grinning from ear to ear. "I always wanted to do that."

"Uh-oh. What is Mom gonna say?"

"Don't worry about it. I told her last night I was coming here."

"Really?"

"She wasn't crazy about the idea, but I convinced her of the importance of a good school. I'm going to check out some schools for you myself. I'll find the one you belong in."

He did. The following week Mom enrolled me in St. Michael's in Flushing. It was a long way from the house, seven or eight miles, but Mom said I could get a bus pass.

The neighborhood around the school reminded me of the Bronx. There were stores and things and it wasn't all fancy.

It looked ordinary. Mom and I went up the stairs of the school and into the building. We found the principal's office.

"I'm placing you in Sister Gerard's class," the principal said. "Grade Four-B."

"Isn't that too high for me, Sister?" I asked.

"Sister Gerard is a good teacher," she said. "She'll give you all the extra help you need until you can catch up to the others. You'll like her."

"All right, Sister, I'll try."

"Fine. I know you'll do all right."

We said good-bye to Mom. The principal showed me which room to go to and I did. My heart was pounding as I entered my new class. Everyone stopped to look at me. I looked back. Their clothes looked ordinary. I felt better.

"What's your name?" Sister Gerard asked.

"Jen . . . uh . . . Michael!" I said.

"Children, this is Michael. Sit here, will you?" She pointed to a seat in the fourth row.

I smiled at myself for my quick thinking. I didn't want anyone making fun of my name anymore. I was sure they wouldn't make fun of the name of their own school. Sister Gerard handed out some paper and pencils.

"We're going to have a spelling quiz. Please put your names on the tops of your papers."

I panicked. I didn't know how to spell Michael. I knew the first thing to passing a spelling test was to be able to spell your own name. I looked around the room to try to find the name of the school written down somewhere. I spotted it on the front of a boy's notebook. I squinted my eyes to read it.

"Michael!" Sister Gerard scolded. "One waits for a question before trying to cheat."

"I wasn't cheating, Sister. I was just, uh . . . looking at that book."

"Well, keep your eyes on your own paper."

"Yes, Sister," I mumbled. I was lucky. I had gotten all the letters I needed before she yelled at me.

Sister Gerard gave out ten words to spell. I did the best I could, but I was sure it wasn't good enough. She collected the papers. She gave out a reading assignment while she corrected them. The boy next to me let me read on with him.

"Michael!" Sister Gerard called out. I looked around to see who she wanted.

The boy next to me poked me in the arm. She wanted me.

"Michael!" she called again.

"Oh, yes!" I stood up.

"Come here, please."

I cautiously approached her. I was sure she was going to yell at me for getting all the words wrong.

"What's your name?" she asked.

The redness rushed into my face and neck. "Uh . . . Michael," I mumbled.

"Well, Michael. Spell your name without the apostrophe *s*." She smiled. She wrote my new name on a piece of paper for me. "Welcome to St. Michael's."

The principal was right: Sister Gerard was a nice nun and I did like her. But I was right, too. I got all ten words wrong.

Sister Gerard kept me after school every day at the convent for extra work. After the Christmas break, she changed my seat to the front row. I concentrated hard on the extra work and the regular work too. It didn't leave me time to make any friends, but I didn't mind. For the first time since the second grade at Our Lady of Mercy, I didn't feel so stupid.

One day after my lesson, I told Sister Gerard my real name.

"I knew your real name, Jennings," she said with a smile.

"You did?"

"Certainly. And if you felt it was important to change it to Michael, well, then, that was perfectly all right with me. Besides"—she smiled brightly—"you couldn't have picked a finer name."

"It was the first one that came to my mind."

"Do you know about St. Michael?" she asked.

"No, Sister, not too much."

"Well, he's a very special angel. He's the Prince of Heaven, God's right hand. He slew Lucifer for the Almighty, when Lucifer wanted to take over heaven."

"Wow!" I said. "He must be strong."

"He is, he's very strong. Did you visit his statue at our church yet?" she asked.

"No, Sister, I haven't."

"Well, you should. Especially now that you've borrowed his name. I think he'd like to meet you, too."

"He's an archangel, isn't he, Sister?"

"Yes, he is."

"Uh . . . can archangels be guardian angels?"

She smiled. "Of course they can. I think asking St. Michael to be your guardian angel is a wonderful idea."

After the lesson, I went up to the church. I pushed open the heavy front door and went in. The smell of burnt candle wax filled my nostrils. I walked up the long dark aisle to St. Michael's altar. The church was completely empty. The altar candles cast long and strange shadows all about St. Michael's statue. I reached the altar rail and knelt. I strained my neck to look up at his face. He was soft and gentle-looking. He was all dressed in black armor. He had a drawn sword held high above his head. His hair was golden blond. He looked strong and powerful.

"Hi, St. Michael," I whispered. "Would you be my guardian angel?"

He didn't answer me.

"I hope you don't mind my borrowing your name," I said. "It's a nice name. Nobody makes fun of it. You know something, St. Michael? I feel awfully lonesome sometimes. I love Doggie and he keeps me company a lot . . . but I sure wish Jerome was home. I didn't know him very long, just two months, but I really got to like him. Do you think you could let him come home soon? Please."

I searched through all my pockets for ten cents to light a

candle. I could only find four cents. I put it in the box and lit the candle.

"I owe you six cents," I said.

I left the church and headed down the hill to catch my bus. I climbed the steps of the bus and showed the driver my school pass. I sat down across from him and looked out through the front window.

"You sure look like you got a lot on your mind," the driver said.

I looked up and saw the bus driver who drove the bus in the mornings. I smiled.

"You've been taking my bus every morning for the last few weeks," he said. "This is the first time I've ever seen you here in the afternoon."

"Uh . . . well, I stayed after school later than usual."

"Oh!" He laughed. "You've been a bad boy."

"No." I laughed too. "I always stay after school, but today I stayed even later."

"You always stay after school, and you're not a bad boy?" He laughed again.

He had such a nice laugh. He sort of boomed it out, with his mouth wide open. He had lots of spaces between all his teeth. He was heavyset and had big hands and a big face. Every so often he would lift his cap and brush back the few hairs he had left on top of his head; then he'd replace his cap. He had dark brown curly hair around the side of his head and in the back.

"I don't stay after school because I'm bad," I said. "I stay because I need to catch up with all the other kids. I got behind."

"How'd you get behind?"

"Oh, it's a long story. I lived in some homes and missed a lot of school. And then when we moved from the Bronx, I was put in the wrong grades. It got all mixed up." I made a face.

"I know how that can be. Living in homes and missing lots of school."

"You do?"

"Uh-hum. I grew up in orphanages."

"You did?"

"Lots of them."

"In Brooklyn?"

"No." He laughed. "In Pennsylvania."

"Pennsylvania, ugh."

"You don't like Pennsylvania?"

"Oh, I like Pennsylvania, all right. It's a word we had on a test and I got it wrong."

He laughed.

"How many homes did you live in?" I asked.

"Oh, I don't remember, lots. I never lived anywhere but homes."

"You were a lifer!"

He laughed. "Yeah. I guess so. What's your name, son?"

"Jen . . . uh . . . Michael."

"Well, Michael, I'm Sal. Put it there!" He stuck out his hand.

I shook it. "Uh . . . my real name is Jennings," I said, "but the kids always make fun of it."

"Jennings! Jennings is a nice name. Why do they make fun of it?"

"I don't know, they just do. They haven't made fun of 'Michael,' so I'll keep it."

Sal pulled the bus up to my stop. I got off.

"I'll see you tomorrow, Jennings." He smiled.

"All right, Sal. I'll see you tomorrow."

I sat behind or across from Sal every morning after that. I even started seeing him in the afternoons. I stopped in the church after my extra lesson to see St. Michael, and then I waited for Sal's bus. I managed to pay Michael the six cents over a period of a few weeks.

124

"How's my son this afternoon?" Sal asked as I climbed aboard his bus.

"I learned to spell three new words today," I told him.

"Three new words!" he shouted. He stopped the bus and turned his head around to me and the other passengers. "Did you hear that?" he boomed out with pride. "My son learned three new words today."

Everyone applauded. I was embarrassed, but I liked it.

"How's your mother and all your brothers?" he asked.

"All right. Larry started going to school again. He hates it. And George . . . I don't know about George."

"What's the matter with him?"

"He's drinking a whole lot. More than I ever seen before. I don't know what's wrong with him."

"Did you ask him?"

"Are you kidding? I can't talk to him. Nobody can. When Mom tries, he gets real mad."

"How about Walter?"

"He wouldn't talk to him, they hate each other."

"I didn't mean that, I just meant how is he?"

"Oh! I don't see him very much. He's always in school."

"What's he going to be?"

"I don't know. I never asked him."

"What do you want to be?"

"Uh . . ." Nobody had ever asked me that before. "Uh . . . a man, I guess."

He laughed. "I know you want to be a man, but what kind of work do you want to do?"

"I know you meant that," I said. "I don't know. Maybe a bus driver."

He laughed loudly.

I liked Sal. I looked forward to seeing him every day and talking to him. I began to miss him on weekends when I didn't take the bus. I knew I could talk to Sal about anything. He always listened to me, and he always answered my questions.

125

One Saturday afternoon Larry, Gene, and I were coming home from the movies. We were playing follow the leader. Gene, of course, was having a hard time keeping up with us. Larry and I decided to stop and wait for him. While we were waiting, I saw a boy kick a shoe box into the street.

"I think I'll see what's in the box," I said.

"Probably nothing. He wouldn't kick it away if there was anything good inside," Larry said.

"Well, it looks like a good box. I might be able to use it for something."

I ran across the roadway to retrieve the box. I shook it and listened. I heard a "mew." I quickly opened the box and found a kitten. He couldn't have been more than two or three days old.

"Hey, Larry! It's a cat."

"Oh, yeah?" He ran over to me. "Let me see."

I showed him the cat.

"Boy, he's little," he said.

"He sure is. I'm gonna take him home to show Mom."

"What about Gene?"

"Wait for him, will you?"

I didn't give Larry time to answer me. I just dashed off. I ran all the way home. I pushed open the kitchen door.

"Maaa," I hollered.

"In here, dear," she spoke softly from her bedroom.

I poked my head in. Mom was in bed.

"What's the matter?"

"I don't feel well, dear. Did you like the movie?"

"Oh, yeah."

"Did Gene behave himself?"

"He went to sleep. What'd ya think?"

"Where is he?"

"Oh, I almost forgot. I found a pussycat." I opened the box and showed her the cat.

"He looks terrible. Where did you find him?"

"He looks okay."

126

"No, dear, he doesn't. He needs his mother. Where did you get him?"

"This kid was kicking the box around, he was inside."

"That's terrible. Poor little thing."

Mom told me how to feed him with an eyedropper, and told me to keep him warm. I was feeding him when Larry and Gene came in.

"Can I feed him?" Gene asked.

"No."

"Maaa. Jennings won't let me feed the cat." He cried as he ran into her bedroom.

"What are you gonna call him?" Larry asked.

"Well, he's black . . . I'll call him midnight."

Larry petted Midnight while I tried to feed him. He only needed one finger to pet him, he was so little. Midnight licked off the drop of milk from the end of the eyedropper with his tiny little tongue. I bundled him up in a facecloth and put him back in the box.

"Mom's gonna buy me my own cat. So there!" Gene said. He then stuck out his tongue and dashed from the kitchen again.

"I liked him better when he slept all the time," Larry said.

"Me too."

Larry made soup for all of us, but Mom didn't want any. She said it would just upset her stomach.

"Should I give some to Midnight?" I asked.

"Oh, no!" she said. "He's a cat. Cats don't eat soup, especially a tiny baby."

"Can I take him to school Monday to show Sal and Sister Gerard?"

"I think you should see how he is by then."

"All right," I said. I left her to help Larry with the dishes.

We finished up in the kitchen and went into the bedroom. I took Midnight with me.

"Can I sleep with him?" Gene asked.

"No. He's too little. You'll crush him."

"No, I won't. I'll sleep light. Then if I fall on him, I won't crush him."

"That's not what light sleep means, dummy," Larry said.

I bundled Midnight up against Doggie. "You'll have to keep him warm. All right, Doggie?" I kissed them both and got into bed.

"Did he answer you?" Larry asked.

"Sure. He said he would."

Larry shook his head. "This whole place is going nuts. Gene wants to sleep light so he won't weigh anything, and you talk to stuffed animals and they answer you."

I awoke early Sunday morning. Rain was falling hard against the window. I laid my head back against the pillow, when I remembered Midnight. I jumped out of bed and went over to the chair where he and Doggie were sleeping. I pushed back the facecloth and lifted him up.

"Good morning, little Midnight," I said. I kissed his fur.

I turned him in my hand so that I could see his little face. His eyes were closed and his body was limp. He was dead.

"Oh, God, no!" I cried. I kissed him a whole bunch of times. "Please don't be dead. Oh, please don't be dead."

"What's the matter?" Larry asked.

"Midnight's dead," I cried.

The whole house was in disorder. Larry and Gene and I were crying. Mom got up from her bed even though she was sick, to settle everyone down. She fixed a small box by lining it with a handkerchief. She told us to bury Midnight in the front yard.

Larry and I made a cross for the top of Midnight's grave. We got Gene's shovel from his pail-and-shovel set and we went into the yard. I let Gene hold Doggie.

We dug the grave and put Midnight in. We covered him over and set the cross in the ground. I couldn't believe my love for him didn't keep him alive. I would have taken good care of him. The tears on my face were mixed with the heavily falling rain, but it didn't matter. I don't think it mattered to Larry or Gene, either. We were all very upset.

Inside, I lay down with Doggie in my arms. He was dripping wet, but I didn't care. I fell asleep feeling very helpless.

"You look like you lost your best friend," Sal said to me the next morning.

"I did," I mumbled.

"Why, son? What happened?"

I sat behind Sal and told him all about Midnight.

"You know, son, just loving something or someone, like Midnight, isn't enough. He was neglected and mistreated long before you found him. By then it was too late."

"But I really loved him, Sal." My eyes filled.

"I know you did. But it was too late. All the love in the world wouldn't have saved him."

I sat in silence as the bus rumbled down Main Street.

"Before he died, he knew you were his friend."

"Do you think so?"

"Of course he did. And isn't that all that really matters now? The fact that he knew you loved him, and he knew you were his friend?"

Sal made me feel a little better. Before I left his bus, he gave me a big hug.

"I'll see you tonight," he said. "And cheer up." He smiled.

I got off the bus and thanked him for talking to me. He winked and closed the door. He drove off.

I walked up the hill thinking about all the things Sal had said to me. When I reached school, I went straight to class. I didn't feel much like standing around in the school yard. Sister Gerard was at her desk.

"Well, you're here early," she said.

"Yes, Sister."

"Don't you feel well?"

"Yes, Sister," I sighed. "I feel all right. I mean, I'm not

sick or anything like that. I just feel a little sad because my cat died.''

"Oh, that's terrible," she said. She stood up and put her arms around me. I cried into her.

She didn't call on me all morning or afternoon. I think she knew my mind was wandering from time to time, and she didn't want to embarrass me. Sister Gerard was like that; she was kind.

Late in the afternoon a boy came into the room from one of the other classes. He handed Sister Gerard a note.

"Continue to read to yourselves," she told everyone in the class. "Michael," she called.

I looked up to see if she wanted me. She did.

"Will you take this note down to Sister Regina for me, please?" She handed me a folded piece of paper.

"Sure, Sister. Should I wait for an answer?"

"Yes, please." She smiled.

I left the room and went down to the principal's office. Sister Regina was in her office talking to a gray-haired man in a dark overcoat. I waited outside.

"Jennings," she called from her office.

"Yes, Sister! I have a note for you," I said as I walked in.

I was a little surprised she remembered my real name. But then, she was the principal and always seemed to know everything.

"Sit down, will you, Jennings. This is Mr. Frazier."

"Hello, sir," I said. I sat down.

"Jennings," she said, "your mother was rushed to the hospital with pneumonia."

"Oh, no." I didn't want to hear what was coming next.

"I'm sorry, son," Mr. Frazier said.

"Mr. Frazier has agreed to let you stay with him until your mother is better. Is that all right?"

I didn't answer her. I was thinking about Mom and going away again. Maybe if she hadn't gotten up to help us with Midnight. Oh, gosh.

"Jennings," she said.

I raised my head just a little. I didn't want the tears I was fighting off to fall.

"If you stay with Mr. Frazier," she said, "you won't have to disrupt your schooling. You can continue with us without any interruptions."

"Uh . . . oh, yes, Sister. All right." I couldn't believe I was going away again. For some reason I just sort of put going away out of my mind and forgot about it. That was a mistake. I should never do that again, I thought. Oh, gosh. I don't even have Doggie with me. What am I going to do? I lost the battle with my tears; they fell all over the back of my hand. I buried my face in my hands. Sister Regina put her arms around me and hugged me. Oh, gosh, first little Midnight, and now Mom. Why?

9

Mr. Frazier turned off the main road and pulled up to a tiny little white house. A man in a brown uniform stuck his head out the door and waved to us. We waved back.

"Who's that?" I asked.

"That's Fred," Mr. Frazier said. "The security guard."

We passed through a set of tall iron gates. The gravel from the roadway made a steady sound against the bottom of the car.

"Are we at some kind of a home or something?" I asked.

"No, son. Why?"

"Well, the iron gates and Fred."

"No." He patted my leg. "We're in Briar Manor. I live here. Fred is there to see that no one comes in who doesn't live here."

"Will he let me in?"

"Of course! Aren't you going to live here?"

"Uh . . . no, sir."

"No!"

"No. I'm just gonna stay here."

"Well, it's the same thing."

"No, it's not! My brother Jerome said staying somewhere and living somewhere was different."

"He's right, son. You're just going to stay here till your mom is better. I'll tell Fred to make an exception in your case and let you in."

We passed many large and beautiful houses. Some of them had long white columns in front, others had bunches of tall trees and neatly trimmed bushes. All of them were pretty. I looked over at Mr. Frazier. His clothes were nice and neat. He was wearing a watch and a ring. He must be rich, I thought. I looked at my own raggy clothes, then did my best to shrink into the seat. I remembered all the rich kids at St. Benedict's and how mean they were to me. I began to get a little nervous. Mr. Frazier seemed kind enough. Maybe all rich people aren't mean. Maybe they're like the nuns at the homes, some are mean and some are nice.

He pulled the car into a driveway and stopped.

"Here we are," he said.

His house was beautiful. It was all gray stone with blue and white trim. There was a birdbath on the front lawn. There was a large boat off to one side of the driveway.

"Is that your boat?" I asked. My eyes were wide open at the sight of it. I had never seen a boat before, except in the movies or in magazine pictures.

"No, son," he said. "That one belongs to my daughter Nancy. She's away at college right now. My boat is kept at the marina."

"How did she sail it into the driveway?"

"She didn't sail it there," he laughed. "We brought it in by trailer."

We got out of the car.

"What's a marina?"

"That's a place where they keep boats when you're not using them."

"Oh, I see. Then this is not a driveway, it's a marina."

He laughed again. "I had forgotten what it was like to talk to a nine-year-old," he said. "We'll straighten it all out later. Right now, Martha is waiting for us, and I have to get back to work."

He held my hand as we walked up to the front door. The door opened and a short, heavyset lady stepped out. She had gray hair that was all pulled back and tied in a knot. Her cheeks were round and rosy. On the bridge of her pug little nose sat a pair of wire-rimmed glasses. She was wearing a green-and-white flowery dress, and a white apron with two big red roses on it. She reminded me of a large bouquet of flowers.

"Hello, Martha," he said. "This is Jennings."

She smiled a wonderful smile and pinched my cheek. "Well, now, Master Jennings," she said, "you sure are the cutest little boy I ever did see." She laughed.

My face flushed. "Hello, Mrs. Frazier."

"Land sakes, no," she laughed. "I'm Martha. I keeps the house 'round here. You'll see Mrs. Frazier at dinnertime."

"Oh. I thought you were Mrs. Frazier."

"Mrs. Frazier is shopping," Mr. Frazier said. "You go along with Martha. She'll show you to your room and get you settled. I'll see you later."

Mr. Frazier walked back to his car, while Martha and I went into the house.

The front room was like walking into one of Mom's magazines. A great stone fireplace set between two windows had a roaring fire blazing away.

"Come along, now," Martha said.

As we crossed the room, Martha started to take off my coat. I let her.

"Are you sleepwalking, boy?" she laughed.

"No, ma'am," I said. "I just never saw anything like this room before."

She laughed again.

Aside from all the couches, chairs, and tables, there was a beautiful white piano in front of a whole wall of glass doors.

In the dining room, there was a shiny table with all the chairs set neatly around it. A ceiling lamp made of a thousand tiny pieces of glass hung just above the table.

"Does anybody eat in here?" I asked.

"Land sakes!" she laughed. "Of course they do. Every night."

"Gosh!"

She took me through a hallway into a bedroom. The room was all blue and green. The curtains were the same as the bed, all flowery and fluffy.

"This is your room," she said.

' "My room!" I thought she was just showing me around the house.

"Over here's your bathroom." She pushed open a small door and switched on a light.

It really was a bathroom. Who would've believed it.

"I never saw a bathroom in the bedroom before," I said.

"I never did either, till I started workin' here." She winked and laughed.

I liked Martha. She was a jolly lady. She reminded me a little of Sal and a little of Sister Ann Catherine at St. Teresa's. I liked the way she laughed.

She slid open what I thought was a frosted-glass wall. It was a bathtub.

"Wow! Would you look at that!" I said.

"Do you take showers or baths?" she asked.

"Uh . . . baths. I never took a shower except in homes or at a swimming pool. You know, before you go in the water you gotta take a shower."

"Well, you can take a shower here if you like."

"Oh, I'd like that." I smiled. "When can I take a shower?"

"Anytime you want to."

"Well, when does Mr. Frazier use the bathroom?"

"Land sakes." She laughed. "This is your bathroom. Mr. Frazier has his own bathroom."

"Really?"

She laughed again as she made her way to the door. "Well, I gots a lot of work to do in the kitchen," she said. "I'll let you freshen up." She closed the door as she left.

After I looked all around the bathroom and bedroom, I sat

135

at the edge of the bed and watched the sun completely set. As it did, the room darkened with it.

"Whatcha doin' in the dark," Martha said as she came back into the room. She switched on the lights. "I thought you'd come into the kitchen and keeps me company."

"I didn't know I was allowed to leave the room."

"What!" she snapped. There was anger in her voice. "While you is in this house," she stammered, "you can go anywheres you want. You hears Martha?"

"Yes, ma'am."

"Now, come along to the kitchen. Land sakes!" she mumbled.

She led the way from the bedroom into the kitchen. There were counters everywhere, sinks, a stove, an icebox, and lots of tables.

"This is really a big house, Martha."

"It surely is. I'm glad Martha ain't gots to clean it up." She laughed. "Would you likes to help me peel some taters?" she asked.

"Oh, yeah!"

She set me down at a table with some newspaper and a potato peeler, and potatoes.

"Do you help your mother at home?"

"Uh-huh. Not peeling potatoes, though. We don't have potatoes 'cept for special times."

"What do you eats most of the time?"

"Oh, soup. Sometimes spaghetti or shells. Sometimes frankfurters or hamburgers. Stuff like that."

"Well," she said, "I'd like to makes something you likes sometime."

"I like pancakes."

"Not for dinner," she laughed.

"No?"

"No. Pancakes is for breakfast. I'll make 'em for you tomorrow."

"I don't hardly eat breakfast, ma'am."

"You don't eats breakfast? But breakfast is important. It helps you get big and strong. Don't you wants to get big and strong?"

"Oh, sure. But we don't got that much food around our house to eat breakfast."

"Land sakes," she mumbled.

Martha set the table in the dining room with all sorts of things. Glasses and plates and lots of silverware.

"Why so many forks and spoons?" I asked.

"Well, some of the spoons are for soup. Some are for dessert or for coffee. Some of the forks are for salad, and the others for the main course."

"How do you know which is which?"

"Watch Mr. Frazier. Whatever he do, you do."

I helped her with the rest of the table, and then sat where she told me to. Mr. Frazier was the first one into the room. He sat at the head of the table in a chair with arms. He set down a stack of mail he had brought in with him.

"Well, Jennings, are you getting all settled in?" he asked.

"Yes, sir. You sure have a nice house here."

"Well, thank you, Jennings. I'm glad we can share it with you."

"Hello, dear," a lady said as she came into the room. She leaned down and kissed Mr. Frazier's cheek. I was sure this was Mrs. Frazier.

"How was your day?" he asked.

"Don't ask," she said. She took a seat at the far end of the table opposite him. She leaned her head back for a moment. "Where's Donald?" she asked.

"Who knows?" he said. He didn't look up from his mail.

She was a very pretty lady. Her hair was black and fell to her shoulders. Her face was thin and all made up with powder and rouge. She wore lots of jewelry. Rings and bracelets and necklaces. She looked like a department store.

"Martha," she called out over her shoulder to the door leading to the kitchen.

Martha pushed open the door with her back. She was carrying a large tray of soup. "Yes, ma'am."

"Where's Donald?" she asked.

"I don't know, ma'am. I tolds him to be home here by six. I tolds him we was gonna have a guest."

"Well, never mind," she said. "Serve the soup."

Martha went around the table pouring the soup into each of the bowls. Mrs. Frazier spoke to me.

"You don't talk very much, do you?"

Before I could answer her, Mr. Frazier interrupted. "Well, the way you come barreling in here . . ." He put his mail down. "You probably scared the hell out of him."

"I did not!"

"You did so," he said. "All that concerns you is that damn kid!"

"Well, I'd like to know where my son is. Is that so frightening?" she asked. "And I'll thank you not to refer to Donald as 'that damn kid.' "

He huffed at her last remark. "You could have at least said hello to Jennings when you came in."

"I was getting to that." She turned to me. "Hello, Jennings. Do I frighten you?"

"No, ma'am."

"There, you see." She sneered. "I didn't frighten him."

"What did you expect him to say?"

"You're impossible!"

She began to eat her soup. I watched which spoon she used and used the same kind.

I was nearing the bottom of the bowl when Martha brought in another tray. This one had all the things I had helped her with. She placed the tray at the edge of the table and began removing the bowls and plates of meat and vegetables. I never saw so much food at one time, except for Thanksgiving, maybe.

"Hi, Mom," a boy said as he burst into the room. He plopped himself down on the chair across from me.

138

"Where were you, Donald? You're late."

"Out!" he said. He swiped a piece of meat off the platter and stuffed it into his mouth.

Donald was about the same age as Walter, fifteen. His face was pimply as well as dirty. His strawlike brown hair jutted out in all directions from under a worn and tattered Yankee baseball cap. His clothes were as raggy as mine. His shirt was wrinkled and tucked in only on one side of his pants. He swiped another piece of meat from the platter with his dirty hands and stuffed it into his mouth.

"Don't you ever wash?" Mr. Frazier asked.

"Sure I do," he said. "Hey, Mom! I'm going fishing tomorrow."

"You have school tomorrow," his father said.

"I know. I'm going down to the pier before school."

"Why not take Jennings with you?" Mrs. Frazier said. "I'm sure he'd love to go."

"Who's Jennings?"

"The boy sitting across from you, stupid."

"Charles! Don't speak to your son that way."

"Well, who the hell did he think Jennings was?"

"Well, that's still no way to talk to your son."

Mr. Frazier mumbled something into the back of his hand.

"Donald, this is Jennings. He's going to stay with us for a while," she said.

"He ain't gonna stay in my room. I don't want no damn kid sharing my room."

"He's going to stay in one of the guest rooms. Now, say hello."

" 'Lo," he mumbled into his plate.

"Hi," I said.

The room fell silent. Only the tinkling of silverware against the plates and some strange gurgling sounds coming from Donald could be heard. He was annoying his father, but Mr. Frazier didn't say a word. He just looked over at him from time to time and shook his head.

Martha poked her head in from the kitchen. "Would you like salad tonight, ma'am?" she asked.

"Yes, Martha," Mrs. Frazier said.

Martha pulled her head back into the kitchen and the door closed.

"Doesn't Martha eat?" I asked.

"The help don't eat in here," Donald snarled. "She eats the leftover scraps in the kitchen, like a dog." He laughed.

"Donald!" his mother snapped. "Be nice."

Mr. Frazier just looked over at him and shook his head one more time.

"Well, she does eat in the kitchen," Donald defended himself.

I felt sorry for Martha. I wished I could eat in the kitchen with her.

We finished dinner and everyone left the table. I stayed where I was. I wanted to help Martha with the dishes.

"Whatcha doin' in here all by yourself?" she said as she came in from the kitchen.

"I was waiting to help you."

"Well, now, that's right kind of you to wanna help poor ol' Martha. But you needn't bother yourself."

"It's no bother. I like helping you."

I cleared the dishes with her. I stacked them up on one of the counters near the sink.

"Martha, do you eat leftover scraps?"

"Mercy no!" she laughed. "Where did you get such a notion?"

"Oh, nowhere. I was just wondering."

"I'll bet it was Master Donald who put such things in your head." She laughed. "He's a bad one, he is."

I didn't answer her with words. I twisted my foot into the kitchen floor instead.

"Now, you listen to Martha," she said. "I'm the cooks around here. I always saves the best pieces for myself, and then I serves the rest of the family." She broke up laughing.

140

"That Master Donald . . ." She shook her head and chuckled. "Hey!" She suddenly remembered something. "If'n you is goin' fishin' in the mornin', you had best get yourself to bed."

"I've never been fishing, Martha. Have you?"

"Land sakes, no!" She chuckled. "You ain't never gonna gets my bones outta bed at no four o'clock in the mornin'. Lessen o' course my money pouch is burnin'." She began to laugh harder.

I reached over and pulled Martha's hand from the counter. I kissed it and scurried from the kitchen. I could still hear her laughing as I went down the hall toward the bedroom.

I lay at the very edge of the bed so I could look out the window. The sky was dark, but the moon was bright. It wasn't quite full, but almost. I was glad it wasn't. George always tried to scare Larry and me when the moon was full. He said werewolves came out and bit you. I didn't believe him, but it was a good idea to be careful, you know, just in case.

I could see the tall trees on the far side of the yard. They looked more gray than green in the light of the moon. I was thinking about Mom. I wondered how she was, and if I was the one who made her sick. I wished now she hadn't gotten up when Midnight died. Poor little Midnight.

Doggie would really like this room, I thought. I know he'd like Martha. I wish I knew some way of getting him. Maybe I could ask Sister Gerard. Or maybe I could ask Sal. Oh, gosh, Sal! I won't be taking his bus anymore. I won't get to see him or talk to him. Oh, gosh. First Midnight and then Mom, and now Doggie and Sal. I wonder why everyone I love always has to go away from me. I turned my face into the pillow.

"Hey! Get up if you're coming with me," Donald yelled.

I pulled my head from under the pillow.

"I'll be in the kitchen," he said. "Hurry up."

I staggered to my feet in a daze. I was still asleep. I had a battle with my left eye. It kept closing on me. I needed some water to help me win. I flipped on the light of the little bathroom.

"Egad!" It nearly blinded me.

I found the water and woke myself up.

"If this is what it's like to go fishin' . . . why does anyone go?" I mumbled.

I finished up in the bathroom and got dressed. I met Donald in the kitchen.

"If you want anything, get it," he snarled. "But hurry up!"

"No, I'm all right."

He picked up an old dented pail with one hand, and the fishing poles with the other. He pushed open the pantry door with his foot.

"Let's go," he said as the door slammed behind him.

I glanced up at the kitchen clock before I slipped out the door. It read ten after four. Wow! I thought. I was never up at this hour before. I was starting to get really excited about my first time fishing.

"Are you sure the fish will be awake by now?" I asked.

"Fish don't sleep, stupid!"

"Never?"

"Never. They take naps once in a while, but they never sleep."

"Gee, I didn't know that. I wonder how they can stay awake so long?"

"Did you ever try to sleep underwater?" he asked.

We reached a rise in the road. The rest of the way was downhill. There at the bottom, breaking the darkness of night, were dozens of tiny lights shimmering off the water. To my left I saw a long string of green lights that seemed to stretch for miles.

"What's that?" I asked.

"What?"

"All those green lights."

"That's the Whitestone Bridge."

"Oh, wow. I never saw a bridge."

"You never saw a bridge? Where you been?"

"I don't know. I just wasn't anywhere around a bridge. That's all."

When we got to the bottom of the hill, I could see a long wooden pier jutting straight out into the water. Our feet made a clomping sound against the old thick boards of the pier. We reached the end and Donald set the pail down.

"This is it," he said.

"It's beautiful," I said.

"What?"

He looked out at what I was looking at and shrugged his shoulders. I stared out at the shimmering lights against the water and the wide open space that lay in front of me. It is beautiful, I thought.

Donald handed me a pole. "I'm not going to bother teaching you how to cast," he said. "Just drop the line straight down."

He helped me unreel my line. I was fishing for the first time. I was very excited.

"I hope I catch something," I said.

"Well, don't expect much the first time," he said.

He filled the old pail by lowering it down to the water with a rope.

"What's the water for?" I asked.

"That's to put the fish in. Just in case we catch any. This way they stay fresh."

I stood by the wooden rail with one foot on top of the other and waited. Donald did the same. As the morning sun began to rise, I could see more and more things. I saw a long row of boats, all tied together.

"Look at all those boats," I said.

"Shhhh," Donald said with his fingers to his lips. "That's the marina," he whispered.

"Oh. That's where your father keeps his boat," I also whispered.

"That's right," he again whispered.

"Why are we whispering?" I asked.

"We'll scare the fish away if we don't," he said.

"Oh."

Donald's reel began to spin with a whine. "I got one!" he shouted.

I was so excited. His pole bent as the fish took his line. My eyes were wide open. He reeled in the line and bent the pole. He did it again and again until he pulled up the fish and swung it over to the pail.

"It's a shark!" I shrieked. "You caught a shark!"

I had seen sharks in the movies, so I knew what they looked like. But I always thought they were bigger. This one was about ten inches long.

"It's a sand shark," he said. "I'll throw him back."

"No, don't do that!" I said. "I want him."

"But it's only a sand shark. I catch them all the time."

"Oh, but I want him. Can I have him?"

Donald chuckled slightly but didn't say anything. He unhoooked the sand shark and slipped him into the pail. I sat back on my heels and watched the fish swim around in the pail.

"You better watch your line," he said.

"Oh, yeah." I jumped back to the rail. I was more determined now than ever. I wanted to catch something, too.

Suddenly there was a tug at my line. "I got something!" I shouted.

"Hook him!" he ordered. "Pull up and hook him!"

I did. I pulled up hard and he was hooked. The reel spun in my hand. Donald shouted orders to me and I followed. I dipped the pole down and reeled as I pulled it up. I did it again and again. I'm sure I got his orders all backwards, but I got the fish. As I started to pull him up, Donald grabbed hold of the line and helped. He pulled the line hand over hand and landed the fish on the pier. It was really big. Much too big to fit in the pail.

"It's a striper," he said.

"A striper? Is that a good one?" I asked.

"Yeah, well, it's okay. It's not as good as a shark, but it's only your first time."

"Maybe next time I'll get a shark," I said.

"Yeah, maybe," Donald said as he started taking apart the fishing poles.

"Are we leaving?" I asked.

"Sure. We gotta go to school."

"Oh, yeah! I forgot. I sure wish we had more time," I said. "Maybe I could catch a shark now."

"I got an idea," he said. "How much money do you have?"

"Money?" I patted my pockets. "I don't got no money."

"Oh, well." He went into deep thought.

"Well, what?" I asked. "What?"

He sighed a great sigh. "Since you're poor," he said, "I'll let you have the shark for nothing."

"Really!" I said. "Oh, wow! Thank you." I looked into the pail at my shark.

"It's too bad you don't have anything to give me," he said. "You know . . . sort of like a trade."

"Well . . ." I thought for a moment. "How about my striper? You can have my striper. I know it's not as good as a shark, but . . ."

"Okay. Let's trade fish," he said. "You say you caught the shark and I'll say I caught the striper."

"Is that all right to do?"

"Sure. It's done all the time. We went fishing together, didn't we?"

"Yeah."

"Well, then . . . I'll just tell everyone you caught the better fish. That's all."

Donald slung the striper over his shoulder and then lifted the poles.

"Come on," he said, "grab the pail."

I took up the pail with both hands and followed him off the pier. As I walked, I watched my shark swimming around. I couldn't wait to show Martha, and tell some of the kids in my class. We walked back up the hill toward the house. The pail kept getting heavier and heavier.

"Hey, wait for me!" I called out.

He had gotten so far ahead of me, I thought I might not find the house if I lost him. I nearly caught up to him, when he started walking again.

"Hey, wait for me."

"The house is right there," he said as he pointed up the road.

It was. I struggled with the pail, setting it down every so often. By the time I had gotten to the pantry door, Donald was long gone. I brought the pail and my shark into the kitchen.

"Whatcha gots there?" Martha asked as she peered into the pail.

"A shark! We caught a shark!"

"A shark! Whats you want with a shark? Ya can't eat 'em."

"Eat him! I don't want to eat him. I want to keep him. You know, for a pet."

"A pet!" She chuckled. "Now I thinks I heard everything. A shark for a pet. Well, set him down in the pantry and gets yourself ready for school. Donald is gonna show where to get the bus."

I put the pail and my shark in the pantry and started down the hall for the bedroom. I heard Martha laughing.

"Land sakes! What'll he think of next?"

Donald showed me where to catch my bus.

I climbed aboard and showed the driver my school pass. I sat down across from him and thought about Sal. I was really going to miss him. The Fraziers lived in a different direction than I did, so there was no way for me to take Sal's bus anymore. Sure, I could talk to Sister Gerard or to Martha, but

146

talking to them just wouldn't be the same. I couldn't tell them how I was feeling or what I was thinking, not the way I could to Sal.

I got off the bus and walked up the hill to school. I went into the yard. The school yard was filled with kids from all the different grades. Each grade had an area where they lined up when the bell rang. I went to the area of my class. I sat at the base of the tall black fence that boarded the yard and I watched the kids play. They were playing tag. Eddie Keegan was playing with them.

Eddie was the boy who sat next to me in class. He was really the only one in school I ever talked to outside of Sister Gerard. I borrowed paper from him sometimes, or asked him the answer to a question I didn't know. He would always lend me the paper or answer the question, but he never talked more than that. I guess he never really wanted to be friends with me.

"Hey, Eddie!" I called as he ran past me.

He stopped and backed up to me. He kept his eye on the kid who was "It"—he didn't want to get tagged. "Yeah?" he said.

"I went fishing this morning."

"Fishing! This morning?"

"Yep."

"Where?"

"In the water. Near the Whitestone Bridge," I said proudly.

He sort of looked at me funny. Like he didn't believe me.

"I did," I said. "I really did."

"Oh, yeah. What did you catch?"

"A shark!" I said. I knew he'd be impressed by that.

"A *shark!*"

"Uh-huh." I smiled.

"Hey, everybody!" he shouted to the others. "Listen to this. Burch caught a shark!"

The kids stopped playing tag and gathered around me.

"Burch went fishing this morning and caught a shark," Eddie told them.

I stood there proud and smiling, but not for long.

They started to laugh at me. None of them believed me.

"I did," I insisted. "I have him in a pail."

"A pail!" one of them laughed. "You put a shark in a pail?"

I was embarrassed. They laughed and laughed. They began to make fish faces at me and call me a liar. I left the yard and went into school. I knew Sister Gerard was in the classroom, so I stayed in the hallway just outside the door. I didn't want her to see me crying.

The kids teased me before the class got under way, but I did my best to close them out. I made believe I was in the dining room at St. Teresa's.

At lunchtime, when all the kids left for the lunchroom, I stayed behind as usual, but this time I had something to eat. I took out a sandwich and an apple. Martha had made me a bologna sandwich with butter and lettuce. "Ech!" I took off the lettuce and scraped off the butter as best I could. I wasn't used to eating butter or lettuce, so I didn't like it very much.

While I was drawing a picture of Doggie and Midnight, the kids started to return from lunch.

"Shark! Shark!" one of them yelled.

"Don't touch Burch's inkwell," someone else said. "You might lose a finger."

Sister Gerard came into the classroom, and the teasing stopped. She gave out a reading assignment.

"Michael," Sister Gerard called.

"Yes, Sister." I folded up the paper as I got to my feet.

She waved her finger for me to come up to her. I was sure she caught me drawing.

"Yes, Sister?"

"Your brother brought you some clothes," she whispered. "They're over at the convent. Remind me after your lesson this afternoon."

148

"Yes, Sister. Which brother?"

"George."

"Oh, okay. Thank you." I started toward my seat.

"And, Michael . . ."

"Yes." I turned back.

"Don't draw when you're supposed to be reading."

After my extra lesson Sister Gerard gave me a shopping bag.

"I think you should see if he brought you everything you need," she said.

I started to take everything out of the bag: there was a pair of pants and a shirt, two socks that didn't match but they were okay. They didn't have any holes in them. A pair of underpants, and Doggie.

"Oh, Doggie!" I cried. I hugged him up to my cheek.

Sister Gerard smiled and left the room.

"Hi, Doggie. I'm so glad to see you. I was afraid I wouldn't be seeing you again for a long time." I hugged him again. "That was really nice of George to remember you."

I repacked the shopping bag, leaving Doggie's head sticking out the top. I left the convent and went up to the church to visit St. Michael. I stopped just outside the front door.

"Now, Doggie," I said, "we're going into church to see St. Michael. He's my guardian angel. He might scare you a little at first, but he's actually very nice."

I took Doggie into church to see St. Michael. I knelt by his altar.

"Hi, St. Michael," I said. I looked up at his peaceful face. "This is Doggie. I know I'm a little too big to have a stuffed dog, but he's not just a stuffed dog. He's my friend. Ever since the Home of the Angels, when I first got Doggie, I haven't been able to think of him any other way but my friend. I promised Sister Clair I'd always love him and take care of him. I will. He's one of those special animals, you know. The kind Sister Clair never wanted to find lying by the wayside."

I left the church and headed down the hill to meet Sal's bus. I waited for a little while, but then it came rumbling along. He stopped and opened his doors.

"Hi, son. Where were you this morning?"

"I couldn't take your bus," I said.

"Well, come on." He made a sweeping gesture with his hand for me to come aboard.

"I can't," I said. I think my face told him something was wrong.

"What's the matter?" he said as he climbed out from behind the wheel. He got off the bus and crouched down in front of me. "What's wrong?"

"I can't take your bus no more," I said. I fought back my tears.

"Why not? What happened?"

"I got lent out. Mom got sick and I got lent out." I couldn't hold back the tears.

Sal put his big arms around me and hugged me. "It's all right, son. You go right ahead and cry. It's all right."

I cried into his chest. "But . . . but . . . boys aren't supposed to cry."

"Anyone who feels hurt or sad is supposed to cry."

"Even boys?"

"Even boys." He hugged me. "Who's this?" he asked. He lifted Doggie from the top of the bag.

"That's Doggie." I sniffled back my tears.

"Well, hello, Doggie." He boomed out a laugh. "Where'd you get him?"

"From the Home of the Angels."

"Oh! So he's one of us." He tweaked his nose.

"Yeah, he's one of us." I smiled. "Hey, Sal . . ." I turned serious.

"Yes."

"I ain't gonna get to see you no more."

"Why not? You're seeing me now, aren't you?"

"Yeah. But . . ."

150

"Yeah. But. Nothing. Your mom won't be sick forever. Until she's well, I'll see you right here. Whenever you get the chance."

"I can see you every day!"

"Sure, why not? You see, you got yourself all upset for nothing." He hugged me once more. "I have to go now. We don't want all these people late for dinner." He laughed. He was referring to the people on his bus.

"No, we don't want that."

"I'll see you tomorrow," he said. He tweaked Doggie's nose again.

"All right. I'll see you tomorrow."

He climbed aboard his bus and slipped back into his seat. He winked as he closed the doors. I watched Sal's bus until it went up and over the rise in the road. Even though I could no longer see it, I had the strangest feeling part of me was still on the bus with Sal. I shook my body. I hadn't ever felt anything like that before. I crossed the street to catch the bus that would take me to the Fraziers'.

"I thoughts I heard someone come in," Martha said as she poked her head into the hallway.

"It's only me," I said.

"Whatcha mean, only you?" She chuckled. "Gets ready for dinner," she said. "We're gonna have Master Donald's fish."

"Oh, yeah! How's my shark?"

"Land sakes!" she laughed. "He's fine. I fed him some bread, and it's like he done never eats before."

"Oh, good!" I scrambled to my feet and went into the bedroom to get ready for dinner.

By the time I reached the dining room, everyone was already at the table. Martha had placed a bowl of soup down for me. I started to eat.

"I saw the shark on the porch, Jennings," Mr. Frazier said.

I beamed with excitement. I was sure Mr. Frazier would be proud of me.

"After dinner, I'll take you down to the bay and we'll throw him back."

I was shocked. My face showed it.

"We can't keep a shark in the house. He won't live."

"I tried to tell him he couldn't keep it," Donald added. "But what can you do? He's just a dumb kid."

"Now, be nice," Mrs. Frazier said.

"A shark needs salt water, Jennings. He won't last in that pail."

"But—"

"Donald will take you fishing again, and he'll teach you how to catch a real fish. Like the one he caught."

I glared at Donald. He put his face into his soup bowl. He made some slurping sounds.

"Better fish?" I said.

"Yes," Mr. Frazier said. "He'll teach you how to catch a better fish."

"We can go tomorrow," Donald said.

"No, thanks."

"Don't you like fishing?" Mrs. Frazier asked.

"Yes, ma'am. But what good is going if you can't tell nobody you went?"

"What's that?" Mr. Frazier asked.

"Nothing," I mumbled. I finished eating my soup.

Martha served the fish. I shot another glance in Donald's direction, but it was no use. His head was still in his food.

We were nearing the end of dinner when my elbow slipped from the edge of the table and my head fell. I was falling off to sleep without realizing it.

"Martha," Mr. Frazier said, "why not take Jennings to bed? I'll take care of the shark myself."

Martha guided me away from the table. My eyes were almost closed. She led me to the bedroom, where I flopped down onto the bed. She began to undress me.

"I unpacked the bag you brought home, Master Jennings."
My eyes popped open.

"Here he is." She chuckled as she handed me Doggie.

I took him from her outstretched hand and cuddled him to my cheek.

"Land sakes," she laughed. "Now I gots me two babies to care for."

I heard her chuckles fade into my dreams.

I saw Sal after school every day. I could only be with him for about five minutes. It wasn't much, but it was better than nothing. I told him about the Fraziers and about Martha. I told him about my room with the little bathroom, and about the fireplace. It was good to share stories with Sal; he understood everything I was saying and everything I was feeling. He remembered what it was like to be alone.

One afternoon Sister Gerard gave me two shopping bags full of clothing.

"I don't recognize any of these things, Sister," I said. "Did George bring them?"

"No, Jennings. I sent a note home with some of the boys in your class who were about your size," she said. "Their mothers sent those things for you."

"Wow!" I said. "They're really nice." I looked through the shirts and pants in the bag.

"They're not new," she said, "but they'll keep you warm."

"They're new to me, Sister. Are all these things for me?"

"Yes, of course."

I'd never had so many things that were mine and mine alone. I always had to share my things with Larry. No doubt I'd share these things, too, when I got home.

My head was full of dreams of how nice I was going to look. I walked the dark streets toward the Fraziers' house. The smell of burnt wood in the air made everything seem wonderful. When I reached the house, I went straight to the kitchen and Martha.

"Well, now," she said as she held up a dark brown coat to

get a better look at it. "Aren't you gonna be the country gentleman."

Martha took both bags from me and sent me to clean up for dinner. I went to my bedroom to talk to Doggie.

"And now I won't have to wear any of these raggy things anymore," I told him. " 'Cept for my shoes, of course."

He was very happy for me. He couldn't wait to see what I looked like all dressed up. I couldn't either.

In the morning I put on a pair of dark blue pants and a green shirt with two little horses on the pocket. The brown coat Martha first looked at had a belt that tied in front. It was warm and fit pretty well.

Martha saw me to the front door and gave me a kiss.

"You be sure 'n remember what everyone says. You hear?"

"I will."

"Martha wants to hears what peoples say about her baby."

I threw her a kiss when I reached the end of the front walk. She laughed and slapped both of her hands on her thighs.

I took the bus to school. I imagined all the people on the bus must have thought I looked real nice. I couldn't wait to show Sal.

I had to wait about fifteen minutes for his bus to come. It finally did. Sal stepped off the bus and walked past me. He put his hand over his eyes as though he were blocking out the sunlight. He strained to find something. He turned around and saw me.

"Oh, there you are!" he boomed out with laughter. "I didn't recognize you."

I couldn't contain my smile.

"Why, you look terrific," he said. "Turn around. Let me get a good look."

I turned full circle.

"You really think I look nice?"

He pinched my cheek and crouched down in front of me. "You look wonderful!" he said. "Now, you go on up to school. I want to watch my son from here."

"All right."

He gave me a hug and held me for a moment longer than he usually did. He didn't know it, but I could have stayed in his arms forever.

I dashed across Main Street and walked up the hill.

There were five or six boys from my class standing by the black iron fence in front of the school. I knew as I approached they saw me and noticed my nice clothes. One of the boys poked another in the ribs and made a gesture with his head for him to look at me. I smiled.

"Hey, Burch!" he yelled. "You're wearing my coat."

"Do you like it?" I asked as I reached him.

Some of the boys began laughing.

"If you like some beggar kid wearing your clothes, I guess I like it."

They all began laughing.

"Look at the beggar boy wearing our clothes," one of the boys shouted to some others in the school yard.

My eyes filled with tears, but I fought them off. I bit down on my lip to keep it from trembling.

"Hey, rag picker! Don't you have anything of your own? You got my pants on," a boy said from the back row.

The kids had me fully encircled. As each kid insulted me, the laughs grew louder. A kid stuck his hand out and grabbed my shirt collar.

"You got my shirt, beggar. Take it off."

I slapped at his hand. He punched me full in the face. As I hurled backward into some of the kids behind me, I bit into my lip. The blood spurted out and down my chin. I regained my feet and lunged at him. Another kid grabbed my arm and spun me around. The crowd parted as I hit the boy who spun me. I caught him on the top of his head. He pushed back at me, knocking me to the ground. I could hear the chants "Beggar! Beggar!" as I toppled backward off the curb into the gutter. My left hand and wrist struck a car's license plate, and a gush of blood shot from my wrist. I gathered myself up

155

and began tearing at the belt tie of the coat until it freed me. I ripped off the coat and flung it into the jeering crowd. My blood splattered over the faces of some of the kids nearest to me. The chanting stopped. I tore open the front of my shirt. Blood was everywhere. I had the shirt half off when Sal's arms closed around me.

"I got you, son. I got you."

He lifted me up and turned me in one motion. I came down with my face flush against his chest. I cried uncontrollably. The blood from my wrist poured all over his shoulder and down his back.

"Get the hell out of my way," he yelled at someone.

He carried me into the school.

"What happened?" I heard the voice of Sister Regina.

"I don't know," Sal said. "I need a towel or something."

"Take him in here," someone else said.

Sal laid me down on a couch. There was a nurse over me. She was looking at my wrist. "This'll need stitching."

I couldn't speak, I was crying too hard. I had a difficult time catching my breath.

"Shhhh. Try to calm down," Sal said. He held me in his arms and rocked me.

A policeman came in with a boy from my class. "This kid said they were teasing him. Calling him a beggar. Who is he?"

"He's my son!" Sal said angrily.

"Let's get him to the hospital," the nurse said.

Sal lifted me in his arms. "This is some damn school you got here," he said. "A bunch of dirty rotten kids."

He carried me out of the school and through a huge crowd of kids. He placed me in the back of the police car and got in after me. We drove off.

Sal stayed with me until Mr. Frazier came.

"Sal . . . why did they do that?" I asked.

"I don't know, son. Sometimes it's just easier to be mean than it is to be kind, I guess."

He held me for a long time in his massive arms.

"I love you," I said into his chest. I said it so softly I was sure he couldn't hear me.

"Come on, son," Mr. Frazier said. "I'll take you home."

"I don't have a home," I said.

"I mean, to my home. Martha is waiting for you. She's very worried about you."

"Come on, son. Go with Mr. Frazier," Sal said. He gave me one last hug.

I got to my feet and left with Mr. Frazier.

As the car pulled into the driveway, Martha came running from the house.

"My baby! My baby!" she shouted.

I got out of the car and into Martha's arms.

"What did they do to my baby?" she cried.

"They didn't like my clothes, Martha," I said. "They called me a beggar." I began to cry again.

Martha held me. "It's all your fault," she shouted at Mr. Frazier.

"My fault!" He was shocked.

"It's not Mr. Frazier's fault," I said. "He wasn't there."

"Martha knows he wasn't there. Buts he shoulda been," she huffed. She was angry. "You think all you gots to do is take a boy in 'n stick him in a spare room, 'n that's enough. Well, it's not! Yous is supposed to see to the things he needs. Ah! Gowan." She huffed again and waved a hand at Mr. Frazier in disgust.

"It wasn't his fault," I said to Martha as she took me into the house.

"It is my fault!" he yelled. He walked toward us with his head down and moving side to side. "Martha's right. It is my fault, son. I'm sorry."

"But—"

"No buts, Jennings. Tomorrow, or when you feel better, we'll go to the store and buy you all the things you need. All right?"

"All right!"

"I'm sorry I talks to you—" Martha began to say to him.

Mr. Frazier put up his hand. He waved at her to stop talking. "You were right, Martha. I'm sorry I didn't see it myself. Thank you for telling me."

"Now, little boy. You gots to get to bed. Martha made you some soup."

She took me into the bedroom.

"Wait a minute, Martha."

I went to the closet and opened the door. I pulled down every stitch of clothing Sister Gerard had given me. I threw them into a pile in the middle of the room. Martha stood speechless. I gathered them up in my arms.

"Does you wants me to help you?"

"No, Martha. I want to do this myself."

I carried the clothes through the kitchen to the trash bin in the pantry. I threw them in.

Mr. Frazier kept his word. A few days later he took me shopping. He bought me pants, and shirts, and shoes, and everything. I knew when I got back to school I was really going to look nice and nobody was going to have a thing to say about it. In fact, I wasn't ever going to speak to anyone in school again, except Sister Gerard. I was an expert. The homes had taught me how to go through the day without talking to anyone. If I could do it there, I could do it in school, too.

It was a week before I went back to school. I met Sal in the morning before I went up the hill to class.

"Well, how are you feeling, son?"

"Fine. Do you like my new clothes?"

"I certainly do," he said. "I liked the other ones, too."

"Well, nobody else did! I like these ones better. Mr. Frazier bought them for me."

"That was very nice of him. Are you all ready for school?"

"I sure am. I'm not going to talk to anybody but Sister Gerard."

"Not even if they talk to you?"

"Nope. And if they make fun of me, I'll shut them out."

Sal crouched down on the ground in front of me. "You known, son, you and I have been through a lot of the same things—living in people's houses, often hungry, never having more than rags to wear, and being made fun of more than most. It could have made me bitter and mean and angry, and for a while it did, but then something happened to change me."

"What?"

"Well, I met an old man one day. He was sitting on a park bench that I used at night for sleeping. I told him to get off my bench. I told him to go and find some other place to sit. Well, he got up and started to walk away, but then he stopped. He turned back toward me and leaned on his cane. He said, 'You know, sonny, all my life I've been bitter and mean and angry. I never went out of my way to be kind to anyone. I never went out of my way to talk to anyone.' He paused a moment and then said, 'That's why I was sitting all by myself.' He then turned and walked away."

"I don't get it."

"I didn't either, at first. But after I thought about what he said, I decided I never wanted to be mean or bitter again."

"So you want me to think about it?" I asked.

"Uh-huh." He pinched my cheek and stood up. "I have to go now, son. I'll see you later."

"All right."

I walked up the hill toward school. I thought about the old man. I still didn't get it. I went straight to my classroom. As the kids came into the room, I ignored them. If they said anything to me, I didn't hear them. I stayed to myself.

At the end of the school day, I was on my way to the convent for my extra lesson when Eddie Keegan stopped me in the hall.

"Hey, Michael," he called.

I turned to see who called me, but then kept on walking. He caught up to me.

"Hey, can you wait up a minute?"

I kept walking.

"I just wanted to say I was sorry. That's all. If you don't wanna talk to me no more, that's okay." He shouted down the hall after me, "I just wanted to say I was sorry before you stopped talkin' to me, that's all." He tailed off his last few words.

I reached the door to leave, then turned back. Eddie was already walking in the opposite direction. The old man was sitting by himself, I thought, because he had no friends. He never talked to anybody, so he was always alone.

"Eddie!" I shouted.

He turned around. He smiled the biggest smile and ran toward me.

Eddie and I were friends from then on. Some of the other kids apologized to me, and I accepted. I still didn't have very much time to do anything but schoolwork and extra lessons, but I did get asked to play tag and Johnny-ride-the-pony at lunchtime.

Sal told me he was very proud of me for not holding a grudge. He told me holding grudges was easier than forgiving. He was right, too. I didn't really like accepting some of the apologies, but I did and I felt good that I did, later.

It was late in March when Sister Gerard handed me a note.

"What is it?" I asked.

"It's for Mr. Frazier."

"Is it a report card?"

"No," she said. "Just give it to him. It's from Sister Regina."

I worried all day about the note. I couldn't wait to find out what it said.

At dinnertime I gave the note to Mr. Frazier.

"He was probably kicked out of school," Donald said into his plate.

160

"If the note came from you, I'd agree," he said.

"Charles! Is that any way to talk about your son?" Mrs. Frazier said.

"Is it all right for Donald to say things like that about Jennings?" he asked, instead of answering her. "Well, never mind." He said, "Jennings is leaving."

"Leaving!" Mrs. Frazier said.

"Yes, he's going home."

"Home! I'm going home?"

"Your brother is coming for you tomorrow. Sister Regina wants us to send you to school with all your belongings. George will pick you up at three o'clock."

"Wow!"

"What's all the excitement about?" Martha asked as she entered the dining room.

"The kid's leaving," Donald mumbled.

"I'm going home, Martha."

"Oh, baby, that's wonderful." She hugged me.

"How about serving dinner?" Donald said in a grumble.

"Donald!" his mother snapped.

"Martha's goin' miss her baby," she said as she continued to hug me.

I was very embarrassed.

After dinner, I said good-bye to the Fraziers and thanked them. Martha took me to my room to help me pack my things. I piled all the things Mr. Frazier had bought me in a separate pile.

"Aren't you going to take them?" Martha asked.

"No," I said. "They don't belong to me."

"Whatcha mean, they don'ts belong to you? 'Couse they do."

Martha stomped out of the bedroom. She returned a few minutes later with Mr. Frazier.

"Now, tells him," she said.

"Don't you want the things I bought you?"

"Yes, sir. But I didn't think they were mine."

"Well, they are, and you're welcome to them." He sat at the edge of the bed. "You know, Jennings, I haven't been as attentive to your needs as I should have been, and I'm sorry. I just want you to know that if you ever need anything, call me. All right?"

"All right, sir. Thank you."

He stood up and gave me a little hug. "Take care of yourself."

"I will, sir. And thank you again. You know, for letting me stay here, and for the clothes."

"My pleasure," he said as he reached the door. "Oh, by the way, I know you caught that striper. Donald couldn't catch a fish in the bathtub." He winked.

"Now, get yourself ready for bed," Martha said. "I'll be right back."

I finished packing my things. I thought about Mr. Frazier and how nice he was to me. Rich people aren't all mean, after all.

I was deep under the covers with Doggie when Martha returned. She turned out the lights and took a seat at the edge of my bed. She brushed back my hair.

"I wish you was my little boy," she said.

A warm tear ran down the side of my face.

"You've had some hard and troubled times for such a little boy," she whispered. "I wants you always to know, you gots someone here who loves you. If'n you ever find youself alone or in trouble . . . you jist get yourself back to Martha. I'll always be here for you."

She began to hum as she rocked back and forth on the side of the bed. She hummed so softly, I almost didn't hear her. I heard her more in my heart than in my ears.

10

George and I sat toward the rear of the bus as it rumbled down Main Street. I had the shopping bag between my legs, and Doggie tucked under my arm.

"Do you have to carry that thing?" George asked. He motioned with his head toward Doggie.

"He doesn't like traveling in the bag. It's stuffy."

"The way you talk about him, anybody'd think he was real."

"He is." I lifted him up to look at him. "At least to me he is."

"Put 'im down," George whispered. He spun his head around to see who might be watching.

"Oh, by the way, thank you for sending him to me."

"That's all right," he said. He patted my knee. "Well, how was it?"

"Not bad. The Fraziers are very rich. I had my own room, and we ate in the dining room. I even had lunch to take to school."

"Speaking of rooms," he sighed, "we moved."

"Moved! You mean we don't live in the house on Coolidge Avenue no more? I won't be near Midnight?"

"No more. In fact, it's better for you. You only have to walk a half a block to the bus."

"What bus?"

"What do you mean, what bus? The one that takes you to school."

"I mean, is it the Q44 or a different one?"

He chuckled. "It's the Q44. You can still see that friend of yours, what's-his-name."

"Sal."

"Hey, what is it with this guy? Why do you like him so much?"

"He's very nice to me. He talks to me and everything. Wait! Someday you'll meet him and you'll like him too."

"I doubt it," George mumbled.

"How do you know?"

"By the way, the new apartment only has three rooms. You, Larry, and Gene will sleep in one bedroom, me and Walter will sleep in the other."

"Where'll Mom sleep?"

"In the front room, the living room."

"Sounds pretty crowded," I said.

"Yeah, well, it's all I could afford."

"How's Mom?" I asked.

"She's okay."

"Hey, George? Why does Mom keep getting sick?"

"I don't know. Maybe it's all in her head."

"What do you mean, in her head?"

"Ah, nothing. Forget it."

"No. Really. What do you mean?"

"I mean, maybe it's all in her mind. Maybe she ain't really sick. Maybe she just thinks she is."

We rode in silence. I didn't understand how someone could just think they were sick and be sick. I remembered trying that sometimes when I didn't want to go to school. It never worked.

We got off the bus at Seventy-seventh Road and walked the half-block to the new apartment. It was on the first floor of a three-story building. Billy pushed open the front door

164

and went in. I followed him. Mom was in bed by the window.

"Mom," I called softly.

She turned her face toward me and smiled. I fell forward and hugged her.

"Oh, Mom," I cried, "I missed you so much."

"I missed you too, dear. I'm sorry I had to send you away."

"It's all right, Mom. The Fraziers were very nice people."

"I'll have to send them a little note," she said. She closed her eyes.

"Are you tired, Mom?"

"A little," she whispered. "But tell me, how do you feel?"

"Fine," I said. "My cut is all healed up."

"What cut, dear?"

"I cut my wrist." I held up my wrist to show her. "I got twelve stitches," I said proudly, now that it was over.

Mom's eyes filled and her lip started to quiver.

"Don' cry, Mom. It's all better now."

She reached out and took my hand and kissed the scar. She started to cry. She turned her face back toward the window.

"Don't cry, Mom. Please don't cry."

"Leave Mom alone," George shouted.

I sat at the edge of her bed for a moment. I brushed at her hair.

"Go inside," George ordered.

I got up and left the room. I went into my new bedroom.

The room was very small. A double-deck bunk bed on one side, a single bed on the other, and a chest across from a window filled the room entirely. I set my shopping bag down on the single bed.

"I heard you come in," Larry said as he stuck his head over the edge of the top bunk.

"Larry!"

"Hi," he said. "Welcome to the phone booth."

"Pretty small," I said as I turned full circle to look at the room.

"What can you expect when George and Walter do things?"

"George said it's all he could afford."

"Yeah, well, maybe if he drank less, he could afford more." He fell back on the bed and stared at the ceiling.

"Which is my bed?"

"That one." His hand flipped over the side of the bed, pointing toward the single bed.

I took Doggie from the bag and placed him by the pillow. I dumped the rest of the things on the bed. "I got some new things," I said.

"Oh, yeah?" He sat up and hit his head on the ceiling. "Ow!"

He rubbed his head as he jumped from the top bunk to the floor. I showed him the things Mr. Frazier had bought me. He held some of them up to see if they'd fit him. They would.

We talked about the homes we stayed in. He'd stayed with a family named Frank. He said they were all right, but he wouldn't want to live there. I told him I wouldn't mind living with the Fraziers.

"You mean, live there for keeps?"

"Well . . ."

"I said once I wouldn't mind living with Mrs. Keys, and you couldn't understand that. Now that you've lived with someone nice, it's different. Isn't it? It's not so hard to think of living someplace else. Someplace where you're not hungry all the time and not treated like a dog."

"I'm hungry here," I said. "But I'm not treated like a dog."

"Well, maybe you ain't. But—"

"Larry." He was interrupted by Mom's voice.

"See what I mean? 'Larry, Larry, Larry.' " He mimicked some strange voice whining out his name as he left the room.

I put my things into one of the drawers of the chest. I tucked Doggie down the side of the bed for safety.

Larry returned in a huff.

"What's up?" I asked.

"I gotta go to the store. Wh'd ya think?" He started to mumble to himself. "This is the last straw. I'm sick of goin' here and goin' there. I'm going, period."

"What are you mumblin' about?"

"Nothin'. I'm sick of this place."

"But we only just got here. How could you be sick of it already?"

"I don't mean this place." He pointed to the floor. "I mean this place where I am." He pointed to himself.

"I don't get you."

He picked up his coat and stormed out.

That night we had soup for supper. Larry, Mom, and I were the only ones eating. George went out, Walter was at school, and Gene was still away. Mom had her soup in bed. Larry and I ate in the kitchen.

The kitchen was as small as the rest of the apartment. There wasn't any room for a table, so Larry and I ate off a chair we placed between us.

"Hey! If we hurry up, we can see *Captain Video*," Larry said.

"*Captain Video!* Where?"

"On television. Where else?"

"But we don't know nobody with a television. Do we?"

He grinned from ear to ear. "George bought a television."

"He did?"

Larry dashed from the kitchen into the living room. He pointed to it. Sure enough, it was a television. It was small, but it was a television.

"When did he get it?"

"I don't know. Sometime while we were away. He said to be real careful with it. He's still paying for it."

"Wow! A television."

"Mom?" Larry called softly.

"Yes, dear?"

"Can Jennings and I watch *Captain Video?*"

"If you keep it low," she said. "I'm trying to get some rest."

Larry and I did the dishes as quickly as possible. When we finished, we put on *Captain Video*. It was a long time since I had seen it. After *Captain Video* we switched the channel to watch *The Lone Ranger*.

"This is terrific," I said. "A television right here in the house."

"Mr. Frank had a television, but he wouldn't let anyone watch it. He only watched it on Sunday, *Toast of the Town* and *The Fred Waring Show*." He made a face.

"Weren't they any good?"

"Singing and dancing and junk like that."

"Who said you could watch television?" George growled as the door slammed behind him.

"Mom said."

"Well, it's my television. Ask me, if you want to watch anything!"

He was slurring his words, and he had a hard time standing up without hitting the wall. He was drunk.

"Can we watch?" Larry asked.

"No," he said, and turned it off. He staggered into the bedroom.

Larry and I just looked at each other, and then went into our room.

"What good is having a television if you can't watch it?" he said. He climbed into his top bunk. "I hate this place," he mumbled.

In the days and weeks that followed, I saw a very different family. Nobody talked to anyone. Everyone seemed to be angry with everyone else. I couldn't understand what had happened. Fights seemed to be about nothing and they never ended. George was drunk or almost drunk every night. He

168

fought with Walter and Mom, calling them terrible names. Walter told him over and over that he hated him and that he was no better than the old man. I thought about the story Sal had told me about the old man, and wondered where Walter might have heard it. After every blowup between Walter and George, Mom always ended up crying. Gene and I fought like cats and dogs. If I was playing with something, he wanted it. If I wanted to do something, he wanted to do something different. He cried to Mom constantly. Even Larry and I didn't talk very much. He was either out or he was crying about having to do everything. I went to bed earlier and earlier every night. It was better just to get in bed and stay under the covers than to listen to all the fighting.

I still saw Sal twice a day, but I didn't tell him about all the fighting. I was a little ashamed of it and thought it was better to keep it to myself. Sal often asked me why I was so quiet. I told him it was my schoolwork.

It was Wednesday, April 25, just two days before my tenth birthday, when I boarded Sal's bus on my way home from school. Sal was quieter than usual.

"What's the matter?" I asked.

"I'm not sure how you'll take it," he said.

"What?"

"Oh, well," he said with a deep sigh. "I've been transferred. To the Bronx."

"Transferred? To the Bronx? You mean you ain't gonna drive this bus no more?"

"I'm sorry, son. I got bumped. Somebody with longer time on the job wanted this run."

I was in shock. I had never thought Sal would go away from me. I was numb.

"Son."

"Uh, yes?"

"I'm trying to work something out so I can get back. I like this run. I have a lot of nice friends here."

"Uh, yeah," I mumbled. "I hope so."

"Son, are you okay?"

"Uh, yeah," I said. I think if I weren't so stunned, I might have cried.

I couldn't think of anything to say. He couldn't either. We reached my stop.

"Are you going to give me a hug?" he asked.

"Sure," I said. "Sure."

I reached over the bar and hugged him. He pinched my cheek.

"Of all the friends I've made on the bus," he said, "you're the best. I'll miss you."

"I'll miss you too," I said. I stepped off the bus.

I watched as his bus pulled out and drove up the hill. I stood staring at his bus and listening to the roar of his engine. It suddenly dawned on me that Sal was gone.

"*Sal!*" I screamed. "Sal." The tears flowed down my cheeks. It was too late. I stood in the street looking out on nothing. Sal's bus was long gone and I was alone.

I crossed the street and walked the half-block home. No one was home but Larry. He was lying in his top bunk reading a comic book. I fell across my bed and cried.

"What's the matter?" he asked.

I gathered up Doggie and cried into him. I heard a thump as Larry hit the floor. He sat at the edge of my bed.

"What happened?"

"Sal is . . . Sal is . . ." I had a hard time trying to catch my breath. "Gone!"

"Gone? Gone where?"

I breathed a few times, then wiped my eyes on my sleeve. "He's gone to work in the Bronx."

"Is that all? I thought it was something awful."

"It is awful. Sal's my friend." I started to cry again. "I like him."

"It ain't no good liking people," he said. He climbed back into his bunk. "I thought you would've learned that by now," he huffed.

"But . . ."

"But, nothing. You get to like someone, and puff! They're gone. It ain't no good liking anybody."

He went back to reading his comic. I lay with my face pressed against Doggie. He's right, I thought. It ain't no good liking anybody. Sal's gone, Midnight's gone, Jerome's gone, Stevie's gone, and Mark's gone.

"Please don't ever leave me, Doggie," I whispered.

"What did you say?" Larry asked.

"Nothing," I mumbled. I closed my eyes to sleep.

My birthday came and went without notice. I didn't mention it, and nobody remembered.

One Friday afternoon I came in from school and found Larry putting all of his things in a shopping bag.

"Is Mom sick?"

"No," he said.

"Then what are you doing?"

"I'm leaving."

"Leaving? Leaving where?"

"I'm leaving here. I've had it. I ain't gonna take this shit no more. I'm tired of being a slave."

"What happened?"

"Nothing more than happens every day." He flipped a piece of paper at me.

It was a note from Mom. She wanted Larry to clean the bathroom and kitchen before he went out.

"Don't go, Larry," I said. "I'll help you clean the kitchen."

"It ain't the kitchen, it's everything. Since we left the Bronx, everything is different. I'm going."

"But, Larry, you're my only friend. Don't go," I begged. "Please don't go."

"I told you," he said, "it ain't no good liking people." He leapt onto the windowsill. Just that quick, he was gone.

"Oh, my God!" I cried. I fell onto the bed. I couldn't believe what was happening. I pulled Doggie up from the side of my bed. "Doggie," I cried. "I can't take no more of this. What are we going to do?"

Mom wasn't home two minutes when she called Larry. I stayed in bed under the covers. She called again. After a long silence she pushed open the door.

"Where's Larry," she snapped. "He didn't do any of the things I asked."

"He ran away," I mumbled into my pillow.

"What? I can't understand you."

"He ran away!" I shouted as I brought my face away from the pillow.

"What! Oh, my God!" She left the room crying.

I pushed my head back under the pillow.

"Where the hell is Larry?" George barked at me from the doorway.

"I don't know," I said from under the pillow.

Suddenly a sharp blow to my back stiffened me.

"Ow!" I yelled. "What did you hit me for?"

"I asked a question. Where's Larry?"

"I answered you," I screamed. "I don't know!"

Everyone blamed me for Larry's running away. They said I should have stopped him. I never heard such carrying on. I'd been sure nobody was even going to notice he was gone, but I was wrong. I stayed in bed and kept my head under the covers.

I had no idea what time it was, but it was late. Gene was sleeping and there were no sounds coming from the other side of my bedroom door. I slipped Doggie into a bag Larry had left and I climbed onto the windowsill. I dropped the bag to the ground, swung my legs over the sill, and climbed down. I had to hang-drop the last few feet, but I was down. I was out. I had taken the first step toward running away. Now what? I didn't know. I didn't have any money. I had to think. I know, I'll go to the Bronx and find Sal. I walked to the corner to wait for the bus.

"Excuse me, sir. Do you know Sal?" I asked the driver as he opened the door.

"Sal who?"

"Uh, I don't know. Just Sal."

"Is he a driver?"

"Yes. He used to drive this bus, but now he's in the Bronx. Do you know who I mean?"

"I think so. Is he a short guy, stocky build?" he asked.

"Yeah. That's him."

"What about him?"

"Could you tell me where he's working?"

He took a piece of paper from his pocket, and wrote down Sal's route and how to get there.

"Thank you very much," I said.

"I suppose you're not taking this bus now. Right?"

"Right." I smiled.

He closed the door and drove off.

By late afternoon I was on my way to the Bronx and Sal. I wonder if he'll let me live with him. If he doesn't, I'll just have to wander around till I get older. Then I'll get a job. . . .

The bus let me off at Tremont and Castle Hill Avenues at about five o'clock. Following the directions, I waited for the bus Sal should be driving. I waited, but no Sal.

"Sir?" I spoke to one of the drivers. "Could you tell me where Sal is?"

"Sal? Sal who?"

"Uh . . . just Sal. He's short and sort of heavy. He used to drive the Q44 along Main street in Queens, but now—"

"Oh, Sal. I know Sal. He's gone, he don't work again till Monday."

"Monday? What time?"

"Let me see." He looked at a piece of paper he took from his pocket. "Five A.M., sonny."

"Five A.M. Oh, boy," I sighed. "Thank you."

I sat down on the bench next to the bus stop to think. It was only five o'clock Friday evening. I had a long wait. As I was sitting there thinking, I hadn't realized I was also reading a sign: "Visit the Bronx Zoo."

"The zoo! What a wonderful idea. Would you like to go to the zoo, Doggie?"

He was very excited.

I asked a lady waiting by the bus stop where the zoo was, and she pointed the way for me. I thanked her and left.

Doggie and I walked down Tremont Avenue until we reached Boston Road. We turned right and walked a few blocks more. There was the zoo. It was closed.

The sign on the front gate said the zoo would reopen on Saturday at one P.M. I decided to walk around the zoo to look for a place to sneak in. I found one almost immediately. There was a low spot in the fence. I checked around to see if anyone was watching, and nobody was. I dropped my bag and kicked it through the fence. Next, I slid under myself. I was in.

I took Doggie from the bag.

"Isn't this great? A whole zoo all to ourselves."

We walked around looking at some of the animals. It was so quiet and still. Occasionally I heard the roar of one of the lions or tigers. I was very excited.

As the sun began to set, Doggie and I sat on a bench to rest.

"We have a small problem, Doggie. We don't have any food."

He agreed that was a problem.

Suddenly I saw a light. We were not alone. I jumped over the top of the bench I was sitting on and scrambled into the bushes. A policeman on a little scooter rode by. Oh, gosh, I'd better be careful. I decided to stay right where I was until morning. I propped up the bag and rested my head against it. I held Doggie close to my cheek and looked up at the darkening sky. I missed Mom.

"I don't like running away too much, Doggie," I whispered. "It's lonely."

174

Saturday morning came up with warm sunshine and the sounds of many small birds. I popped my head through the top of the bushes to look around. There were a number of workmen in the area. I ducked back into the bushes.

"I think we should stay here until the zoo opens, Doggie," I whispered. "There are lots of men out there."

I took out some comic books and reread them. I was trying to get my mind off food, but it wasn't working. I had an Archie comic that showed Jughead eating bunches of hamburgers. I decided to look at my baseball cards. I'll have to get some new ones, I thought. The 1951 season's started already.

I was lying back against my shopping bag and dreaming about how nice it would be to go to a baseball game someday when I heard a kid's voice. I popped out of the bushes and saw some kids with their parents.

"Oh, great!"

I ducked back into the bushes and began packing up my things.

"Come on, Doggie . . . food!"

I stashed my bag in the bushes and left. With Doggie tucked under my arm, I headed for the main restaurant. I stood Doggie up on a table near one of the trash baskets. I figured the best place to get anything to eat for nothing was at the trash basket. We waited a long time. Finally a lady threw away half a bag of popcorn. I swiped it out of the basket.

I finished the popcorn but was still very hungry.

"Hey, sonny. Who you waitin' for?" a man with a white paper hat asked me. He was sweeping the floor around the basket.

"Uh . . . I'm waiting for my friend Sal."

"Oh. 'Cause the boss don't like no one hangin' around that ain't eatin'."

"Oh."

"What time is he comin'."

"About five o'clock."

"We close at five oclock. You can't wait here all that time without eating nothin'." He turned his head in all directions. "Wait here," he said.

He swept his way back toward the restaurant and then disappeared. I wondered if I was gonna get in trouble. Maybe I shouldn't wait, maybe I should leave. I was about to leave when I saw him backing out of the restaurant door. He turned toward me. He was carrying a frankfurter, a soda cup, and a bag of potato chips. He had the chips tucked under his arm. He looked both ways as he approached me.

"Here, kid. Eat 'em slow. You gots three hours to wait."

"Thank you," I said. "But why?"

"My boss is a mean guy. I don't like chasin' people away, and I don't like gettin' yelled at." He smiled and left.

I shared my food with Doggie.

"He sure was a nice man."

Doggie agreed.

I took my time eating. I had a lot more than three hours to wait, but the man didn't know that. He thought I meant five o'clock today. After I finished eating, I slipped out of the restaurant.

Doggie and I visited lots of animals. We saw the seals, the monkeys, and the lions. We liked the monkeys the best. We were in the area of the bears when a zoo keeper told everyone it was closing time.

Doggie and I made our way back to our bushes and slipped in.

"Wasn't that fun?" I asked.

He thought it was terrific. He wondered why the zoo didn't have any doggies.

"I don't know," I said. "Maybe some zoos are only for animals you can't keep as pets. You know, like a lion or a giraffe."

He figured I was right, but he still wanted to see at least one doggie in the zoo.

"Well, you're here," I said.

176

He couldn't argue with that.

I took out my comics and my baseball cards. I read to Doggie from the backs of the cards. It wasn't long before I fell asleep.

Sunday was more of the same. We waited in the bushes until visitors arrived. We walked around and saw the animals. We stayed clear of the main restaurant because we didn't want to run into the nice man again. He might get suspicious if he saw me waiting two days in a row. I hung around the area of one of the smaller food stands. Late in the afternoon people started throwing things away. I retrieved half a frankfurter and some more popcorn. I found an empty soda cup and filled it with water. None of what I found was very filling, but it had to do. Before the zoo closed for the night, I found some Cracker Jack and another half of a frankfurter. I washed it off and wrapped it in a napkin to save for later.

The sun was long gone and the night sky was filled with stars. I lay with my head against the bag, Doggie tucked under my arm.

I fell asleep thinking about how nice it was when I had friends, and when all my brothers talked to each other, and when Mom wasn't sick. I thought about how long ago it was when I only cried because I hurt my knee or didn't want to go to bed. I wished things were like that again.

11

"Jennings!" Sal bellowed out. "What are you doing here?"

"I ran away," I mumbled. I stood on the top step of his bus. He held out his arms for me to come to him. I fell into his arms and started to cry. I didn't want to, but I couldn't help it.

"What's the matter, son?"

I cried hard against his chest. He kissed the top of my head and patted my back.

"Shhhh," he whispered. "You're here now with me. Don't cry."

He pulled his handkerchief from his back pocket and started wiping my eyes and nose.

"Blow!" he said.

I did. He wiped my nose and tucked the handkerchief into my top pocket.

"Now, sit down and talk to me."

I sat down behind him and hung over the back of his seat. I told him it wasn't really my schoolwork that had made me so quiet. I told him it was all the unhappiness at home. I told him about George's drinking and about Larry running away. I asked him if I could live with him.

"What would your mother say? Don't you think she'll miss you? Don't you think she misses you now?"

I didn't answer him. I knew he was right.

"Are you hungry?"

"Oh, yeah!"

"Good!" he said. "We'll stop after this run and get something to eat."

I watched the people getting on and off Sal's bus. I let my chin ride on the bar in back of his seat.

At the end of the run we went to a diner for breakfast. Sal ordered bacon, eggs, and pancakes for me. I propped Doggie up alongside the salt and pepper shakers and fed him some bacon.

After we ate, Sal ordered another cup of coffee.

"What are you going to do next?" he asked.

"Well . . . I guess I'll go back to the zoo."

He laughed. "I got a better idea. I'll take you home."

"Do you have to?"

"Yes, son." He got serious. "I have to."

"Oh, gosh, that's not a better idea."

"How about . . . if I take you home and ask your mother if I can come to visit you every so often. Is that a better idea?"

I thought about it for a long moment. "I guess that's not a bad idea."

He laughed. He leaned over to pinch my cheek.

"Sal . . ." I said.

"Yes?"

"What good is it to like people?"

"What?"

"What good is it—?"

"Yeah, I heard you. I just wanted to know where that came from."

"Larry said it ain't no good to like people 'cause they're always going away. Especially the ones you really like."

"Like me, for instance?"

"Uh . . ."

"Listen, son. Larry's wrong. There's a lot of good in liking people, even if they do go away."

"What?"

"Well, you at least enjoyed liking them, knowing them, and being with them when they were there. Didn't you?"

"But it hurts."

"Of course it does. And the more it hurts, the more you know just how special they were to you. If you never liked anyone because you were afraid they'd go away, you'd never know the joy of friendship. You would always be alone."

"Like the old man on the bench?"

"Just like the old man on the bench. You see, son, friendship is when your path crosses someone else's. For however long a time that may be, if you like talking to and being with that person, there's a joy in that. And when you part company, your sadness will only be as great as the joy you shared."

Sal took me home.

Mom hugged and kissed me. She cried and yelled at me.

"Where were you?" she asked. "I was worried sick."

"I went to the zoo."

"For three days!"

"Uh . . . I like the zoo."

She hugged me again. "Don't ever do that again!" She cried. "And thank you, Sal, for bringing him home."

Sal scratched the top of my head. "I'd like to talk to you, Mrs. Burch," he said.

"Rita. Please call me Rita," she said. "I feel I've known you for some time. Jennings has spoken of you so often."

"Why, thank you."

"Would you like some coffee?" she asked.

"Yes. Yes, I would."

Mom made Sal some coffee. They sat at the small table in the living room. Mom sent me into the bedroom so they could talk in private.

"Hey, Doggie," I said, "this is too important not to listen."

He agreed, but thought it wasn't nice to listen.

180

"If it was about just any old thing, I'd agree, but this is about Sal seeing me or not."

We listened. I pressed my ear against the crack in the door. I couldn't hear everything, but I did hear Mom say yes, it was all right for Sal to see me once in a while on weekends.

"Why do you want to do this?" she asked him.

"Well, when a boy travels that far and waits three days to see me, he's really telling me he has a need. I'd like to try to help him fill that need, if I could."

"That's kind of you," she said.

"Well, I'm not trying to be kind," he said. "I'm trying to be responsive."

"But you don't owe him anything."

"Don't I? Doesn't everyone who has something to give owe a little to those who need? He just needs a little time, and I have it."

"I don't understand all that stuff, Doggie," I said. "I just know we're gonna see Sal. Yippee!" I threw Doggie in the air and caught him as I landed on the bed.

I wish Larry was around. He'd change his mind about not liking anyone. He'd like Sal.

Sal started to come on the weekends. He took Mom, Gene, and me to bunches of places. He took us to Alley Pond Park for picnics, for drives in the country, and swimming at Jones Beach. Once in a while Walter came with us. Sal started to teach him how to drive the car. It was really nice having Sal around; he made a difference in the family. He came during the week sometimes and brought lots of food. He cooked dinner, or took everyone out. Occasionally he and Mom went out by themselves.

Sal made Mom forget her problems. She laughed a lot more and cried a whole lot less. She had a friend. Walter liked driving Sal's car, he liked playing Scrabble and other games with Sal and Mom, and he liked having some fun for a change. And Gene was absolutely crazy about Sal. He couldn't sit down without Gene climbing all over him.

Only George didn't like him. Anytime Sal came into the house, George left. He never did anything with us and never wanted to. I couldn't understand it. When George got drunk, which was often, he said ugly, mean things about Sal. I didn't care that he didn't like Sal, but when he said mean things, I got angry.

I asked Mom once why he didn't like him. She just said he had a sickness with alcohol and that it wasn't his fault. I didn't agree. He never tried to like Sal. He didn't even try to get to know him.

It was a Saturday morning. Sal was coming over to take us to the beach. I was looking for my bathing suit. George came out of his bedroom. He had a hangover. He went into the kitchen to get some coffee. I followed him.

"We're going to the beach. Wanna come?" I asked.

"No."

"You never go anywhere with us. Why not?"

"Leave it alone, kid," he said. He lit a cigarette.

"George, why don't you like Sal?"

"I just told you to leave it alone, and you ask me that!"

"I just wanna know, that's all."

He poured a cup of coffee and sipped it.

"I don't understand it," I said.

"Kid, I don't like anyone coming in here and taking over."

"He's not taking over."

"Bullshit! I break my ass for this family, and what do I get for it? Nothing. He comes along, and everybody loves Sal. He didn't have to carry this place when Mom was down. He didn't have to feed everybody and take care of the bills. He just comes in and laps up everyone's attention. Well, he ain't getting mine. Now, ain't you glad you asked?" He spilled his unfinished coffee in the sink and left the kitchen.

There was something in what he said. He did give a lot to the family, but he took a lot, too. I think the bitterness and meanness made everyone forget he was doing good things, or was it the other way around? Was he bitter and mean because nobody gave him credit for the good things he was doing? I was confused.

The water at Jones Beach was warm, but the waves were too big. Mom wouldn't let Gene or me go in any farther than the edge of the water. We played in the sand. Mom and Walter waded in up to their waists. They called Sal to come in, but he didn't want to. He wanted to lie in the sun.

"I'll be right back," I told Gene. I headed over toward Sal. "Hello," I said. "Can I ask you something?"

"Sure, son. What is it?" He lifted himself up to his elbows and shaded his eyes.

"Do you know why George don't like you?"

"I think so." He laughed. "Where do you get all these questions?"

"Is it because he did lots of things for the family and nobody thanked him? And then you—"

"That's part of it."

"What's the other part?"

"Well, George has a problem that none of you other boys have."

"He drinks."

"Besides his drinking. George is being pulled in two different directions. His heart is telling him one thing, while his mind is telling him something else."

I looked at him and scratched my head.

"It's something George has to work out. In time he will. Do you want a soda?"

"Uh . . . no, thanks. You know, Sal, talking to adults is tough."

We had a wonderful summer. All but George, that is. I couldn't remember when we spent so much time together. I wished Larry hadn't run away. I'm sure he would have had a good time too. I wondered where he was and what he was doing.

In early October, Sal took us all upstate to see the leaves

changing colors. We were all very excited, especially Walter. He had a chance to drive the car a really long distance.

He followed Sal's instructions and soon we were out of the city. The trees along the highways were beautiful, reds and yellows, oranges and browns.

Sal told Walter to make a turn. He did. We passed through two great stone pillars onto a narrow road. Along the sides of the road tall leafy trees overhung each other. It was as though we were riding through a tunnel of leaves. At the end of the tunnel there was a large red brick building with huge white columns holding up a balcony.

"Where are we?" I asked.

"I thought we could all use a rest," Sal said.

"I want a hambugga," Gene said.

"Let's get out and stretch our legs," Sal said.

We got out of the car. I saw a few people toward the rear of the building.

"What is this place?" I asked.

I no sooner asked than I spotted a boy running toward us. He shouted, "Mom!"

It was Jerome. I couldn't believe my eyes. It was Jerome. He hugged Mom and cried. Walter, Gene, and I gathered around to take our turns at greeting him. When it was my turn, I hugged him.

"How ya been?" he asked.

"Gosh," I said. "I had no idea we were coming to see you."

"You look kinda shocked," he said.

"I am. I am."

We walked around the grounds for a while. Sal told us he and Mom had planned the trip for some time. Only Jerome knew we were coming. We ate lunch in the main dining room. There were lots of other parents, brothers, and sisters, all visiting.

"This doesn't look too much like a hospital," I said.

"It's not," Jerome said. "It's called a convalescent home."

"Oh."

Jerome laughed. He knew I didn't know what he was talking about.

"Want to see my bed and my new models?" he asked.

"Sure."

"Can I go too?" Gene asked.

"No, dear. You stay here with us," Mom said.

We left the others at the table and went to his dormitory. It looked a lot like the homes I'd been in, except there were no bars on the windows.

Jerome showed me his model planes and ships. They were really something to see. Jerome handed me a baseball card.

"Yogi Berra?" I said.

"Yep! If he wins the MVP, put it up." He laughed and made a gesture with his thumb toward the wall.

"Right!"

He took out books of stamps. "I have a collection."

"Wow!" I began to look at all the pretty stamps.

"So George didn't come," he said. He seemed a little disappointed.

"Well . . ."

"I guess I didn't really expect him to," he said. "I was hoping, but not expecting."

"He don't get along too good with Sal."

"Well, what can you expect? With the old man twisting up his brains, how could he do anything else but hate Sal."

"What old man?"

"Your father. Who else?"

"My father!"

"Oh, boy . . . don't tell me you don't know nothing about the old man."

"You mean the old man on the bench?"

"What bench?"

"Never mind, never mind! Tell me about my father."

"Oh, boy." He sat down. "I really put my foot into it."

"Is my father alive?" I asked. My heart pounded.

"I can't believe nobody ever told you."

I sat back on the bed next to his. I had a million questions running through my mind, but none of them would come out.

"He's a drunk," he said. "He lives in the Bronx on 149th Street and Third Avenue with his mother. Your grandmother."

"I got a grandmother too?"

"Oh, boy," he mumbled. "Mom's gonna kill me."

"Jerome, you just gotta tell me more."

"I don't know what else to tell you."

"Uh . . . uh . . ." I couldn't form any words. "Uh . . . does everybody know?"

"I don't know. I thought you knew!"

"Well, I didn't!"

"Obviously. Hey! You can't tell Mom I told you."

"Why not?"

"She'll kill me, that's why not."

I sat thinking for some time.

"So, is that why George don't like Sal?" I asked.

"Sure. He likes the old man. They go drinking together. The old man tells him all this junk about Mom . . ."

"What about Mom?"

"He tells him she's crazy, junk like that. George believes him."

"How do you know all this?"

"Mom tells me some, and Walter tells me the rest. Walter really hates the old man."

"Is that why Walter and George hate each other?"

He nodded his head yes.

"Wow!" I said. "This sure answers a lot of questions. Things make a lot more sense now."

"Yeah, well, now forget it!"

"Did you ever meet him?"

"No, and I don't want to. He never did a damn thing for me or you or anybody. He's nothing but a drunken bum."

"I wonder why George likes him."

" 'Cause he's a drunk too. Drunks like each other. They help each other stay drunk."

"Maybe if George didn't drink, he'd see the old man never did anything for anybody. Maybe then he wouldn't like him either."

"Maybe."

"It's gonna be hard for me not to say anything."

"Well, try."

"I'll try. It sure messes up all my dreams, though."

"What dreams?"

"Oh, I don't know. I guess I wanted Sal to marry Mom and be my father someday, that's all."

"Forget it. Mom can't marry Sal until the old man's dead."

"Yeah, I know. Look at that. I only found out he was alive ten minutes ago, and already I wish he were dead."

"Join the crowd."

Jerome and I looked through his stamp collection. I tried to keep my mind on what he was saying about the stamps, but it was hard. So many things ran through my mind. So many questions and so many answers. Questions I wanted to ask, and answers I now understood.

The ride back home was fairly quiet. Gene fell asleep on Mom's lap.

"I'm leaving the bus company," Sal broke the silence.

"What!" Mom said. "Why?"

"I got a better job."

"Doing what?"

"Driving a tractor trailer from one state to another."

"Will you go away for long periods of time?" Mom asked.

I perked up to hear the answer.

"Three or four weeks at a clip."

"Really?" I asked.

"It'll be all right, son. You'll be in school and busy with your work. I'll see you each time I get back."

I sat in the back and sulked. I didn't want Sal to go away. I didn't want him to go away at all! He reached back and started to tickle me.

"Stop!" I laughed.

"As soon as you get rid of the sour puss, I'll stop."

He continued to tickle and I continued to laugh.

"Next summer," he said, "I'll take you with me."

"On a truck trip!"

"Yep!"

"Oh, boy!" I said. Suddenly it wasn't such a bad idea. I would love to go on a trip with Sal. "Okay," I added.

"Okay, what?" he asked.

"You can take the job."

Sal burst out with laughter.

Sal went on the road. I missed him from the moment he left.

I kept my word to Jerome. Even though he hadn't made me promise, I kept my word. Knowing my father was still alive sure made a difference with understanding why George did and said the things he did. And when Walter and he argued, and Walter said he was no better than the old man, I knew who he was talking about. I guess what bothered me the most was: why hadn't Mom told me about him?

Mom, Gene, and I were watching *Rama of the Jungle* one Saturday. Rain was falling heavily and there was plenty of lightning. It made the picture on the television jump all over the place. Walter had gone to do some extra work at school before the term started. George was getting ready to go out. The television picture went totally fuzzy. Mom tried fixing the buttons, but nothing happened.

"George," she called, "could you fix this?"

He came in from his bedroom in a huff. "What?"

"Can you fix the picture?" she asked.

"It's the antenna," he said. "It has to be adjusted."

"Can you adjust it?"

"For Christ's sake. I gotta go. I don't have time to screw around on the roof."

"I only asked. You don't have to get so angry."

"Why don't you get Sal to fix it? He seems to be able to fix everything."

"If he weren't on the road, he probably would," she said.

George stormed out of the house.

"I'll fix the antenna," I said.

"No you won't. You're too little."

"I'm not too little," Gene said. "I'll fix it."

Mom laughed. She went to the closet and put on her coat. I was angry at George for what he said about Sal. I wondered how long it would be before I said something.

"I'll be right back," Mom said as she left for the roof.

Gene and I sat in front of the television and watched the fuzzy screen. A few minutes later it started to clear.

"That's pretty good," Gene said.

"Yeah, not bad."

I was watching Rama's friend feed his parrot, when I heard a crashing sound.

"That sounded like it came from the hall."

I opened the front door and listened. Other people on the floors above us had heard it too. Some of them were opening their doors. I heard a scream. I dashed up the stairs and reached the third-floor landing. A number of people were already in the hall; others were still coming out. As I turned onto the last flight toward the roof, I saw Mom. She was lying faceup on the stairs. She was bleeding from her nose and mouth. Her eyes were closed.

"Mom!" I screamed.

I reached down. I wanted to hold her or something, when a man grabbed me.

"Don't touch her," he yelled. "I think her neck is broken."

"Oh, my God!" I cried.

"I think she's dead," somebody said.

"No, no. She can't be dead. She isn't dead."

I struggled to free my arms, but I couldn't. "Let me go!" I screamed.

"No, son, I can't."

Two policemen rushed past me.

"Get these people outta here," one of them yelled.

"Let me go!" I yelled.

"Who's he?" the policeman asked the man holding my arms.

"I think he's her son."

"Now, son, calm down," he said. "We're gonna help your mother."

"Is she dead?"

"No, son. She's not."

Two more policemen rushed past us. They were carrying blankets. My knees started to wobble. I was feeling weak all over.

"Where's my brother?" I asked.

"He's in my apartment," someone said.

The policemen lifted Mom. They slowly carried her down the stairs. When she was within reach of me, I wanted to touch her.

"Let me go, please," I begged.

The man released his grip and I staggered forward. I managed to touch her hand. I kissed it.

"I love you, Mom," I cried.

They carried her away.

12

The lady from the Child Welfare Bureau got out of her side of the car and came around to mine.

"Well, here we are," she said cheerfully.

I looked up at the cold gray stone building. As far up as I could see, the windows were covered with either wire mesh or bars. We were somewhere in Brooklyn.

She pushed open the entrance door and motioned for me to go first. I touched the brown paper bag I had tucked under my arm to assure myself I had it. I went in through the door and she followed.

The front hallway was tiled an ugly green, the center of which had worn down to a sick pale yellow by a million shuffling feet. She pushed open the second door and again gestured for me to go first. Inside, there was a fat lady with a polka-dot dress sitting at a desk. On the front of her desk was a sign that read "Stop here!" The lady's hair was pulled back and pinned.

"Good afternoon," the lady who brought me in said.

"Name?" the fat lady said without looking up at us.

"Tell the nice lady your name."

"Jennings."

"First name?"

"That is my first name."

"Last name?"

"Burch."

She scribbled my answers on a paper.

"Age?"

"Ten and a half."

"Residence?"

I hesitated to think.

"Where do you live?" she asked. She was impatient.

"Nowhere," I said.

"Any clothing?"

I touched the bag under my arm. "A shirt."

"Wait a minute," the lady who brought me interrupted. "He lives at—"

"It doesn't matter," the fat lady said. "His records will be here soon enough. Wait in there!" She looked at me but pointed to a door on the far side of the room.

I left the desk and headed for the green metal door.

"'Bye now," the lady who brought me called out. "Have a good time."

I didn't bother to answer her or look back. She was either very new at her job or blind. I pushed open the heavy door and went in.

The room was large and bare. There was one metal bench and a small wooden table along one wall. A few children's books were scattered on the tabletop and one on the floor. I picked up the book from the floor. It was dog-eared and torn. I put it on the table. Someone has scribbled something across one of the pages. I turned it around to see what it said. "God dam lier" was written in crayon across the faces of a man, a woman, a boy, and a girl. The page was the letter F for "family."

I sat at the edge of the bench and opened my bag. I took out Doggie.

"Here we are."

I looked around the room. The frosted-glass window was covered by a rusted old wire-mesh grating. A radiator beneath the window sputtered out steam and some dirty brown water.

The paint on the wall was worn away in the area of the water. Little chips of paint had fallen from the ceiling over the years but were never swept away. Only one of the two globe lamps that hung from the center of the ceiling was lit. The room was dark and gloomy.

"I know I'm going to be sorry I brought you here, Doggie," I said to his nose as I held him next to my lips. "But I can't make it through these places without you." I started to cry into his fur. He didn't mind.

After waiting a long time and scratching another inch of paint off the arm of the bench, I put Doggie back into the bag and lay down at one end of the bench with the bag tucked under my head. I closed my eyes and listened to the sputtering radiator hiss and spit out its insides. It sounded angry.

"Sonny," a voice called softly.

Someone tapped me on the shoulder to wake me, but I had already been awakened by the voice.

"Yes," I said to the back of the bench. I turned my head to see who it was.

"What are you doin' here, darlin'?" a lady asked.

I shielded my eyes from the light of the overhanging globe lamp so I could see her face. She was an elderly lady with gray hair. She had something tied around the top of her head, and was wearing a flowered dress, all faded and worn.

"Darlin'?" she repeated.

"The lady at the desk told me to wait here."

"Damn son of a bi . . ." She swallowed her last word. "Well, come along."

She took my hand and led me down a number of dark hallways. It was obviously late and past everyone's bedtime. She pushed open the dormitory door. The smell of pee rushed at me. I gagged. She took me over to a row of small cabinets. She rummaged through a number of them until she found an empty one. She handed me a pair of pajamas.

"Your number's fifty-one, darlin'. Don't forget it," she whispered.

"I won't," I said.

"Change and find your bed," she said, and left. She mumbled something about having to do everything. She reminded me of Larry.

I changed into the pajamas. They were about forty sizes too big. I positioned Doggie in his usual spot under my arm and held my pajama pants up with my free hand.

"Now to find my bed," I said aloud to myself.

The room was huge. There were windows on three walls. I checked the numbers of the beds as I walked. I reached bed number fifty-one. It was against the right wall near one of the windows. The shadows of the bars were cast across my bedcovers. It was like climbing into a cage.

There was a smell of bug spray in the blanket and the bed was clammy and damp. I didn't know if the pee or the bug spray smelled worse. I laid my head against the pillow and closed my eyes. I held Doggie against my cheek and listened. I heard a car passing on some nearby street. I heard an occasional cough and a few sniffles. I heard Mom crashing down the stairs. I fell asleep.

I was jolted awake by someone bumping into my bed. I popped from beneath the covers to see two boys fighting. I returned my head to the darkness beneath the covers and felt around for Doggie. He was safe under my pillow.

When the fighting quieted down, I came from beneath the covers again. I pulled Doggie from under the pillow and stuffed him under my pajama top. The pajamas were so big he was well hidden. I crossed the room. I reached cabinet number fifty-one and slipped Doggie inside. I stripped off the pajamas and dressed.

"I'll see you later," I whispered into the cabinet before I closed the door.

Doggie was well hidden behind the pajamas and a laundry bag. I followed some kids into the bathroom.

The room was very much like the bathrooms at the other homes, except there were no numbered hooks. I wet my face and wiped it dry on my shirt sleeve. I saw some kids brushing their teeth, but I wasn't about to ask them where they got their toothbrushes from. Until I learn the rules, I thought, I'm not going to ask anyone anything.

I stood beside bed number fifty-one and waited. I studied boy number fifty.

"Line up!" shouted a lady in a gray dress as she pushed open the dormitory door.

Kids scrambled to their places.

"Walk!" she shouted, then clapped her hands.

The line started moving. At first, the sounds of the shuffling feet were disorganized. But as the line moved from the room into the hallway, the shuffling feet became organized, rhythmic. We marched into the dining room. Girls shuffled in from the opposite side of the room, adding to the sound. On the command "Stop," we did. I was standing in front of chair number fifty-one.

Breakfast was a lump of lukewarm sticky stuff served in a heavy white bowl with a thin green line running around the outside. Hot cocoa was served in the same dented metal cups that were used at St. Teresa's. As soon as the lady poured the cocoa into my cup, I looked down at the floor. It was tiled and couldn't splinter even if it wanted to. I felt better.

All the ladies in the dining room wore the same kind of gray dress that the dormitory lady wore. There were no nuns anywhere.

I ate a little of the white sticky stuff but then decided a piece of bread and butter would taste better. It did.

We were taken from the dining room into a playroom. There were actually two of them side by side, with a large doorway between them. Girls stayed in one room, while the boys stayed in the other. Along one wall of each playroom were two sets of glass-paneled doors, opening out into a courtyard.

I drifted over to one of the doors and looked out. A number of kids had already gone out and were playing. The yard was made of the same gray stone, with the same wire-mesh fence, only this fence had barbed wire running all across the top. It frightened me. For the first time, I felt as though I were a prisoner. I kept staring at the barbed wire.

"Jennings!" someone shouted.

Mark was standing not ten feet away from me. Chills ran all over my arms and legs.

"Mark," I said weakly.

I couldn't believe my eyes. My hands met his.

"Mark."

I couldn't say more and risk crying. I think he felt the same. His eyes filled with tears. They were magnified by his big owllike glasses. We stood looking at each other.

"You got taller," he said.

"And you got fatter."

We laughed. The laughing seemed to make talking easier.

"What are you doing here?" I asked.

"Same thing you are," he said. "Waiting."

We laughed again.

"I got sick at the Home of the Angels, so they sent me to the hospital."

"What's wrong?"

"I don't know. You know nobody talks to us kids. When I got out of the hospital, they sent me here."

"How's this place?"

He shrugged his shoulders. "Sloppy. There's never anyone around."

"They don't need anyone around," I said. I looked out toward the fence and the barbed wire.

He followed the path of my eyes. "Oh, you mean the wire?"

I nodded my head. "I feel like a prisoner."

"You are. I mean, we are."

"I know," I mumbled. "I just never thought about it until now."

"When did you get here?" he asked.

"Uh . . . last night."

"What's your number?"

"Fifty-one. And yours?"

"Seventy-two."

"They sure got a lot of kids in here."

"They sure do."

"Where are we?" I asked.

"You know, every time I meet you, you don't know where you are." He laughed. "Don't nobody tell you nothing?"

"They don't talk to us kids, remember?"

We laughed.

"Well, you're in the Brooklyn Shelter. It's in Brooklyn."

We laughed again.

"Hey, Mark! I got something to show you."

"What?"

"I can't tell you. I wanna show you."

"Come on, then. Show me."

"Can I? I mean, now?"

"Of course."

We left the playroom and went to the dormitory. I opened cabinet number fifty-one and pushed back my pajamas. I removed Doggie and placed him into Mark's arms.

"Oh, Doggie," he whispered. He held Doggie to his cheek and closed his eyes. A tear ran down the side of his cheek.

"They took Brownie away from me," he said almost to himself. "I got sick and threw up in bed. They got real mad at me and took away Brownie." He seemed to be somewhere else while he talked, so I didn't say anything in response.

I stood alongside him as he replaced Doggie and covered him up. We were walking past the cabinets toward the door when he remembered something.

"Hey, wait!" he said. He went over to his own cabinet. He opened the door and pointed.

I walked over and looked in. There on the door was the angel I had made for him.

"I still got it," he said. "Sister Frances came to visit me in the hospital, and she brought it to me."

"Sister Frances?"

"I was surprised too."

We talked on the way back to the playroom. He'd been at this shelter for three months. He told me the food was lousy and the shower water was too cold. We went out into the courtyard.

"Is your mother sick again?" he asked.

I nodded my head yes. "She fell down the stairs and broke her neck and back."

"Oh, wow," he gasped.

I closed my eyes and tried to shake off the sight of her all twisted up on the staircase.

"It's good to see you again, Jennings. I missed you," he added. "I never thought I'd hear myself say that, but it's true, I missed you."

"I missed you, too," I said. "I thought about you a lot, especially after meeting Jerome."

"Jerome?"

"He's the brother who was in the hospital."

"Oh, yeah, I remember now. You met him?"

"Yeah, he came home for about two months. Let me see, now . . . it was just about a year ago. Gosh, he was nice. He reminded me a lot of you."

"Was he fat?"

"No," I laughed. "He wasn't fat. He was just nice, like you."

"I made believe you were my brother after you left," he said.

"Did you?" I smiled.

He nodded his head, but then lowered it. He was embarrassed.

"I sure would like it if we were brothers," I said.

"Well, that's impossible. That's just make-believe."

"Why? Why is it just make-believe?"

" 'Cause we're not brothers. Simple as that."

"No." I waved my hand in front of his face. "That's where you're wrong. Jerome once told me just having the same last name didn't make two people brothers."

"It's a good start, though." He laughed.

"Wait! He said it's what you feel inside about someone that makes you brothers, not the last name."

Mark didn't say anything. He just pushed his glasses back on his face and sort of stared off into space.

"What do you think?" I asked.

"If that's true, and it sounds pretty good, then we could be brothers."

"Sure! Why not?"

"Yeah," he said. "Why not!" He put his hand out to me. We shook hands.

"What's your last name?" he asked.

"Uh . . . Burch," I said. I wasn't expecting the question. "What's yours?"

"Burch!" he shot back. "What else?"

We laughed.

"Actually"—he got serious—"I don't know if I have a last name. At least I don't know what it is."

"There! You see? It could be Burch, couldn't it?"

He laughed. "Yeah, I guess it could be."

"Then we could have the same last name too, couldn't we?"

"Yeah, we could."

"Then let's say we do. All right?"

Mark got very quiet all of a sudden. His eyes filled and his lip quivered.

"What's the matter?"

He shook his head. I understood that meant he couldn't talk, so I waited.

"Until now," he broke the silence, "the only present I ever got was the angel you gave me." He sighed deeply. "Now I got a brother and a last name."

A bell rang.

"What's that?" I asked as I jumped to my feet.

"Relax," he said. "It's just the lunch bell."

"Already?"

"What do you mean, already? I'm starving."

We had franks and beans for lunch. They weren't too bad.

After lunch, the lifers went to class while the rest of us went into the playroom or the courtyard. I sat at one of the tables in the playroom and played checkers with myself.

"Burch Jennings," a lady called me from the doorway.

"Yes," I said. I stood up.

She motioned for me to follow her. I did. She led the way to the classroom and stopped just outside the door.

"You're to attend class each day."

"But . . ."

"But what?"

"I thought, uh . . . I thought class was only for lifers . . . I mean, orphans."

"Ordinarily that's true," she said. "But there's no telling how long you'll be with us. According to our records"—she held up a folder—"your mother has received some very serious injuries."

"And I'll be here a long time? Is that it?"

"I'm afraid so."

"Oh, gosh." I pouted. "Uh . . . could I ask a question?"

"Make it brief."

"Well, I once stayed with a family named Frazier . . ."

"Frazier?" she said. She opened the folder and looked through it. "I don't see any Frazier here. Was it arranged privately?"

"Sister Regina arranged it."

"Who's Sister Regina?"

"She's the principal at St. Michael's. My school."

"Well, that was a private placement. I'm afraid there's nothing I can do about that."

"You mean I can't stay with them again?"

"I'm afraid not."

"Oh, gosh. Why not?"

"Well, if the Fraziers, or anyone else for that matter, wanted you, they'd request you."

"Request me?"

"Ask for you. They'd want you, and ask for you."

"Oh, they want me, all right." I smiled. "Martha wants me."

"Son," she said. She crouched down. "I think you should forget about the Fraziers."

"Forget about them?"

"Please. Listen. I've experienced these things for a great many years. It's better if you just make the best of it here and forget about anyone coming for you. When your mother gets well . . ."

"Even Sal?" I asked.

"Sal? Who's Sal?"

"He's my friend. He used to drive the bus I took to school, but now he drives a truck. I left him a note to come for me. I shouldn't forget about Sal coming for me, should I?"

She looked away for a moment. "Son," she said, "I don't know how else to explain this to you except straight out. If someone really wanted you, like this Sal or the Fraziers, you wouldn't be here. Do you understand that?"

"You mean, they don't want me?"

"I'm sorry. Try to make the best of it here. Your mother . . ."

I didn't wait for her to finish. I pushed open the classroom door and went in. I sat down in the first empty seat I saw. She couldn't be right. Sal does want me. I tried pushing the thought of him not wanting me out of my head. I tried to pay attention to what was going on in the class. I couldn't.

"Hey, what's up? Whatcha doing here?" Mark asked.

Class had ended and I hadn't even realized it.

"Uh . . . I'm a . . ."

Mark sat down in the seat across from me. "What's the matter, Jennings? Did something happen to your mother?"

"No, no," I said. "It's nothing like that."

"Oh, good." He touched his chest with his fingers. "When I saw you come in, I thought . . ."

"Oh, no. It's not my mother. They just think I'll be here a long time. And . . ." My eyes began to fill at the oncoming thought.

Mark tapped my arm gently. "I know," he said. "It's hard to think of having to stay here a long time."

"You don't understand," I said. I began to tell Mark about Sal and about the Fraziers. I told him about Martha and about the note I had left for Sal. Mark listened. I told him what the lady in the hall had said about nobody wanting me.

"You know, Jennings," he said, "it's possible Sal's still on the road and hasn't found your note yet."

"Now, why didn't I think of that?"

" 'Cause the lady got you all upset."

"I'll bet you're right. I'll bet Sal is still on the road." I smiled and squeezed Mark's arm. "And I'll bet the Fraziers don't even know I was lent out again."

"There you go," he said. "You're probably right." He wiped his hand across his upper lip to remove sweat.

"Why are you sweating?" I asked. "It's not hot in here."

"Sez you! It sure is."

"No, it's not." I put my hand up to feel the air. I touched my forehead and then I touched Mark's. "Wow! You're burnin' up. Are you sick?"

"Naa. It's just hot in here." He got to his feet, but he staggered. He held on to the desk.

"What's wrong?"

"It's nothing."

"Don't you think you should go to the nurse or something?"

"No!" he snapped. "It's nothing."

We left the classroom and went into the playroom.

"Wanna go in the yard?" he asked.

202

"Ah . . . I don't think so. Maybe we should just sit in here for a while."

"I'm all right," he said.

"Are you sure?"

He made a funny face as if to say: "Don't be silly." He pushed open the door and walked into the yard. I followed.

We sat near the fence on the far side of the yard.

"This guy Sal, he sounds awfully nice."

"He is," I said. "Wait till you meet him. You'll like him."

"How will I get to meet him?"

"When he comes, I'm gonna ask him to take you with us."

"Naaa. Don't do that. Forget about it."

"Why?"

"Just forget about it."

"I'm gonna."

"Jennings, would you just forget about it, please?"

"Why, Mark? Don't you wanna come with us?"

He ran his finger along one of the cracks in the gray stone beneath his feet. "Jennings, I've been here a long time. Forever. Nobody's gonna take me anywhere."

"Sal will. When he comes for me, he'll take you too."

"Nobody wants a fat slob!" he said. His eyes filled. He put his head down to pay more attention to the crack.

"I thought you was my brother," I said.

"That's just for in here. Not for real."

"I thought it was for real. I'm gonna tell Sal it's for real. And I'm gonna tell him to take you too." I got up and walked along the fence. I didn't want to give him another chance to tell me no.

After dinner Mark got me a towel and a toothbrush. We washed, brushed, and changed into our pajamas. There weren't many kids in the dormitory, so I was able to carry Doggie over to my bed in the open. I slipped him under my pillow. Mark and I sat on my bed. He wanted to hear more about the outside. I began to fill him in on everything that had happened to me since I had seen him last. I told him about school and being left back. I had to explain to him what being left back meant. I was up to the part about St. Teresa's and Stevie when he yawned.

"Is this boring to you?"

He laughed. "No. I like to hear about new things. I'm just very tired."

He hopped down from my bed. "I'll see you tomorrow," he said. "I wanna hear the rest of what happened."

"Are you sure?"

He laughed and started to leave.

"Hey, wait! Where's your bed?"

"Not far," he said. "Watch me."

He was right, his bed wasn't far away at all. We waved to each other.

I slipped beneath the covers and pulled Doggie out from under the pillow.

"Isn't it nice to be with Mark again?" I whispered.

He agreed it was.

"I'm sure Sal will take him home with us, aren't you?"

He was sure.

After the lights had gone out and the room quieted down, I slipped out of bed. The room was dark and shadowy. I got down onto the floor and crawled under the beds. I made my way over to Mark.

"Hey, Mark," I whispered.

"What? Is that you?" He sounded a little groggy.

"Yeah," I whispered. "I got something for you."

"What?"

I placed Doggie in his arms. "I want to share him with you. You take him one night, and I'll take him the next. What do you think?"

I took his silence for a "yes" and crawled away.

I was sure Mark needed Doggie as much as I did. Maybe more.

After breakfast Mark and I were in the playroom. Rain had spoiled any outdoor activities, so the rooms were filled with kids all trying to play with the same games. Mark and I sat off to one side near the glass doors. I was telling him about Jerome.

"Did you ever learn to play chess?" he asked.

"Naaa. Not too good."

"I'll teach you."

"Really? I didn't know you knew how to play chess."

"Oh, yeah. I could teach you. Let's get the set."

"Now? With all this going on?" I said as I motioned toward the disorder around the room.

"Sure now. Nobody here is gonna be playing chess."

"You're right."

We got the board and pieces without any problem whatsoever. Finding a spot to play in was another story. We left the playroom and went into the classroom. We set up the board.

"You look pale," I said. "Are you all right?"

"I'm just tired. Let's play."

He showed me again how the pieces moved. I had forgotten. The longer we played, the worse Mark looked.

"I think you should go to the nurse."

"Listen, Jennings! I don't wanna go to no hospital again. Okay?"

"Okay. I was just suggesting—"

"Forget it. If I see a nurse, she'll put me in the hospital, and then I'll never see you again."

We played in silence for a while.

"Why would they put you in the hospital?"

" 'Cause they just would. They did last time."

"Are you feeling the same way?"

He nodded his head yes. "It's just a cold or something," he said. "It'll go away."

"Suppose I go to the nurse and tell her I got a headache. When she gives me an aspirin, I won't take it. I'll save it for you. What do you think?"

"That's not bad. Think you could do it?"

"Sure," I said, and jumped to my feet.

I left the classroom and went into the hall to find the nurse's office. I did. There was a white door with a big glass window next to it. I knocked on the door.

"Come in."

I pushed open the door and stuck my head in.

"Hi," she said. "Come on in."

"I have a headache," I said from where I was standing.

"Well, come in and I'll give you something for it."

I went in. "It's right here." I tapped on my head.

"What?"

"My ache."

"Oh." She laughed. She went over to a cabinet and fussed with a few things. She returned to me with a tiny little glass with some brown liquid in it. She handed it to me. "Drink this," she said.

"What's this?" I asked. "Don't you have any aspirin?"

"It's castor oil. If you still have a headache after dinner, I'll give you some aspirin."

"Oh. I have to drink this first?"

"Yes."

I drank the stuff. It tasted awful.

I returned to Mark and sat down.

"Did you get the aspirin?"

"No, but I'm working on it."

After dinner Mark told me not to bother getting him any aspirin. He said he felt better.

"Oh, good," I said. "For some reason I have to go to the bathroom again."

"That's the third time."

"Yeah, I know. It must be something I ate."

"Or drank." He laughed.

We changed into our pajamas early and sat on his bed.

"I've been thinking about what you said. You know, about Sal."

"What about him?"

"Do you really think he might take me too?"

"Oh course he will. I'm telling you, he will!"

Mark sort of drifted off a little. "You know," he said, "I never told nobody this, but . . ." His cheeks flushed. "I'm only telling you 'cause we're brothers now."

"Okay. I won't tell nobody."

"Promise?"

"I promise."

"Well, I dream sometimes of belonging to somebody. You know, having them tuck me in bed, and even kiss me good night. It's dumb, I know, but I dream about it sometimes."

"Didn't anyone ever tuck you in or kiss you good night?"

He shook his head no. "When you were telling me about Martha, I was dreaming about it then."

"Oh, Martha's wonderful. She would even hum to you."

We drifted off somewhere, he in his thoughts and me in mine. I'm sure we were both thinking of the same thing, Martha.

After the lights were turned out, I made my way across the darkened room to Mark's bed.

"Hi," I whispered. "I brought you Doggie."

"But it's not my turn," he said. "I had him last night."

"I know. But what can I do? Doggie said he wanted to sleep with you." I placed Doggie alongside him.

"Thank you," he whispered. He said it so softly I could hardly hear him.

I brought his blanket up to his chin and then smoothed it out. I took the loose end and folded it under his mattress.

For the next few days Mark and I stayed in the playroom. We played chess together. He was almost always tired, and so never felt like going out into the yard. I didn't mind. I liked being with him, so it didn't matter where we were or what we were doing. We never spoke about how he was feeling, because I knew he didn't like talking about it. We talked about the things we were going to do together on the outside. I think for the first time Mark was really happy about something. So was I.

We were in the dining room one afternoon. We were having spaghetti and meatballs. That was Mark's favorite. I looked over to see how he was doing. He was pale and weak-looking. I was about to turn back to eat my lunch when he slipped from his chair to the floor.

"Mark!" I screamed.

I raced from my place to Mark's table. Kids were around him; others were getting out of the way. Some of the kids nearest the doorway were calling for help. I reached Mark.

He was wet and clammy. His eyes were half-open and half-closed. I cradled his head in my arms and rocked him.

"There's help coming, Mark," I cried.

"I tried to wait for Sal," he whispered. "I tried."

"Don't worry, Mark, wherever they take you, we'll come for you."

"Will you?" he gasped.

"Oh, yes. Yes! I promise. We'll come for you."

I leaned down and kissed his forehead.

"Get out of the way," a lady yelled to some of the kids.

She pushed her way through the crowd.

"Give him air," she yelled. She pushed me down and lifted Mark in her arms. I grabbed up at his dangling arm and hand, but missed.

"Mark!" I cried.

She carried him through the crowd. I caught only a glimpse of the back of his head before the legs of the kids standing around encircled me.

"Mark!" I screamed. The tears flowed down my cheeks and into my mouth. I spit out the salty taste. I tried getting to my feet, but I couldn't. The kids were pressing in on me. Suddenly a sharp blow to the back of my head sent me sprawling. I landed facedown on the floor.

"Get up from there!" one of the ladies yelled.

As I struggled to get up, she yanked on the back of my shirt.

"What the hell is going on? A kid faints and you start some big commotion."

She pulled me to my feet by my collar, dragged me across the room, and flung me into the corner.

"Now, stand there till you learn to behave yourself!"

"But . . ." I turned to tell her Mark was my brother.

She slapped me hard across the face, slamming my head into the wall.

"Shut up!" she screamed.

I buried my face deep into the corner and cried. She clapped her hands together twice and the room fell to a dead silence. It was as though the clapping of her hands made everyone disappear.

I stood in the corner for the rest of the afternoon and on into the night. I heard the dining-room ladies setting the tables for dinner. They were whispering among themselves. I was sure it was about me. I kept my eyes to the wall and thought about Mark.

As I watched the tiny spots on the wall in front of me, and listened to the ladies' quiet chatter, I began to hear the sound of the oncoming feet. It came on like the roll of thunder. It grew louder and louder until the vibrating wall and the sound were one. Then suddenly, silence. One last explosion followed the command to "Sit." The tinkling and clinking began. During the course of the dinner, it built from tinkle to clatter, then fell back to silence. As the thunder moved out of the room, I began to think of how to see Mark. I had a plan.

After what seemed forever, the dining-room lights were switched off. I wanted to leave the corner, but I was afraid to.

I was startled when the lights went back on.

"What are ya doin' here, darlin'?" the lady asked.

"I'm being punished," I said.

"Well, git along with ya," she said in a gentle way. "Git yourself ta bed."

I left the dining room but went straight to the nurse's office. I sat in the dark hallway outside to think. The light from her window projected a small boxlike square on the opposite wall. I stared at it.

"Can I help you?" the nurse asked.

My heart stopped. I didn't expect her to be in the hall. I expected her to be in the office.

"Sonny?"

"Yes."

"Are you all right? Do you have another headache?"

"No," I said. "I'm looking for Mark."

"Mark who?"

"The boy who got sick in the dining room."

"Well, why not come in?" she said as she pushed open her door. "Are you friends?" she asked.

"Well, a little more than friends."

"Oh, you're buddies!" She smiled. "Well, Mark is a pretty sick little boy."

"What's wrong with him?"

"We're not sure."

"Is he gonna die?"

"No," she said. She gave my shoulders a hug. "They'll just keep him until they find out what's making him sick. He'll be all right. Now, don't worry about him." She handed me a lollipop.

I took the lollipop to bed with me. I gave Doggie a lick.

"Doggie," I whispered, "here's the plan. Tomorrow we gotta stash away some food. We're gettin' outta here. After lights-out tomorrow, we're going over the fence."

Doggie was worried about the barbed wire.

"I am too," I whispered. "But it has to be done. We gotta get out to see Mark.

I finished the lollipop and put the stick on the windowsill. I slid beneath the covers.

210

"Gosh, Doggie, I miss him," I whispered. "I love him, too."

Doggie felt the same. He wondered why I hadn't told him.

"Tell him I love him? I couldn't do that. I only told you, and . . ." I paused to think. "Sometimes Mom. I told Sal once, but I made sure he didn't hear me."

Doggie wondered why.

"Why? I don't know why. I guess people don't wanna hear that stuff. I never hear nobody say it. The only ones who ever said it to me, outside of you, and Mom sometimes, was Sister Ann Charles and Martha. Ah, Doggie, why don't you go to sleep?"

The following day I collected a roll or some bread at each meal. I stuffed them inside my shirt and then hid them in my cabinet. By nightfall I was ready to go. Instead of changing into my pajamas, I just slipped them over my street clothes. My pajamas were so big, nobody noticed I was fully dressed. I lay beneath the covers and waited. Rain began to fall heavily against the barred window.

I slipped out of bed and stripped off my pajamas. I took my shoes from beneath the pillow. Doggie and I were off.

I crouched down on the floor. The night sounds were loud. There were coughs and sniffles, creaks and squeaks. I was sure everyone was awake and could see me. My heart was pounding. I crawled across the dormitory floor toward the door. I reached the door. So far so good.

I crawled down the darkened hallway toward the playroom. I was just outside the door when I heard someone singing in the playroom.

"Oh, my gosh," I whispered. "I don't know any other way out of the building."

I decided I would lie in the shadows of the hall and wait. A long time passed before the Irish lady opened the playroom door. I pressed close against the wall and held my breath. She wasn't three feet from me. She set down her pail. She nearly laid it on my fingers. She closed the playroom door, lifted her pail with a grunt, and went on to the next door. She fumbled for the knob, then found it. She pushed open the door and went in. I began to breathe again. I slipped into the playroom.

I stood by the glass door and watched the rain beat against the glass. I looked far across the courtyard at the high fence and the barbed wire.

"Well"—I took a deep breath—"here goes."

I opened my laundry bag and placed Doggie inside.

"Now, don't go and eat everything up," I told him. "We need that stuff for Mark and for us, for later."

He said he wouldn't.

I slid the bolt back and pushed open the door. The wind whipped the rain hard into my face. It was cold and stinging. I closed the door behind me and stood flat against the glass door.

The yard seemed to be about a million miles wider than it was this afternoon. The rain splashed heavily against the gray stones and into puddles. I started running. I ran as fast as I could. The rain pelted against me. As the fence drew nearer to me, I prepared myself to leap. I did. I managed to dig my fingers around the small wire boxes of the mesh fence about a third of the way up. I held on. I pressed my arm against my laundry bag to keep it against my body. I strained to pull myself up farther. I wedged the toes of my shoes as far into the tiny boxes as I could. I was slipping off the fence.

Suddenly the yard was flooded with light.

"What the hell are you doing up there?" a man yelled.

He scared me. I couldn't move anywhere but down. I tumbled off the fence. The man was on top of me before I could even turn to look in his direction.

"I gotcha," he growled.

And he did. He had my coat collar so tight in his grasp I could hardly breathe.

"Stop!" I choked out. "I can't breathe!"

"Who's there?" a lady yelled.

"Some damn kid's trying to escape," the man yelled back.

"Let go!" I said as I yanked myself away from his grip.

"Bring him over here," she said.

He regripped my collar and pulled me to my feet. I grabbed my laundry bag as he dragged me toward the lady. I stumbled but managed to stay on my feet. We reached the lady.

"Take him to Mrs. Garrison, John," she said.

"Come on," he growled. He yanked me into the playroom.

It wasn't until I was in the hallway that I realized just how wet I was. My feet sloshed inside my shoes. We reached Mrs. Garrison's office. I was frightened. He knocked lightly on her door. I didn't think he could do anything lightly.

"Come in," she called through the door.

He pushed open the door. Mrs. Garrison was sitting at her desk behind a stack of papers.

"Yes, John?" she asked.

"I caught this kid trying to escape," he said rather proudly.

"It's not 'escape,' John, it's 'run away.' Thank you. You can go back to your duties now."

He nodded his head and began to back out the door. He backed right into the dormitory lady, who was coming in behind him.

"Ow!" she hollered.

He had stepped on her. I started to giggle, but it faded quickly. I knew it wouldn't be a good idea to laugh right at this time.

"Sorry, Rose," he said, then disappeared out the door.

"Well?" Mrs. Garrison asked me.

"Well, what?"

"Don't 'well what?' me," she snapped. "Where were you going?"

"Uh . . ." I wiped away a runaway trickle. "I was trying to find Mark," I mumbled.

"Mark? Who's Mark?"

Before I could answer, Rose interrupted. "That's the boy who got sick yesterday afternoon."

213

"Oh," Mrs. Garrison said. She moved some papers around her desk. "Rose, would you ask Margaret to come in, please?"

She nodded her head and left.

I wondered who this Margaret lady was. Was she going to be the one to punish me?

"Sit down," Mrs. Garrison said. She pointed to a chair near her desk.

I sat. I pulled my wet laundry bag closer to me.

"Oh, there you are, Margaret," she said.

I turned and saw the nurse who gave me the lollipop.

"This young boy was trying to slip out to see—"

"Yes, Mrs. Garrison. Rose told me."

"I thought it would be better if you talk to him."

"My, but you're wet," she said as she crouched down on the floor in front of me.

She attempted to take the laundry bag from me, but I pulled it back.

"Don't be frightened," she said. "I just wanted to get these wet things out of your way."

I pulled it back again. "Can I put it on the floor myself?" I asked.

"Sure, if you want to. I wasn't trying to take it. I was only trying to make you comfortable."

I placed the laundry bag by my foot. I was still very nervous about what the punishment would be. I was hoping they wouldn't take Doggie away from me. I had to know.

"Are you going to take Doggie?" I asked.

"Doggie? Who's Doggie?"

"Oh, gosh," I said. I hoped I hadn't put my foot into it and told them about Doggie without having to. "Oh, he ain't nobody."

"Is he your pet?" she asked.

"Uh-huh."

"Is he in the laundry bag?"

I thought maybe I'd just make believe I didn't hear her.

"Is he?" She smiled.

214

I nodded my head yes.

"Well, you don't have anything to worry about. We're not going to take him away from you. Can I see him?" she asked nicely.

"You promise you won't take him?"

"I promise," she said. She placed her hand over her heart.

"All right," I said. I reached down and undid the string on the bag. I lifted out Doggie.

"Oh, he's cute," she said. "But he's soaking wet."

"He fell in a puddle."

I still didn't know what the punishment was going to be, so I asked, "Are you going to hit me?"

"Hit you? Of course not. I just want to talk to you."

"Talk to me? Is that all?"

"Listen, son. Your friend was very sick. He had a bad heart."

"Is he going to be away for years and years?" I asked.

"I'm afraid your friend has died. He . . ."

I know she was still talking to me, but I couldn't hear her. Pins and needles ran all over my body. My lips felt light and my hands felt funny. The floor came rushing up at me.

"He's going to faint." A loud voice boomed in my ears.

"Are you all right?" I kept hearing over and over again like an echo in a long tunnel.

I wanted to answer the voice, but I couldn't. The words just wouldn't come. I tried to see who was talking to me, but the room was all black.

Suddenly I was jolted by a sharp pain deep inside my nose, somewhere behind my eyes.

"Mark!" I screamed. The words finally came. I blinked open my eyes and tried to pull from somebody's grasp.

"Shhh, now. Lie still," Miss Margaret said.

I was lying on the floor of Mrs. Garrison's office. Miss Margaret was wiping my forehead with something. Doggie was clutched in my arm. She put a white thing under my nose. I jolted back again. It was the thing that burned my eyes.

"Let's get him into my office," Miss Margaret said.

I was lifted as though I weighed nothing. I was floating out of her office and down the hall.

"Mark," I whispered over and over. I was hoping what she said wasn't true.

I was placed down on a white bed with a soft pillow. I saw Miss Margaret above me.

"Is Mark dead?" I asked.

"Shhh. Try to get some sleep," she whispered.

I started to cry. I brought Doggie up to my face and cried into him. Miss Margaret moved him aside and lifted me. I pressed my face into her stomach and cried. I stayed in Miss Margaret's arms for some time. A million thoughts ran through my mind. Mark was dead. He was gone. He was never ever coming back. He'd be like Midnight, buried somewhere in the ground, all cold and alone.

"I'm going to give you something to make you sleep," Miss Margaret said.

If Mark was dead, I thought, would he be with Midnight? I wish Sal were here. He'd tell me. I thought about what he told me about Midnight: "All that really matters now is that he knew you loved him, and he knew you were his friend."

Gosh, I hope so, I thought. I wish now I'd told Mark I loved him, even if people don't go around saying those things. Mark didn't know I loved him.

Miss Margaret stuck me in the arm with a needle. It pinched a little, but I didn't cry. There were no more tears left inside me. I wanted to think about Mark, but I couldn't. I started to fall headfirst down a dark and endless well.

The days that followed were lonely ones. I stayed to myself. I took Mark's angel off his cabinet door and put it on mine. I sat in the same spot in the yard where Mark and I used to sit. I thought about him, about how happy he was for just a little while.

The days ran into weeks and the weeks into months. I never made another friend because I didn't want any. The kids called me "Dummy" and "Weirdo" 'cause I never talked. I just had nothing to say, and nobody I wanted to say it to. I had Doggie. He loved me and he wanted me. And the lady in the hall was right. If I was wanted by anyone, I wouldn't be in here.

I was in the dining room one afternoon. We were having spaghetti. Remembering it was Mark's favorite, I looked over to chair seventy-two. There was another boy there, but it didn't matter. I only saw Mark. I saw him smile and push his glasses back on his face.

"Jennings Burch," the lady called from the doorway.

I stood up and pointed to myself. She gestured for me to come to her. The room was so quiet as I crossed over to her, only my footsteps could be heard.

"Get your things," she said. "You're going home."

Her words cracked the silence of the room like a whip. Goose bumps ran all over me. The hair on the back of my neck stood up.

"Is Sal here?"

"No," she said. "I think his name is Walter. He's your brother."

"Oh."

As I reached the dining-room door, I turned back to look at chair seventy-two. I didn't see Mark. I saw the boy who now owned that number. He was staring at me. All the kids were staring at me. Their faces were drawn and blank, but I could read their thoughts. I knew every one of them was wishing he was me.

13

"Was it awful?" Walter asked.

"It's a prison," I said.

He tightened his grip on my hand at the word "prison." Walter was lucky. He never had to know what one of these places was like.

I looked back over my shoulder toward the building and the memory of Mark. Some people were walking by. A man with his dog on a leash and a lady with an armful of bundles. I wonder if they know what's in that building and, if they do, I wonder if they care.

As soon as we boarded the train and took our seats, I took Doggie out of the bag. I let him look out the window.

"You still got that ratty thing?" he asked.

"He's all I got," I said.

I looked over Doggie's head as the train sped through the tunnel.

"You're very quiet," he said.

That was a kinder way of saying "Dummy" or "Weirdo," I thought. I wanted to talk, but it was hard to find words. I had been silent for so long, I was getting used to it.

"Jennings, are you there?" Walter asked with a smile.

"Yes," I laughed, "I'm here."

"For a moment I thought you might have left me."

"No. How's Mom?" I asked. I wanted to ask about Sal

too, but I was afraid of the answer. I was afraid he might not be around anymore.

"Not very well. She's in traction."

"Traction? What's that?"

"Well, that's hard to explain." He paused to find the words. "I'll describe it to you. It'll sound awful, and it is awful, but it's important. It's necessary to keep her back and neck in one place until it gets better. All right?"

"All right."

"She has a brace—that's a metal thing—around her chin. It's connected to some ropes to hold her head toward the top of the bed. Okay so far?"

"Okay."

"Then she has some belts around her waist, hips, legs, and feet that are attached to some other ropes to hold the rest of her toward the bottom of the bed. Attached to those ropes are weights."

"Weights? What are the weights for?"

"That's the traction. The weights pull her back and neck straight so she heals better."

"Oh, gosh!" I said. "That does sound awful. How long will she be like that?"

"A long time," he said. "A very long time."

"Will she stay at home?" I asked.

"Yes."

I breathed a sigh of relief. If he said no, I really would be a lifer.

"Larry came back."

"He did?" I perked up.

"He shouldn't have bothered," he said dryly.

"Why? What's the matter?"

"He's a drunk like George and the old man."

"Is he?"

"He's changed."

Gosh, I hope not, I thought.

"Walter?"

"Yes."

"Is the old man you mentioned my father?"

"Uh . . ." He hesitated.

"I know he's alive. Will you tell me about him?"

He thought about it, then said, "He's a drunken bastard!"

We rode in silence for a while.

"That's it?" I said.

"What else do you want to know?"

"Oh, I don't know. I thought there was more."

"No, there's no more. He'd rather take a drink than to see his kids have food, or clothes, or a place to live."

"Did you ever meet him?"

"Meet him? I lived with him. So did you, but you don't remember him. It's a good thing, too."

"Why?"

"He beat everyone up all the time. Never kept a job. He didn't have any education. He's a bum. George and Larry are following him right into the bottle. They'll end up just like him."

"George works," I said. "He helps Mom with money. Doesn't that make him different?"

"No! He's still a bum. He didn't have to quit school. We could have stayed in the Bronx. Things would've worked out. And maybe better, too."

"But nobody knew it wouldn't work out too well, did they?" I asked.

"I don't want to talk about it anymore," he said.

Again we rode in silence. I leaned my head into Doggie and closed my eyes.

"Education is the most important thing you can have," he said.

I sat up.

"If you have that, it's yours. Nobody can take it away. You can make a place for yourself, and nobody can hurt you."

I looked up at him. He was staring straight ahead. He was

talking to himself. I put my head back down on Doggie and closed my eyes.

We came out of the subway at Elmhurst Avenue. I remembered seeing or hearing that name somewhere, but I couldn't remember where it was.

"Where are we?" I asked.

"Oh!" He laughed and tapped his hand against his forehead. "I forgot to tell you. We moved."

"Moved? Where?"

"Here. Elmhurst."

"Elmhurst. Is that near St. Michael's?"

"No, I'm afraid not. I registered you into St. Bartholomew's."

"Where?"

"St. Bartholomew's. It's just a few blocks from here. You'll like it."

"I liked St. Michael's."

"Well, it's too far."

"Gosh. I liked St. Michael's." I pouted.

"Right here," he said. He was pointing the way into a huge apartment building.

"Here?"

"Apartment 5G. It's on the fifth floor."

The building was beautiful. Fancy gold lettering above the door read "Wingate Apartments." He used a key to open the lobby door. He walked to the right, and I followed. He climbed a few steps and stopped.

"What are we standing here for?" I asked.

"We're waiting for the elevator."

"Elevator? Like the one in Macy's?"

"Well, it's not as big as the one in Macy's."

"Can I tell the man the floor?"

"There is no man. It's automatic."

"What's automatic?"

"You just push a button and it goes by itself."

"Without a man?"

"Right."

"How does it know where to go?"

"It's automatic."

"Oh, gosh," I said. "We're back to that again. Can I push the button?"

The elevator door opened and we stepped in.

"Push five," he said.

I was amazed at the elevator going all by itself. It stopped at the fifth floor. We got out.

The apartment was very big. There wasn't much furniture, so maybe it just seemed big. Off the front hall was a kitchen and a living room. There was nothing in the room but a couch and the television. They looked lost.

We walked down a long hall to a back bedroom. We passed the bathroom, a closet, and another bedroom.

"Is Mom in there?" I asked.

"Yes," he whispered.

We went into the back bedroom. It looked like a dormitory. There were two single beds, a double-deck bunk bed, and an army cot.

"Who sleeps there?" I asked. I pointed to the army cot.

"You do."

"Oh, great!" I said.

"You won't think it's so great when you try it," he said. "And don't . . ."

I plopped down on the cot and it collapsed.

". . . plop down on it," he tailed off.

We laughed. He helped me put it back together.

"When can I see Mom?"

"When she wakes up. Now, let me give you some of the rules."

He told me a nurse would be in three times a week to bathe Mom. I had to make sure I was home to let her in. I was never to touch the bed, never to tell Mom bad things or complain to her. And I was never to turn off the light.

"Do you understand?" he asked.

"Why can't I turn off the light?" I asked.

"Because she's afraid of the dark."

I took Doggie from the bag and placed him on the cot. "Where is everybody, Walter?"

"Well, Gene is still away. I'll get him on Friday. George is working, and Larry's out. I have to study now, so be quiet."

I wanted to ask him about Sal, but again, I was afraid of the answer. I cautiously sat down on the cot and lifted Doggie.

"Hi, fella," I whispered. "We got a whole bunch of new stuff to get used to."

"Stop whispering!" Walter snapped.

"Walter?" Mom called out. Her voice was low, sort of muffled.

Walter jumped to his feet. I stood up.

"Can I come?"

"No, stay here."

I sat back down and hugged Doggie. "I hope I can see Mom soon," I said.

"Jennings," Mom called.

I looked around the corner of the door to see if it was all right to see her. Walter motioned for me to come in.

Mom was all covered up except for her head. Walter was right when he described how she looked. She looked awful. The tears welled up in my eyes as I got near her. She was staring at the ceiling.

"Jennings," she called again. The brace around her chin prevented her from opening her mouth all the way. That's why her voice sounded muffled.

"I'm right here," I said.

"Oh, I'm sorry, I can't see you," she said. "I can't turn my head."

"I'll come closer, all right?"

"Don't touch the bed," Walter said.

I got as close as I could.

"That's better," she said. "How are you, dear?"

I couldn't talk. The tears would fall if I did, and I didn't want to break the rule about upsetting her.

"Don't cry, dear," she said. "I know I look terrible, but I'll be all right."

"I'm not crying," I said as I backed out of range and wiped my eyes with Doggie. I stepped back to her.

"Are you going to be my little helper?" she asked.

"Yes," I said.

"That's good. I'm going to need someone I can depend on. Walter can teach you how to feed me. Do you mind helping me?"

"Of course not. I'll help you."

She closed her eyes. The room was silent. I didn't know if she fell asleep or what. I started to back away.

"Are you still there?" she asked.

"Yes." I stepped forward. "I'm still here."

"Please be a good boy. Don't drink like George or run away from me like Larry did." She started to cry.

"I won't," I said.

Walter tugged at my shoulder. He pointed toward the door. He wanted me to leave. I went back into the bedroom and sat down. Walter came in right after me.

"I didn't mean to make her cry."

"You didn't," he said. "She gets that way sometimes. She just starts crying."

I lay back on the cot and closed my eyes. I was awakened by Walter.

"Do you want some soup?" he asked.

"Okay," I said. I sat up and stretched.

Walter had the soup already in the bowl when I got to the kitchen. I no sooner sat down than I heard the front door slam.

"Who's that?" I said.

"George or Larry, I guess."

It was both of them. Larry zipped past the kitchen door and

went right on down the hall. George stuck his head in the door.

"Hi," he said.

"Hi. How are you?" I replied.

"Fine. Fine." He was a little glassy-eyed.

"Where's Larry going?" I asked.

"He's a little under the weather," he said. "Well, I'll see you later. I'm gonna watch a little of Uncle Milty."

"Who?"

"Milton Berle, *The Texaco Star Theater*. Come and watch with me." He left the doorway.

"Well, what do you think of Larry now?" Walter asked.

"How can I think anything? I didn't see him."

"Well, he's drunk."

"Is that what 'under the weather' means?"

He nodded his head. We finished the soup in silence, except for the tinkling of the spoons against the bowls. I was sorry to see Larry under the weather. I was looking forward to seeing him again.

I finished eating and joined George in the living room.

"The ventriloquist is Jimmy Nelson," George said, "and his dummy is Danny O'Day." He was explaining who I was watching.

"Oh. I thought you were watching something about an uncle."

"I am. Uncle Milty. That's Milton Berle's nickname. This is his show."

"Oh, I get it now."

During the commercial George went into the kitchen for a beer.

"You want anything, Mike?" he called from the kitchen.

"No, thank you," I said.

George was the only one who called me Mike. Everyone knew I had changed my name at St. Michael's, but nobody called me anything other than Jennings.

George returned with his beer and lit a cigarette. "It's not my fault," he said.

"What?"

"That Mom fell down the stairs and got hurt," he said. "It's not my fault."

"I didn't think it was your fault," I said. "I was mad when it first happened, but I got over that."

"Were you mad at me?"

"Sure."

"Why? I didn't push her down the stairs."

"No. But she asked you to fix the antenna. What difference does it make now?" I said. "I'm not mad no more."

"It makes a big difference," he said. "I want you to know it wasn't my fault."

"I know it wasn't. It was just an accident, that's all."

"Okay," he said. "How was the home? Rough?"

"Yeah, pretty rough."

"I want you to know I tried to get you almost as soon as you got there."

"Did you?"

"They wouldn't let me take care of you. They said seventeen wasn't old enough. I had to be twenty-one."

"Twenty-one! Egads. Nobody's twenty-one, 'cept Mom and . . . Nobody's twenty-one."

"Well, let's just hope there's no more homes," he said.

I nodded my head in agreement. "How's Larry? When did he get home?"

"He's all right. He just drank a little too much, that's all. As far as when he got home? Let me think . . . I'd say about a month or so ago."

"Walter's real upset that he's drinking."

"What's a few beers? That's not drinking. Walter's a pain in the ass."

"Walter thinks he's gonna end up like . . . ." Uh-oh, I said to myself. Now I did it.

"Like who? Me?"

"Uh . . ."

"Son of a bitch! I break my ass to hold things together, and what do I get for it?" He shook his head and dashed out his cigarette. "Doesn't anybody see anything but my drinking? Maybe I should be like Larry and run out when things get tough. Or like Walter, just take and keep on taking. Make a place for myself and screw everyone else. It ain't fair," he said. "I'm tired of it." He got up and left the room.

I sat by myself for a few minutes. I turned off the television and went into the bedroom. George was sitting on his bed. Larry was lying across his bed, fully clothed, and snoring. Walter was reading at the desk. I sat on George's bed.

"I see other things," I said. "You once brought me Doggie when I needed him. You tried to get me out of this home, and you're the only one who calls me Mike."

"Thanks," he said, and scratched the top of my head. "I'm just blowing off steam. Don't pay no attention to me."

I went over to my cot and lay down. I hugged Doggie and fell asleep. Sometime during my dreams I felt someone taking my clothes off. I was much too sleepy to help them. They covered me up and replaced Doggie in my arms.

"Good night, Mike," George whispered.

Walter woke me up in the morning. I dressed and watched him feed Mom.

Part of the morning, for about half an hour, I rode up and down the elevator. It was fun. I stopped on all the floors. I returned to the lobby for about the fifth time, when Larry got on.

"Jennings! What are you doing here?"

"I live here," I said.

"I know that," he laughed. "I meant when did you get home?" He got into the elevator and pressed the button.

"Yesterday afternoon."

"You got home yesterday? I didn't see you."

"I saw you. You were drunk."

He laughed. "I had a couple. I wasn't drunk."

"Larry. What are you doing?"

"What do you mean, what am I doing?"

"I don't know. I just remember you complaining about George's drinking, that's all."

"Well, I changed my mind."

"You changed more than that," I mumbled.

The elevator stopped at the fifth floor and we got off.

"You haven't seen me in a year, and all you got to talk about is how much I drank last night. Don't ask me how I am or where I've been."

"I was gettin' to that."

"Well, don't bother," he snapped. He pushed open the apartment door, then slammed it in my face.

Larry wouldn't talk to me for the rest of the day. I guess I couldn't blame him. I should've asked him how and where he was, and then asked about his drinking. This way, I would've known how and where he was before he stopped talkin' to me.

I fed Mom some soup and some tea. To feed her, I just put whatever she was eating in a glass and then held it up to her cheek. She did the rest by sipping it down through a funny-looking crooked straw. I asked her if I could use one of her straws to drink chocolate milk or something, but she said no. She was afraid I might break it. After she finished eating, I started to read a comic book to her and Doggie. I didn't get to the end of the first story before she fell asleep. I kissed her hand as lightly as I could before I closed the door. I made sure not to turn her light off.

After supper Doggie and I watched *Captain Video* and *The Name's the Same*. Larry had gone out, so we were alone. Doggie said he was tired.

"I am too," I said, and staggered down the hall toward the bedroom and fell onto my cot, carefully, so it wouldn't collapse.

The next morning, I went down the hall to the kitchen. As I turned at the doorway, there was Sal, sitting at the table reading the paper.

"Sal!" I cried. I flew into his arms. I knocked his paper to the floor.

"Hey! Take it easy. Take it easy." He laughed.

He kissed the top of my head as I hugged him.

Suddenly I jumped back from him.

"Why didn't you come for me? Didn't you get my note?"

"I got your note, but I couldn't come for you."

"Aren't you over twenty-one?" I asked.

He laughed. "Sure I am. But there's more to it than that."

"What?"

"I wasn't ready to make a commitment to you."

"What's that?"

"I wasn't ready to take care of you on a full-time basis."

"Don't you care about me?" I asked.

"Sure I care about you. But, there are other ways to show someone you care."

"Like what?"

"Like not lying to them, for one thing. I couldn't come for you and say I'll take care of you and then just leave you someplace, could I?"

I pouted a little before answering him. "I just missed you. I've been gone seven months," I said. "I missed you a lot."

"I missed you too, son." He hugged me. He held me in his huge arms.

"Son, isn't it better to know I won't lie to you? Isn't it better to know when I come for you, it'll be for keeps?"

I had to think about that for a moment. "I guess so," I mumbled. "But sometimes lying's better. It makes me feel good."

"But only for a little while. When the lie has to stand up as the truth and doesn't, it hurts twice as much." He raised his eyebrows as if to ask me: What do you think?

"I guess so," I mumbled.

Sal tickled me to make me laugh, then held me.

"How was it, son?"

I told him. I told him about Mark. He was pleased I had

remembered what he had told me about Midnight. I didn't tell him I felt bad about not telling Mark I loved him, because I loved Sal too. I figured nobody went around saying those things.

I told Sal I thought a lot about Jerome. "Do you think we might arrange to visit him again?"

He laughed. "I think I can manage that," he said. "But it'll have to wait until I get back."

"Get back? Back from where?"

"I have to go on the road tonight."

"Oh, gosh. For how long?"

"A few weeks. I'll try to arrange it when I get back. All right?"

"All right." I gave Sal a hug and he left.

I fed Mom some soup.

"Want me to read to you?" I asked.

"That would be nice, dear."

I got my baseball cards and read the backs of them to her. When I got to Yogi Berra's card, I said, "Oops!"

"What is it, dear?"

I told her about the deal Jerome and I made about Yogi winning the MVP. Then I had to explain to her what MVP meant.

"You have to get out more, Mom," I said.

She laughed. "Don't make me laugh, dear. It hurts."

"I'm sorry."

"I think I want to sleep now," she said.

In the weeks that followed, one day ran into the next. I fed and took care of Mom. I talked to her when I could, but it was hard. She would either cry or fall asleep.

No one was ever around, so I was very lonely. Gene had made some friends in the building, so I only saw him at suppertime. We would fight over television, but then he would fall asleep. Then I'd watch what I wanted.

One afternoon I found Larry packing a suitcase.

"Where are you going?" I asked.

230

"Away?"

"Away where?"

"Just anywhere," he said. He picked up his comic books and then threw them on the floor. "You can have them if you want them."

I didn't say anything. I just sat on my bed and watched. I thought about the first time he had run away and how I felt. It's different now. He was different. The Larry who ran away a long time ago never came back.

"You ought to run too," he said.

"Oh, yeah? Why?"

"You're just the damn slave around here," he said. "I'd be a slave too, but I'm too smart for them. You're stupid."

"Why am I stupid? Because I take care of Mom, I'm stupid?"

"That's right!"

"Well, if I don't do it, who will? You?"

"Not me, buddy."

"I'm not your buddy."

"Look! Don't give me any of your crap. If you don't wanna run, don't!"

"I don't."

"But don't give me any of your crap. I ain't nothin' around here. So I'm going. I'm going to where I can be somebody."

"What are you talking about?"

"I'll tell you what I'm talking about. George's the breadwinner. Walter's the brains. You're the goody-two-shoes, until they don't need you no more, then you're out! And Gene's the baby. Where does that leave me?"

"I don't know. Where?"

"Nowhere! I don't belong here." He slammed down the suitcase lid and stormed out of the room.

I sat by the window and looked down on Elmhurst Avenue. I saw Larry come out of the building lugging his suitcase. I hope he finds what he's looking for. I wished he could've found it here. I wished he never would've started drinking. I laid my head across my arms and cried. I was mixed up. I wanted to be angry with Larry because he had changed so much, but I wasn't. I was sad for him. Under all his growling and complaining, he was as lonesome as I was. He was looking for someplace to belong. I could understand that.

"Good-bye, Larry," I whispered.

I didn't tell Mom Larry had gone. She asked for him a couple of times, but I said he was out looking for work. I didn't tell Walter until maybe a week or so later. "So what?" was all he had to say.

My eleventh birthday came and went without notice. I didn't tell Mom it was my birthday because she would just start crying. I didn't want that.

Sal finally returned. I told him about Larry.

"That's too bad," he said. "He's getting used to running away, and that's no good.

"What do you mean, he's getting used to running away?"

"When someone runs from something once," he said, "that's one thing. But when they continue to run, it becomes a habit. They learn to run all the time instead of facing things. That's bad."

I told him not to tell Mom about Larry. He understood.

He talked to Mom. He told her he was looking for a new job.

"I'd like to be around here more," he said.

"I'd like that too," she said.

"I think Jennings and Gene need someone around. Besides," he said, "I'm getting tired of this job. I'd like to get something with less hours on the road. Maybe then I could stay in the living room."

"That would be nice," she said.

"I'll have to ask the boys," he said.

"I don't mind," I said, smiling.

"I know you don't mind. It's George and Walter I'm talking about."

"Oh, them," I mumbled.

"Yes, them." He laughed. "I'll ask them when it gets a little closer."

"When will that be?"

"Oh, I don't know. Maybe the late fall."

"The fall! That's years away," I said.

"No, it's not. It only seems that way."

Sal went back on the road the following day. I missed him. Fall was years away, and I knew it. I also knew George wouldn't like Sal staying in the living room. Walter might think it was all right as long as he could drive the car. But George. Uh-uh.

I was home one afternoon sitting by the bedroom window. Mom was asleep and I was alone. I saw what I thought was Sal's car pull up. I watched. Sal got out.

"Oh, Doggie, look! It's Sal!"

He was excited.

I held him up to see better. We watched Sal go around his car and open the other door. Jerome got out.

"Jerome!" I cried. I ran from the window and out of the room. I ran down the hallway and out of the apartment. I pressed and pressed for the elevator to come, but it wouldn't. I ran down the stairs. I almost fell over my own feet. I was just coming out of the stairwell when Jerome came down the hall.

"Jerome!" I yelled.

We threw our arms around each other.

"What are you doing here?" I asked.

"They let me come home."

"For how long?"

He shrugged his shoulders. "I don't know. For keeps, maybe."

Jerome was put to bed immediately. The apartment was like a little hospital, Mom in one room and Jerome in the other. But at least now I had someone to talk to. I was glad to be with Jerome again. I'd missed him. We talked about all sorts of things: stamps, models, baseball, and chess.

"You're really getting good," he said.

"I had a good teacher. Mark."

"Mark? Who's Mark?"

"He was a boy I knew at the home," I said quietly.

"You talk as if he were dead."

"He is."

"Oh. Well, we all have to go sometime."

He spoke so matter-of-factly, I was startled.

"Doesn't it bother you?" I asked.

"What? Death?"

"Yeah."

"No. When you've lived your whole life in one hospital or another, you get used to things like that."

"Oh, wow," I said.

"Are you afraid of death?" he asked.

"Uh . . . I never thought about it, really, not until Mark died. Now I think about it sometimes."

"It's nothing," he said. "For people like me, it's only the end of sickness and pain, that's all."

"And for people like me?"

He laughed. "People like you are better off not thinking about it at all. You get along better that way." He pushed his glasses back on his nose.

Jerome reminded me so much of Mark. If they had met, I thought, I'm sure they would have liked each other.

We talked about the family. We talked about Larry running away. He agreed with Sal.

"Running can become a habit," he said.

We talked about George wanting to be thanked for carrying the load by himself.

"I don't think he wants to be thanked as much as he wants to be recognized," he said.

"What?"

"He wants Mom and Walter to see he's doing good and

appreciate him," he said. "When all they see is his drinking, he drinks more."

"How do you know all this stuff?" I asked.

He laughed. "I pay attention," he said. "And I ask questions. Asking questions is how you learn, and learning is how you grow."

"Will I grow if I ask questions?"

"Sure."

"Then will you tell me what it means to have a brother, and to be one? I've been thinking about this for a long time."

"Sure," he said.

"Well?"

"Well, what?"

"Aren't you going to tell me?"

"Sure I am."

"When?"

"In time," he said. "In time, Jennings, you'll tell me."

"I was afraid of that," I mumbled.

"Now," he said, "tell me what Walter thinks about all this stuff going on."

I told him Walter thought education was the only thing that was important. The only thing you could count on. I told him Walter thought George and Larry were nothing but bums.

"That's too bad," he said. "Walter sees everything as black and white."

"What do you mean?"

"Walter only sees things from his point of view. He doesn't see George and Larry have created a whole different set of problems for themselves. Walter can only *spell* 'compassion.' "

I scratched my head. Jerome laughed.

"You see, it's like this. Walter, with all his intelligence, doesn't realize all of you have the same problem. You're all trying to belong, you're all trying to survive. He's found one way, and it's a good one. George and Larry found another, and it's bad. Someday maybe Walter will see how lucky he is. He could have just as easily gone a different way. Their way."

"Someday I'm gonna learn how to talk to adults," I said.

He laughed. "It's not all that difficult," he said. "All you have to do is say what you feel and learn to listen. It's called being open. There's two sides to everything."

"I'm glad I asked. Want to play checkers?"

He laughed.

After school each day I was anxious to get home and be with Jerome. He was my only friend—outside of Doggie, of course.

"Don't you ever go out anywhere?" he asked.

"No."

"Why not?"

"Well, I just take care of Mom and you. That's all. I used to go to the park across Broadway when the nurse came," I said. "She didn't want me around when she bathed Mom." I made a face.

"Well, why don't you go to the park now?"

"Now? But I want to stay with you."

"I want you to go to the park! You can't just keep staying indoors all the time. I stay in because I have to. But you don't have to."

"But—"

"No buts. *Go!*"

I went to the park. I sat on the bench and waited. I figured I'd wait a little while and then go back. I watched the kids playing on the swings and the slide. My eye caught sight of a blond-headed girl on the far side of the park coming toward me. I watched her. She came closer and closer. Her eyes caught mine. She stopped in her tracks and stared. I looked behind me to see who she was staring at. There was no one there. I turned back. Suddenly she started running toward me. I got nervous.

"Jennings!" she shouted.

236

It wasn't until she got very close to me that I realized who it was. It was Stacy.

"Stacy," I said. Chills ran over my arms and legs. "Stacy."

I started to stand as she reached me. She nearly tackled me back down onto the bench. She kissed me.

"What are you doing here?" I said.

"I live here. I've been away at school, but I'm back now. What are you doing here?"

"I live here too."

"Where?"

"Right there." I pointed up Elmhurst Avenue. "So that's where I heard the name."

"What?"

"The name Elmhurst. When I first got here, I was sure I had heard of Elmhurst, but I couldn't remember where I heard it. You told me Elmhurst, back at the home."

"Oh, wow!" she said. "I can't believe I'm seeing you! So, tell me." She grabbed hold of my arm and wrapped both her arms around it. "Where've you been?"

I felt the redness rise in my face and the back of my neck. "Everywhere," I said.

She asked me a million questions. She hadn't changed at all. Well, at least not in how fast she could talk. She had changed in appearance a little. She was taller and prettier. She was wearing a light blue dress with white lace around her collar and sleeves. Her hair was still golden yellow and shone in the sunlight. She was becoming a real young lady. She smelled wonderful.

"You know, I loved you when we were kids," she said.

I turned a bright red. The heat rushed into my face. "Oh, gosh," I said.

She laughed. "You still say 'Oh, gosh.'" She leaned forward and kissed my cheek. "You know, I still love you," she said.

"Oh, gosh," I mumbled.

She started to laugh again. She tucked herself close into

me. "I wasn't glad when I first got home," she said. "I wanted to stay at school for the summer. But now I'm glad."

"Oh, gosh."

Stacy and I walked to the edge of the park. She held my hand. Her hand was soft and warm. I hadn't realized how soft someone's hand could be.

"Will I see you here tomorrow?" she asked.

"Uh . . . yes," I said. "I'll be here tomorrow."

She leaned toward me and kissed me. She no longer kissed me on the cheek, but on the mouth. I was frozen where I stood. I watched her walk up the street. She turned back and smiled. I didn't see Stacy as forward anymore, I saw her as open. She was what Jerome was talking about. You didn't have to guess what Stacy was thinking or feeling, she told you.

I walked up the hill toward home. I was rushed with new feelings. When I got into the bedroom, I sat on my bed.

"What's wrong with you?" Jerome asked. "Fresh air too much for you?"

"Uh . . . I . . . uh . . ."

"Well, that's a good start. What else?" He laughed.

"I . . . uh . . ."

"You said that." He laughed again. "Want to play cards?"

"Yeah." I got up and went over to him. I sat on the cards.

"What's the matter with you?" he asked. "Are you in love or something?"

"What? No!" I said. "I'm not in love, I'm not in love."

He really started laughing. "I think you're in love," he said.

"Really?"

"Could be. I looked like that when I was eleven and in love," he said. "Who is she?"

"Uh . . . Stacy," I mumbled.

"Stacy. That's a pretty name. Tell me about her."

I told him. I told him when I first met her, about the home, everything.

238

"I think you're in love."

"How do you know?" I asked.

"You just know," he said. "You get all these tingly feelings. It's puppy love."

"Puppy love?"

"Yeah." He smiled. "Like two little puppies having a wonderful time playing together. Enjoy it."

"I've never been in love before. I'm a little afraid of it, I think."

"What?"

"I think I'm afraid of love."

"How can you be afraid of love? Love is the nicest thing in the world."

"Yeah, but . . . if it's the nicest thing, how come nobody talks about it or says anything about it?"

"We're talking about it, aren't we?"

"That's true."

"Well . . ."

I started to tell Jerome what I thought and felt about love. How I wished I had told Mark what I felt about him. And about Sal.

"Mark and I pretended we were brothers," I said.

"Is that why you asked me about brothers?"

I nodded my head yes.

"Well," he sighed, "I still think you'll work out what it means to have and to be a brother all by yourself. But as far as love is concerned, I think people are just afraid of the words. Take Mom, for instance."

"Mom?"

"Yeah. Mom never says it, but she feels it."

"How do you know?"

"Well, she could have put everyone in a home and not come back at all, but she didn't. As hard a time as Mom was having, she kept trying. She kept trying to keep us all together. Sure, everything's a mess, but she tried. That's love."

"Why don't you think she says it?"

"It's the words," he said. "So many people think their love won't be accepted or returned, so they don't say it. They think by not saying it, they won't be hurt. They're wrong."

"They're wrong?"

"Sure they are. By not saying it, they build a little wall around themselves. They lock all that love up inside. That hurts more than rejection."

"I want to say it sometimes," I said. "But it don't come out. I want to tell Mom and Sal, but it just don't come out."

"Well, when you want to say it, you should just say it. Let it come out."

"Gosh. I don't know if I can," I said. "I always thought nobody wanted to hear that stuff. Now I got to think about saying it."

"Say it!" he said. "If everyone went around thinking nobody wanted to hear it, 'I love you' wouldn't exist."

I sat on the park bench and looked around. I didn't see Stacy anywhere. I waited. I ran my fingernail along a crack in the bench and waited.

Suddenly two hands were clasped over my eyes. Both my hands went up to hold hers.

"Guess who?" Stacy said. Her voice was soft and sweet.

I hadn't realized how nice her voice was. My fingers ran over her hands and her fingers. She felt warm.

"Stacy," I said.

"You win." She leaned over the top of me and kissed my cheek. She slipped her arms around my shoulders and pulled me close to her. My head pressed against her chest. "You win me," she said.

We walked around the outside of the park. I held her hand. We talked about all sorts of things. I told her about Mark. She remembered him. She stopped walking and cried. I held her around her waist as she leaned into me. She put her head against my shoulder and her arms around my neck. I thought I should be bright red in the face, but I wasn't. I liked being near her. She was wearing a pink sweater to match her pink slacks. Her blouse was white and lacy. Her hair was pinned back over each ear. The words were stuck in my throat. I kissed her above her ear.

I walked Stacy home after the park. She lived in a small private house on the street just behind the building I lived in.

"Can you believe how close we are to each other?" I asked.

She had her hands around my waist. "I can believe it," she said.

"No, I mean that's my house," I said. I pointed to it.

She looked up at the huge building.

"The whole thing?" she said.

"No," I laughed, "just one little apartment."

"Want to go to the movies Saturday?" she asked.

"All right," I said.

"All right," she said. "I'll see you Saturday." She leaned forward and kissed me.

I kissed her back.

I left Stacy and sort of floated down the street toward Broadway. My head was filled with new thoughts, I was filled with new feelings. I laughed a little when I thought of how I acted toward Stacy three years ago at the home. As I walked along, I had the strangest feeling I could hear music. That's really weird. I was sure only people in the movies heard music when they were in love. I was right. I passed a little wooden shack by a building under construction. I heard the music coming from inside. I stopped near the door. Someone was playing the harmonica. I listened.

"Why don'tcha come in?" a voice said as the music stopped.

I hesitated for a moment, but then pushed the door open.

"Hi, young fella," the man said.

He was an elderly black man with white curly hair. He was sitting by a small potbelly stove. He was wearing a dark brown sweater pulled over a plaid shirt. He had a big hole at his elbow. He needed a shave.

"Sit yourself down," he said. "Takes da chill from ya bones."

"It's not cold," I said.

"Well, it's cold fo me," he laughed. "Whatcha calls yourself?"

His laugh was raspy and deep.

"I calls myself . . . I mean, my name is Jennings."

"It's a pleasure ta meetchu," he said. He put his hand out. "Dey calls me Clarence."

"How did you know I was outside the door, Clarence?" I asked as I shook his hand.

He chuckled. "Instinct, me boy. Instinct."

I scratched my head. I didn't think I smelled bad, but I guess if he could smell me through the door, I must. I'll have to take shower, I thought.

Clarence played his harmonica for me. He closed his eyes when he played. He swayed back and forth with the music. Clarence was drifting off somewhere. He played beautifully.

"Does anybody live here with you?" I asked.

Clarence laughed. "I don't lives here. I works here. I'm da night watchman."

"What do you watch?"

"I jist see dat nobody fools wit da building till mornin'. Dat's all."

"Oh. So you just sit here all night and play your harmonica?"

"Dat's all." He grinned. "Play me harp 'n make me friends."

"Do you make a lot of friends?"

"Millions of dem. Millions." He smiled. He had as many teeth as he had friends.

"Millions? How do you have room for millions of friends?"

He laughed. "Dat's easy," he said. "I only needs enough room for da friend I'm wit. When dey go . . . I gots room for another." He started to play another song. In the middle of his playing he stopped. "Don't ever worry 'bouts havin' too many friends, son," he said. "Jist enjoy who yo is wit."

"There's a girl I like to be with. Her name is Stacy."

"Stacy! Why, dat's a beautiful name. I'll bet she's a lovely girl."

"She is."

"And is she yo foist love?" he asked.

"I think so. It's puppy love."

"Puppy love." He laughed, showing all his teeth. "Well, ain't dat somethin'. Why, I 'member when I was 'bout your age." He closed his eyes and dreamed. "I was in love wit a little girl name o' Milisa." He made sort of a humming sound.

"What happened to her?"

"We grews up," he said. "She wents her way 'n I wents mine. I always thinks of her, dough. She was my foist love and dat's very special."

He started to play his harp again. He stopped.

"If'n yo and Stacy should ever drifts apart," he said, "don't ever forgets her. She will always be da one who started yo heart to beatin'. Dat's important." He smiled.

He started to play. He winked at me as I made my way out the door. It was getting late and I had to get home.

I got to see Stacy nearly every day. I had to take care of Mom and Jerome first, but after that I got to see her. We went for walks, and once in a while to the movies. It was nice just being with her.

Stacy showed me things I hadn't seen before. Things I knew were always there, but just never saw them, like flowers. She loved flowers and trees and birds. If I were with her in the evening, she would name some of the stars for me. I never knew stars had names; I thought they were all just stars. For that matter, I never knew grass had a special smell, or leaves felt the way they did. I hadn't realized a sunset could be so much prettier when you watched it with someone else. I never knew rain was sometimes warm. Stacy had a

243

way of making everything seem wonderful. If I could say "I love you" to anyone, I thought, it would be to Stacy. So many times I came close to finding the words. And just as many times I swallowed them. Someday I'll say it, I thought. I know I will.

It was early in July when Stacy and I were out walking. We stopped to rest in a triangular-shaped park with benches and trees. It was a small park, so it didn't have any swings or anything. We sat on one of the benches.

"I have to go, Jennings," she said.

"Go? Go where?"

"Away. I have to go away with my parents and my sister."

"Oh, gosh. I don't want you to go away."

"I don't either," she said, "but I have to."

She leaned her head into my chest and started to cry. I brushed her hair back with my hand and kissed her forehead.

"Don't cry," I said. "I'll see you when you get back, won't I?"

"I won't be back until September. Then I go away to school."

I flicked my thumbnail against my pointer finger. Love hurts, I thought. It's like friendship; even if you don't say it, you feel it.

"Can I write to you?" she asked.

"Sure," I said. "I never wrote to nobody, but I'll write to you."

"Then maybe we'll see each other next summer," she said.

I looked out over the park toward my school. The building was empty now. But in a couple of months I'd be back there. I'll be in the sixth grade. Next summer's a long time from now.

"Jennings," she said quietly.

"Yeah."

"I won't see you next summer, will I?"

"I don't know," I said. "So many people I liked have come and gone in my life. I don't hold out much hope for next summer. It's too far away to plan."

"You still live by the rules of the home, don't you?"

"I don't have no choice, Stacy," I said. I looked into her eyes. The edges of her lids were lined with tears. So were mine. "I made the mistake once of forgetting it all could end tomorrow, and I paid for it."

"How?"

"It ended, and it hurt twice as much."

We sat on the bench as a light rain started to fall. At first we didn't move.

"We're getting wet," she said.

We left the bench and dashed toward the school. We stood in the doorway.

"When do you have to go?" I asked.

"Tomorrow."

I brought her wet hand up to my lips and kissed her fingers. There wasn't anything left to say. Jerome had told me when you feel it, say it. But I couldn't. The words just wouldn't come. They were there, but I couldn't get them out.

The rain let up and we walked. I took her to her house.

"I'll write to you," she said.

I nodded my head.

"And if we see each other next summer," she said, "that will be wonderful."

"And if we don't," I said, "I'll know from how much I miss you just how special you are to me."

She kissed me, then ran into the house.

The pins and needles faded after a few minutes and I could walk. I passed Clarence's shack and heard the music. I leaned my head against the side of his door and cried.

I went straight to bed when I got home. I took Doggie from under my pillow and hugged him. "You never let me down, do you, Doggie?" I whispered.

I guess I moped around a bit for the first few days. Jerome

didn't say anything to me. He sort of knew something was wrong, but he didn't say anything.

When I was back to being myself a little, he talked to me.

"You've grown up a lot," he said. "Love will sometimes do that to you. Even more than questions."

"Do you really think so?" I asked.

"I do," he said. "I don't know what happened, but whatever it was, you seem to be taking it all right."

"She went away."

He made a face like he was sorry.

"There'll be others," he said. "Stacy is just the beginning."

"Do you think I feel real love for her?" I asked.

"Sure you do, don't you?"

"How come it's different than what I feel for Mom or Sal or Doggie? I love them too."

He laughed. "Love comes in all sizes and shapes. You'll see. Did you ever tell her you loved her?"

I shook my head no.

"Can't get it out yet, can you?"

"No."

"You will," he said, "and when you do . . ." He paused. "You'll know what it feels like to say it, and you'll never stop. It becomes a habit."

Jerome didn't talk much after that day. He got sick a few days later. I called a number that was put by the phone in case of an emergency. His doctor came from Bellevue Hospital. She made arrangements for Jerome to go back.

"I'm gonna miss you," I said. "Please come back soon."

"I will," he mumbled. "I promise."

I laid my head by his arm as the men prepared to take him.

"Promise me something," he said.

"Yes, what?"

"Promise me you won't stop asking questions."

"I won't stop."

"Good. And if it all goes wrong for you, don't give up. Hang in there." He closed his eyes.

"Jerome," I whispered.

"Yes."

"To feel what I feel for you is to have a brother, and to be able to tell you about it is to be one."

"Simple, isn't it?" He smiled.

The men lifted him onto a stretcher and took him.

I lay in bed with Doggie. I cried out all the tears I had. There were none left. I was tired. I had given Mom her medicine and she was trying to sleep. Walter and Gene were watching television. George was out.

"Mom is taking it badly, Doggie," I said. "I never saw her cry so much."

I heard Walter go into Mom's room.

"Jerome is gonna die," she screamed. "I just have to lie here and take it."

I heard a crash. I leapt from the bed and ran into Mom's room. She had cut the weight, letting it fall to the floor.

"Oh, gosh!"

"Grab that rope," Walter said.

He tried to retie the weight. Mom was screaming. Chills were running all over me. I was scared.

"Give her another pill," Walter said.

"Do you think I should?" I said. "I gave her three already."

"Three!" he snapped. "I gave her two."

"I gave her four," Gene said.

"Did you?" Walter asked.

Gene nodded his head.

"Oh, my God!" he cried. He ran from the room, dropping the weight back to the floor. He called the police.

"Keep her awake," he said. "The police are on the way."

"Will she die?" Gene asked.

"God! I hope not," Walter said. He ran from the room. "Keep her talking," he yelled.

"Mom, talk to me," I said.

"Yes, dear. Is Jerome dead?" she asked.

"No, Mom. He's not gonna die. He promised."

"I know. I promised things too, and I couldn't keep them," she cried.

"It's all right," I said. "You tried."

"No one thinks I tried. They all blame me for what's happened. I tried to make a good home, but I couldn't do it alone. I just couldn't do it."

"What's she talking about?" Gene asked.

"Nothing. Go see if Walter needs you."

"Walter needs me?" Mom said. "Walter doesn't need me. Walter doesn't need anyone. George only needs drink, and Larry . . ." She cried. "Oh, Larry! Why did you go away again?"

"He didn't go anywhere. He's at work."

"No, he's gone. I know he's gone. You're all gone. I'm alone. I can't do it alone."

I couldn't help finding more tears. I talked and cried at the same time. "You'll be all right, Mom. You'll see. You won't have to do it alone. I'll help you."

"It's too late," she said. "I tried to keep everyone together. I didn't want my children to grow up hating each other, but now they do. I lost them."

The policemen pushed me aside.

"Outside, son," one of them ordered.

I backed out through the door. Two ambulance men came rushing down the hall. Walter pulled me close to him and folded his arms around me. He had Gene holding on to one of his pants legs. They wheeled Mom past us.

"Is she dead?" Gene asked.

"No," a policeman said. "She'll be all right."

He called Walter over to one side to talk to him. He kept looking over his shoulder at Gene and me. I knew what was coming. I went into the bedroom to be with Doggie.

"I can't take much more of this, Doggie," I cried into him. I hid my head under the pillow.

Walter nudged me. "Jennings," he said softly.

"Go away!"

"I can't," he said. "You have to go."

"I don't want to!" I screamed. I brought my head from beneath the pillow. "I don't want to!"

Walter sat on the bed and held me. "I'll come for you just as soon as they let me," he said.

I got to my feet and went to the closet. I took my laundry bag out. I started to stuff some things into it. Walter left the room. He knew there wasn't anything else to say. I kissed Doggie and put him in on top of my clothes. I took a piece of paper from Walter's desk. I wrote Sal a note.

> Dear Sal,
> Please come for me and Doggie. We need you.
>
> Your son,
>
> Jennings Burch

I crumpled up the paper and threw it in Walter's wastepaper basket.

"Come on, Doggie," I said as I lifted my laundry bag.

14

We sat in the dark shadows on a wooden bench in the precinct station house. Gene was half-asleep lying up against my side. His feet were pulled up. I'm glad now that Stacy went away. It would be awful for her to be waiting somewhere for me to show up, and I didn't. She'd understand, I know, but it would hurt.

"Gene Burch," the policeman behind the desk called out.

There was a lady standing in front of the high wooden desk. She was here to take Gene.

"Come on," I said.

I got Gene to his feet.

"Where're we going?" he asked.

"You have to go with that lady."

We started to approach her.

"I don't want to go with her. I wanna stay with you."

"Can we stay together?" I asked anyone who would answer me.

"I'm afraid not," the lady said. "We only have room for him at the moment."

"You can go back and sit down," the policeman told me.

"I want to say good-bye first."

"I ain't going!" Gene yelled.

The lady took his hand.

"I ain't going!"

I crouched down to talk to him. "Look, it won't be for long," I said. I didn't believe myself. "I'll see you real soon." I kissed his cheek. His tears were salty.

He was crying too hard to form the word "good-bye." He went with the lady. I watched through the blur of my tears as he left. He kept looking back at me to stop her, but I couldn't. There wasn't anything I could do. I sat back down and took Doggie from the bag.

I curled up facing the back of the bench. I drifted off, thinking about Mom and Jerome. I wonder if Jerome had known things would get worse. He had told me not to give up. That's easy, I laughed to myself, to say "I won't" before it happens.

I was awakened by a policeman.

"There's a lady here from Child Welfare," he said.

I sat up and cleared my eyes. I swung my feet to the floor and lifted Doggie. I put him in the bag.

The lady took me out to a car. She didn't ask me my name or anything. I guess she already knew everything she wanted to know.

After an hour or so of riding in silence, we stopped in front of an old red brick building. There was some ivy growing up one side near the door.

"Are we in Brooklyn?" I asked.

"No, Yonkers," she said. "Let's go."

She was cold and abrupt. I knew she wasn't going to say "Have a good time" when she left. She pushed open the front door. The hall was dark, but she knew exactly where she was going.

She brought me through the darkness to an office. She switched on a light.

"Sit there," she said. She dropped a folder she had tucked under her arm on the desk. She left.

I sat on a rickety old chair and waited. The room was painted the same light and dark green. Who paints all these places? I wondered. They must have millions of gallons of green paint.

A lady in a dark blue dress pushed open the door.

"Oh!" She was startled. "I didn't know anyone was here," she said.

"I'm here."

"Well," she said as she stepped behind the desk and picked up the folder. "Let's see who you are."

I could have told her who I was, but by the way she spoke, she didn't seem to want to know who I was from me.

"Burch Jennings," she said. "Burch surely is a strange first name. What kind of name is that?"

"It's my last name," I said. I smiled weakly.

"Oh! Well, let's get you settled, Jennings." She put out her hand for me to take.

I got up and took her hand. She brought me through the same darkness to a dormitory. She brought me to a bed and left me. It was too dark to see my number, so I didn't know who I was. One number is as good as another, I thought. I'll find out tomorrow who I am.

I felt around the side of the bed and found a cabinet. I opened it up and took out pajamas. My bed was against the wall, near a window. The window had bars, of course, and their shadows crossed my bedcover.

I changed into the pajamas and put my things in the cabinet. I put Doggie alongside the pillow. I climbed into bed.

I lay back against the pillow in a sitting position. I heard the usual night sounds, a cough, a sniffle, and a cry. The blanket was heavy and itchy, and not necessary. It was hot. I pushed the blanket down toward the bottom of the bed. I smelled pee. Funny, I hadn't smelled it when I first came in. Maybe I'm getting used to these places. I slid down beneath the sheet and hugged Doggie.

"I'm sorry, little fella," I said. I kissed his nose. I pushed him under the pillow for safety and closed my eyes. I thought about Clarence playing his harmonica, or harp as he liked to call it. If I lay real still, I could almost hear him.

I was awakened by a sharp pain to my stomach. I popped open my eyes and sat up. There was an ugly kid with his fists clenched standing alongside the bed. Three or four other kids stood nearby. I slipped my hand beneath my pillow to feel Doggie. He was there. It was morning, and for some reason this ugly kid hit me.

"What do you want?" I snapped.

"Who's the toughest kid in here?" he growled in a raspy hoarse voice.

His brown hair was all ratty and stuck up in every direction. He had a scar that ran from the top of his forehead, across his left eye, down his cheek, to the corner of his mouth. He frightened me.

"Who's the toughest kid in here?" he repeated.

"I don't know," I said.

That was the wrong answer. He hit me flush in the mouth, cutting my lip. Blood spurted all over my chin and pajama top.

"Who's the toughest kid in here?" he said. He was now more determined than ever.

I thought back to the Home of the Angels and Butch. I drew back my right foot, then shot it forward. I caught him full in the stomach. I heard the gush of air leave him. He doubled up and fell to the floor. I leapt from the bed, bringing the sheet and blanket with me. I dug my feet into him as I landed. He was much bigger than me, so I took every advantage. I covered his head with the blanket, then tried to get him into a head lock. His fist came from nowhere and struck me on the top of the head. I saw stars. Before I could shake the starry feeling off, he was on me. He pinned me to the floor. I brought my legs up behind his head and grabbed hold of him. I pulled him backward toward the floor. We rolled and wrestled around the floor and under the bed.

"What's going on here?" a lady shouted.

She grabbed me by one of my sideburns and lifted me straight up. She did the same to him.

"You again!" she huffed. "Don't you know how to do anything but fight?" She was apparently talking to him.

"And you!" she said. "If this is how you're going to begin your stay with us . . ." She paused to catch her breath. ". . . you're in big trouble."

I said nothing. I glared at the kid who started it all. He glared back.

"See me after you dress!" she said. "The two of you!"

I went about putting my bed back together. I took my clothes from the cabinet and put Doggie inside. I crouched down to talk to him.

"I'm in trouble already," I whispered.

I took my things and went into the bathroom. The scar-faced boy and his friends were there waiting for me.

"Who's the toughest kid in here?" he said again.

He sounded like a broken record. I looked him straight in the eye. "I don't know," I said. "I haven't met everyone yet."

"Well, I am!" he said in his toughest voice. He jammed his thumb into his chest on the word "I."

"Maybe you are and maybe you're not," I said. I took off my pajama top.

Redness flushed into his cheeks. He started to change into his clothes. I continued to do the same.

"What's your name?" he muttered.

"Jennings," I said. "And that's my first name!" I jammed my thumb into my chest on the word "my."

"I'm Ronny," he said. He extended his hand to me.

I was surprised. We shook hands. He smiled and I smiled back.

We stood in different corners of the dining room through breakfast. None of the kids poked fun or laughed at us. If Ronny was the toughest kid in here, they knew he wouldn't be in the corner forever. As far as I was concerned, they didn't know anything about me at all, except that I took on the toughest kid in a fight. I had a funny feeling about that. I hoped I wasn't going to get a reputation as a bully. But it was good knowing kids were afraid to tease you.

After breakfast the dormitory lady yelled at us. She was dressed in the same dark blue clothes as the first lady I saw the night before. I guess that was their uniform. She took us to the playroom and left us.

The playroom looked like every other playroom I was ever in. Shelves of toys and games, tables and chairs, and glass-paneled doors leading to the courtyard.

All the kids stared in our direction as we came into the room, but nobody laughed.

"Let's go outside," Ronny said.

We stepped into the gray-stone courtyard. If I didn't know I was in a different place, I'd think I was in Brooklyn. The high wire-mesh fence had the same barbed wire running along the top of it. As we crossed the yard, the kids parted in front of us. There was something to being a bully, I thought. Nobody would ever bother you. But then, what good is it to have kids being nice to you only because they're afraid of you? We sat down beside the fence.

"How'd you get the scar?" I asked.

"I fell off a train."

"You fell off a train?" I gasped.

"Yeah. I was runnin' away from a home in Texas. I hitched a ride on a train and fell off. I gots two hundred stitches."

"Oh, wow!" I said.

I showed him where I got stitches. He thought it was a neat scar.

"I saw Texas in the movies," I said. "Are there really a lot of cowboys and Indians there?"

"Naaa. That's just movies. There ain't none of that stuff in Texas. It's just a regular place."

"It must be nice being in a home in Texas," I said.

"You been in these homes long?" he asked.

"Yeah, pretty long."

"Were any of them nice?"

I understood. The homes in Texas weren't any better than here.

We talked for a while about the rules of this home and about some other stuff. He told me the dormitory lady was called Frog Face, but her real name was Mrs. Abbott. He told me he was a "juvenile delinquent" and that his parents didn't want him anymore.

"What's a juvenile delinquent?"

"That's a bad kid," he said. "Someone who's been in jail."

"Have you been in jail?"

He nodded his head yes.

"Oh, wow!" I said. "How was it?"

"Are you kiddin'? You take the worst place you ever been to—"

"The Carpenters' or maybe St. Ter—"

"It don't matter where," he interrupted me. "You take that place, and it would be like heaven compared to jail."

"Oh, wow!" I gasped. "And now your parents don't want you no more?"

He laughed. "They didn't want me before I went to jail."

"What was you in jail for?"

"Trespassin'. I was sleeping in this guy's barn and he didn't like it."

"That's all?"

"It was his barn," he said as he shrugged his shoulders.

Ronny reminded me a lot of Stevie. I saw he wasn't as tough as he made himself out to be. I saw he was just as alone as everyone else was.

"Whatcha in for?" he asked.

"My mother's sick."

"Ain't you got no father?"

"Naa. I got one, but he's a drunk. I don't know him."

256

He nodded his head as though he had heard the story about a thousand times. He probably had.

"I'm gonna crash out of here," he said. He eyed the barbed wire along the top of the fence. "Wanna come?"

"Naa. I tried bustin' out once," I said. "That's a tough fence."

"Oh! You been in here before?"

"Not this place. Another place. They're all the same."

"Yeah," he muttered.

"When are you going?"

"Tonight, or maybe tomorrow."

I nodded my head. He stood up and stretched.

"I think I'll go pick on somebody," he said as he walked off.

I smiled and shook my head. I looked around the yard. The old red brick building looked sort of nice with the ivy crawling all over it. It's too bad it wasn't so nice on the inside.

Just before lunch I went into the dormitory. I wanted to check on Doggie and get my number. With all the commotion, I hadn't gotten it.

Doggie was fine. A little cramped, maybe, but he was fine. My number was forty-seven.

I started toward the door, when I heard someone crying. I looked around but didn't see anyone. I stood up on my tiptoes and stretched my neck. On one of the beds in the far corner there was a large bulge under the blanket. I approached the bed and the bulge.

"Hi," I said to the whimpering blanket. "Are you all right?"

The crying stopped and the blanket became still.

"Hello, under there. Are you all right?"

A small head popped out from under the covers. He was about eight years old. Tears wet his pale cheeks. His hair was dark brown and all messed up. He had the biggest, widest brown eyes I had ever seen.

"What's the matter?" I asked.

"I'm ascared," he cried.

I sat on his bed and touched his thin frail hand. "Ascared of what?" I asked as nicely as I could.

He looked around the room with his big eyes. I'm sure he saw more than I ever could see. He blinked away some of his tears; others got away and rolled down his cheek. "This place," he sobbed.

"Is this the first place you been to?" I asked. I knew it was a dumb question as soon as the last word fell off my lips.

He nodded his head yes.

I remembered back to the Home of the Angels and my very first day. I got cold shivers.

"What's your name?" I asked.

"Aldridge," he said. He huffed back his breath as he tried to breathe normally.

"That's a nice name," I said. "And what's your last name?"

"That is my last name. My first name is Kevin."

I laughed a little to myself. I told him my name and went through the same old first-name, last-name business.

"Listen, Kevin," I said, "I ain't gonna say it's good in here, and I ain't gonna say it's bad. 'Cause it ain't nothing at all."

"What do you mean?" He asked. His eyes were wide open.

"It's nothing," I said. "It's just a place to wait, and you gotta make the best of it. You eat and sleep and remember your number, and that's all."

"That's all?"

"That's all." I shuffled myself where I sat. "But listen!" I pointed a finger at him. "One thing you don't do," I sighed, "is go around all day thinking about leaving, thinking about going home." I took a deep breath. "Just forget about that!"

"Forget about that," he echoed.

"Yeah," I said quietly. "Forget about that."

"You been here a long time?" he asked.

I nodded my head. "Well, not this place, but others." I told him my mother was sick. I told him I had to stay until she was better. He stared at me the whole time I talked. He didn't say a word.

"Is your mother and father sick or drunks, or what?" I asked.

"They're dead," he said with the blankest of looks. "My father killed my mother, then he killed himself."

I was shocked into silence. I didn't know what to say to that. All I could think was: This kid better learn the rules real fast. He was a lifer and didn't know it. I felt bad for him.

I helped him out of bed and took him into the bathroom. I washed his face.

"Now, doesn't that feel better?" I asked.

He smiled. It was his first smile, and with his big eyes his smile nearly brought tears to my eyes. I looked away and pinched the bridge of my nose.

As we walked to the playroom, Kevin leaned into me. I put my arm around his shoulder. We went into the playroom. As I moved toward the center of the room, some of the kids moved away from me. The "bully" reputation had already started. There wasn't anything I could do about that. In fact, I was about to make it worse.

"What's your number, Kevin?"

"Fourteen," he said shyly.

"Who's thirteen?" I shouted.

The room fell silent. A boy raised his hand.

I cleared my throat. My heart pounded. "See that kid, Kevin?"

He nodded his head yes."

"Well, anytime we line up for anything . . ." I paused to make sure he understood me. ". . . you make sure you're standing behind that kid. Got that?"

He nodded again.

"And you!" I pointed at number thirteen. "Make sure he's behind you."

I took Kevin into the yard. This place would only be a stopover for me. But for Kevin it was the beginning of his days on the inside. I wanted him to at least have a chance at making it. Mark did it for me; it was time I paid him back.

For the next several days Kevin stuck to me like glue. I knew it wasn't a good idea for him to be with me and me alone, I had to break him away. I was getting to like him too much. In the end it could only hurt him.

We sat below the ivy against the building.

"Listen, Kevin," I said. "You gotta start playing with other kids."

"What other kids?"

"Any other kids. I want you to start playing with other kids."

"Why?" He blinked his big brown eyes at me.

"Oh, gosh," I said. "Uh . . . it's the rules."

"The rules? What rules?"

"There's a rule around here that says you gotta play with different kids every day." I avoided his eyes as I spoke. "Do you understand?"

"No," he said quietly. "I like to play with you."

"Oh, gosh," I mumbled. "That's the problem."

"Problem? Why's that a problem? Don't you like me?"

I wiped my face from my forehead to my chin to try to gather some words. "Sure I like you. But if you only like one person in this place, you're gonna have a problem."

"I like you," he said. "I don't see no problem."

I searched through my memory for the words Mark used to explain it to me. I was forced to turn my head and look at him.

"You see, Kevin, if you pal around with only one person all the time and that person leaves, then you're more lonely than before. Understand?"

His big eyes welled with tears. "Are you leaving?" he asked.

"No, I'm not leaving," I said.

"Oh, good!" he said as a tear fell. It rolled down his cheek to the corner of his mouth. His tongue flicked out and licked it away.

"But that don't matter, Kevin. I'm gonna leave someday and you're gonna have to stay. I want you to have other kids to play with when that happens. Do you understand?"

He did. The tears built in his eyes and his lip quivered. A few tears fell, rolling to the corners of his mouth.

"Don't cry, Kevin. I'm not saying these things to hurt you." I put my arm around his shoulder. "I'm telling you this stuff to help you."

We sat quietly for a few minutes.

"So I should go and play with somebody else now?" he asked.

I nodded my head yes.

He got to his feet and looked at me. He wiped his face in one great swipe with the back of his dirty hand. He smeared his tears and the dirt all across his nose and cheeks. I wanted to hug him, but I didn't. He blinked his eyes and turned around. He started to walk away. I watched him as he walked toward a group of kids. He turned twice to look back at me. I waved my hand for him to keep going. He shuffled along in his baggy pants over to the kids. Kevin was going to make it, I thought. At least for now he would.

The ivy turned brown as the weather turned colder. It wasn't long after that before the leaves shriveled up and fell to the ground. The wind blew them around for a while, but then, a little at a time, they sort of piled up against the wire-mesh fence in one of the corners of the yard.

It was late in November; Doggie and I were sitting at the edge of the bed in the dark. I was looking up through the bars at the sky and some of the stars. I couldn't remember their names. Doggie and I were wondering if Thanksgiving had already passed or was it about to come. I swung my feet into bed and thought about Jerome. I slid beneath the covers. I was able to keep one of his promises, the one about not giving up. But I couldn't keep the one about asking questions. There wasn't anyone in here who knew anything. They were all just kids. Half of them were afraid of me, and the other half just plain forgot how to talk. I fell asleep hugging Doggie.

I was jolted awake by a warm feeling all over me. I suddenly realized I had wet the bed.

"Oh, gosh," I mumbled out loud to myself. "How did that happen?" I got out of bed. I was very embarrassed. I hadn't wet the bed in years and years. Now I added to the smells of the room. I started to remove the sheets and the blanket.

"What's going on here?" Mrs. Abbott, the frog-faced dormitory lady, asked.

A chill ran the length of my spine. "Uh . . . I wet the bed, Mrs. Abbott."

I barely finished speaking when she cracked me across the back of the head.

"I expect this from the little ones," she screamed. "But I'll be damned if I'll take this from kids your size."

"I'm sorry," I said. "I don't know what happened."

"You pissed the bed, that's what happened. Grab your sheet," she snapped, "and follow me."

She stormed across the dormitory floor. I stuffed Doggie into the cabinet and grabbed the wet sheet. I caught up to her in the hallway just outside the playroom. She pushed open the playroom door and flipped on the light. She grabbed my pajama collar and threw me into the room.

"Strip!" she ordered.

"Why?"

She slapped me hard across the face. "Strip!" she yelled.

I started to unbutton my pajama top, when she grabbed hold of it and tore it off.

"When I say strip," she screamed, "I mean fast." She slapped me again.

The tears ran down my stinging cheek as I untied the string

262

on my bottoms and dropped them. I covered myself with my hands.

"Sit on that table," she ordered.

I sat on the table. She threw the wet sheet over my head.

"Stand up," she snapped.

"On the table?" I asked.

"Of course on the table, you dumb bastard."

I got to my feet with the wet sheet draped over me. The light went out.

"Don't sit down till I tell you to," she ordered.

The door slammed. I stood in the dark. The longer I stood, the colder I got. I was sure she wasn't in the room, but I listened anyway. I didn't hear anything, just some outside street noises. I sat on the table and drew in my legs. I wrapped my arms around the top of my knees. I was freezing.

I sat on top of the table for the rest of the night. Each time I thought I heard someone in the hall, I stood up. By morning the sheet had dried. I was tired. The sunlight poured in through the glass-paneled doors, casting shadows on my sheet. My embarrassment turned to fear. The kids would be coming soon. They'll see me here. I wondered if maybe I shouldn't get off the table and sneak into the dormitory. "She'll know I'm not here when she comes in," I talked out loud to myself. "She'll see me and the sheet aren't on the table. I better stay here."

I heard the awful sound of the marching feet in the hallway. The thunderous sound of the feet got louder and louder. The door opened. As the kids filed in, they laughed. I could hear the girls giggling. Some of the boys poked at me through the sheet.

"Now, kids," Mrs. Abbott announced, "this is a bedwetter."

The kids erupted with laughter. I guess it didn't matter to them who was under the sheet, bully or no bully. This was funny to them, and they were going to laugh.

"And here's what he looks like." Mrs. Abbott snapped the sheet from me.

I lunged off the table to their laughter, only to be caught by the arm and hurled against the table by Mrs. Abbott.

"I didn't tell you to get down!" she snarled. "Get back up there." She slapped me hard across my thigh.

As I climbed back on the table, she slapped me across my bare behind. The kids roared with laughter. I stood on the table with my hands covering myself. I jammed my eyes closed. I refused to cry.

"Put your hands on top of your head," she barked.

I opened my eyes in shock. I looked directly at her. Her face was red with anger. She pulled a thin strap from her waist.

"Put your hands on your head," she said slowly and angrily.

I closed my eyes and put my hands on my head. The girls giggled. Mrs. Abbott whipped me hard across the leg, behind, and back on one shot with the strap. The sting stiffened me. I clenched my teeth together. Her second shot caught me across my stomach and chest. The laughter and giggles died down. I stood vowing not to cry or flinch, no matter how many times she hit me. I kept my eyes closed tight. I didn't want to see anyone. This way I could shut them out and make believe they weren't there.

I was dead tired. I stood on the table in the darkness of my closed eyes and my own mind. I didn't move. Hours passed, but still I didn't move.

Suddenly someone tapped me on the leg. I stiffened.

"Get down from there," she said.

I opened my eyes. It was the lady who was in the office the first day.

"Get dressed," she said.

Without a word I jumped from the table. I left the play-room and went straight into the dormitory. Apparently everyone was at lunch. I got dressed, put all my things into the laundry bag, including Doggie, and left the dormitory. I pushed open the playroom door and then the yard door. I crossed the gray-stone courtyard and scaled the wire-mesh fence. I pulled myself to the top with my laundry bag tucked tightly in my belt. I carefully climbed over the barbed wire, then dropped to the ground. I was out.

I didn't know where I was going. I only wanted to get away from there. I walked for about an hour along some highway. I was tired and hungry, but I wouldn't stop. I wanted to get as far away from that place as possible. I took Doggie out of the bag.

"We're out, fella," I said. The tears ran down my cheeks, and I wiped them away on my sleeve. "I don't know exactly where we're going, but it'll be away from there."

He was happy about that.

We walked for at least another hour before I saw a sign for Boston Road.

"Doggie!" I shrieked. "Maybe we're near the zoo."

I followed the highway to the Boston Road exit. When I reached the street, I stopped. I asked a man where the zoo was and he pointed me in the right direction. I held in my excitement until I walked a good distance away from him.

"Wow!" I yelled.

Doggie was very happy, and so was I.

"We don't ever have to leave the zoo, Doggie. We can stay there till I get big."

The sun was nearly down by the time we got there. The zoo was closed, but not for me. I went to my old door and slipped in. I carefully avoided the guards on patrol. I made my way on and off the path until I found a clump of pine bushes. I remember Stacy telling me that pine bushes would always stay green. That meant they would give me enough cover for hiding. The pine bushes were very soft underneath; they made a great place to rest. I was starving, but I was more tired. I propped the bag under my head and brought Doggie to my cheek.

"We'll get some food tomorrow," I whispered. I closed my eyes. "I know Jerome and Sal think running away can be a habit, but they weren't on that table."

I was listening to a strange scratching sound as I woke up. I lay perfectly still. I opened my eyes and looked around. There was a gray squirrel about five feet from me.

"Hi there," I whispered.

He looked up at me and stood on his hind legs for a moment. Then he went back to his scratching.

"Look, Doggie," I said. "That's a squirrel. He's looking for nuts."

Doggie said he wished he had some nuts. He was starving.

"I know. As soon as some people start coming in," I said, "we'll get some food."

I didn't have any comic books or baseball cards to pass the time with, so I just sat and waited. Hours passed before I saw the first visitor.

"Come on, Doggie," I said. "Let's follow some people around and hope they're not too hungry."

We left our hideout and wandered. The weather was getting so cold, there were hardly any people around, and no food.

"We got a real problem, Doggie," I said.

He knew we did.

Finally a kid dropped a whole bag of popcorn. He reached down to pick it up, but his mother wouldn't let him. I waited until they were out of sight before I scooped up the popcorn. I ate most of it before I put any in the bag. As hungry as I was, I needed to save some for later.

We didn't find any more food by the time the zoo closed. We went back to our hiding place. I gave some popcorn to Doggie and ate some myself.

"I think we'll have to go someplace else, Doggie. We could starve to death right here if we don't."

He agreed.

I sat back against the trunk part of the bush. I was tired.

Not sleepy-tired so much as I was body-tired. I lifted Doggie up near my cheek.

"You know, Doggie," I said, "I honestly don't think I could have come this far without you. You've been my friend through an awful lot of things. Thank you." I kissed his nose.

I slid down to the ground and put the laundry bag behind my head.

"I wish Sal would come for us and take us home."

Doggie wished that too.

"I know he can't, Doggie. There ain't no use in kidding ourselves into thinking he will. Remember, it hurts twice as much when it doesn't happen." I cuddled up to Doggie. I wrapped my arms around him and myself as best I could. I was cold. I fell asleep.

I woke up to the same scratching sound.

"Hi, Bushy," I said. "Do you mind if I call you Bushy?" He didn't mind.

"I wish I could dig up some nuts like you do," I said. "I could eat anything right about now."

Snow started to fall.

"Uh-oh," I said. "I think we got big trouble."

Doggie agreed.

"What'll we do now?"

Bushy scurried up a nearby tree.

"I think we better go, Doggie." I tucked him into the bag and popped my head out of the bushes. The coast was clear. I ran for my exit, ducking in and around bushes and trees along the way. The last thing I needed was to get caught. I reached the fence and slipped under.

I walked along Tremont Avenue for miles. I stopped here and there in doorways. I was cold, tired, and hungry. I couldn't think of anywhere to go, or what I should do.

I stopped under the awning of a shop across the street from a cemetery to shake some of the snow off and think. I leaned against the shop window and looked out over the tops of the gravestones toward the dark sky. The lights from a bridge seemed to twinkle as the snow swirled and blotted them out from time to time. It looked pretty.

"Doggie!" I shouted. "I got it!"

I pulled him out of the bag.

"Do you know where we're going?"

I made him shake his head no so I could tell him.

"We're going to Martha, Doggie. We're going to Martha."

I walked along the street looking for someone to ask about the bridge. I saw a man parking his car. I ran up to him.

"Sir," I asked as nicely as I could, "is that the Whitestone Bridge over there?"

He looked in the direction I was pointing. "Yes," he said. "Are you lost?"

"Lost? Me lost? Naaa. I'm visiting with my mother and I was just wondering, that's all."

"Yeah, that's the Whitestone," he said, and walked off.

"Whew," I said, then uncrossed my fingers. "So far, so good."

I dashed across the street and hopped over the cemetery wall. I ran up and down the sloping hills toward the bridge. The snow had wiped away the paths, so I headed in as straight a line as I could. My excitement soon gave way to tiredness and I walked. From time to time the snow would swirl away the lights of the bridge altogether. I would stop then and wait for them to reappear. I took Doggie from the bag.

"Martha's on the other side of that bridge," I said.

He wanted to know what bridge.

"Well, it was there a minute ago."

I walked a little farther, then stopped near a tree to rest. The tall leafless trees stretched high into the dark night sky. Their arms dipped and swayed with the swirling wind. I was getting scared.

"I don't think we should have come this way, Doggie," I said as my eyes darted in all directions.

I started walking in the direction I thought the bridge was. I was lost.

"Oh, gosh, Doddie. What are we going to do?"

He thought we ought to get back to the road.

"The road! That's a good idea."

I headed in the direction I thought the road was. As I walked, the night sky seemed to get lower. The long arms of the trees seemed to dip down at me, trying to grab me. The arms had hands, and the hands fingers. I ducked around the reaching fingers and started to run. The wind swirled and whistled. I ran faster and faster, trying to find my way out. I tripped over a small gravestone. As I tried to regain my feet, I was grabbed by the fingers of a wiry bush. I screamed.

"Who's that?" a deep and gravelly voice asked from nowhere.

My heart stopped as I looked around and saw no one.

"Who is that?" the voice asked again, this time slower and louder.

"Oh, gosh," I mumbled as I squeezed Doggie's stuffing into his head and his tail. If it's a ghost, I thought, I better answer him.

"Jennings," I said in the clearest trembling voice I could find. Doggie was at my cheek. He was shaking so hard my knuckles were hitting me in the jaw. My teeth chattered.

"What are you doing here?" the voice asked.

"I'm a . . . I'm a . . . running away. I'm a . . . trying to find Martha."

"Is she dead?" he boomed out.

"Gosh, I hope not," I said. I looked all around, but only saw darkness and the fingerlike branches trying to reach me. "Are you a . . . a ghost?" I asked.

"Yes."

"Oh!" I squeezed Doggie harder.

"Boo!" he said as he came at me from a thicket of bushes.

I ran so fast my feet couldn't catch up with me. I ran in and around gravestones and reaching branches. I fell two or three times, but stayed on the ground no more than a second. I heard the ghost's laughter fade in the distance as I ran. I saw the wall of the cemetery and went for it. I leapt over the wall and into the open arms of a policeman.

"Whoa. Slow down."

"There's a ghost in there!" I said as I peeked back under his arm.

"A ghost!" he laughed.

"Yeah! A ghost!"

"Well, maybe we'd better go take a look."

"Oh, I don't think so. I don't think we'd better."

He laughed again. "What's your name, son?"

"Uh . . . I don't remember."

"His name is Jennings," the ghost said. He was leaning against the wall of the cemetery.

"The ghost!" I screamed.

The policeman held me in one spot. He and the ghost laughed.

"So you're the ghost, Pop?" the policeman said.

"Only when I have to be." He laughed. "Only when I have to be." He left the wall and disappeared into the darkness.

"Is he your father?" I asked.

"No," he chuckled. "Pops is the night watchman. He's there to scare off little boys like you."

"Oh."

"Now, sonny," he asked, "where do you live?"

Oh, gosh, now they'll send me back and I won't ever get to Martha's. The tears welled up in my eyes. I tried to fight them off, but I couldn't.

"Son," he said.

"Huh?"

"Where do you live?"

"Nowhere," I said.

"Nowhere? Everyone lives somewhere."

"Well, I don't."

He brought me over to his police car and opened the door.

I sat in the front seat and squeezed Doggie's stuffing back to where it belonged.

"That's a nice dog," he said. "He looks like he's been through a lot."

I turned Doggie over in my hands. You have been through a lot, haven't you, fella? I said to him from my heart. I'm sorry.

"What's his name?" the policeman asked.

"Doggie."

He reached over toward him; I pulled him close to me.

"I'm sorry," he said. "I only wanted to shake his paw and say hello."

"Oh," I said. I brought Doggie near him and stuck out his paw.

"Hi," he said to Doggie. "My name is Daily. Officer Daily."

"He says hi."

"Oh, he talks? That's really something. Where do you live, Doggie?" he asked.

"He lives with me," I said. I kissed his nose and put him in the bag.

Officer Daily started his car and we drove off. I listened to the wet slushy snow slap against the underside of the car as we rode along Tremont Avenue. The side window was fogged up. I wiped it with my fingers. The droplets of water on the other side of the glass made the lights along the avenue spread out and run into each other.

"Have a rough time, son?" he asked.

I didn't answer him. I just kept thinking about being sent back. Mrs. Frog Face is going to kill me.

He patted my knee. "I'll see that you're all right," he said.

I knew he meant well. I knew he was just saying that to make me feel good.

As he drove the car, I looked up at him. He had chubby cheeks with a dimple near each corner of his mouth. His hair was bright red and his face was freckled. A shock of his hair curled down on his forehead. He had his cap set back on his head.

We arrived at his station house. It looked like all the others I'd been in. Two green lights outside the front door, ugly gray stones halfway up the building, and a rickety old door. The inside wasn't any different, either. The high wooden desk, the iron rail running along the front of the room, and the single wooden bench. I sat down.

Officer Daily went behind the desk and talked to a policeman without a hat. They spoke in low voices. I strained my neck to try to hear, but it was no use. When someone doesn't want you to hear, you don't. I held my laundry bag close to me. I looked around at the cracked walls and the chipped paint, and I waited.

"Are you Jennings Burch?" the policeman without the hat asked.

They know who I am, I said to myself. Rats!

"I don't wanna go back," I said.

Neither of them said anything to me. They continued to talk to each other and read some papers.

"I don't wanna go back!" I said louder.

"Don't worry, kid. You don't have to," the hatless policeman said gruffly.

"Oh, good," I mumbled.

"They don't want you back," he added. "We're sending you to Martin Hall."

"Martin Hall?" I said.

"You're a juvenile delinquent now, kid," he said. "You're going to jail."

"Come on, Frank," Officer Daily said to him. "Do you have to scare the kid?"

"Well, it's true!" he snapped.

They went back to whispers. I was stunned. I hugged the laundry bag to my cheek. The tears rolled down my face.

"Damn!" I said. I was angry at the tears. I wiped them

away on my sleeve. Think of the worst place you been in . . .
That's what Ronny said. Oh, gosh.

"Oh, no!" Officer Frank said with a wave of his hand.

"But Frank!"

"No way! Not me! Talk to the captain."

"He ain't here."

"Sorry," Officer Frank said with a grin. "Take him down.
Now! And when you get back I got some mail for you to run
over to the borough office."

"Okay," Officer Daily said. He came around the desk,
then over to me.

"Am I going to jail?" I asked.

"I'm afraid so," he said. "But it ain't so bad. It's not like
a real jail, it's for kids."

I got to my feet. I wobbled.

"Are you all right?" he asked.

I didn't answer him. We walked out of the station house
and got into his car.

"Damn," he said as he hit the steering wheel with the side
of his fist.

"What's the matter?" I asked.

"Oh," he sighed, "it's nothing." He started the car.

"Was it what Officer Frank wouldn't do for you?"

He smiled. "You're pretty sharp, kid. Yeah, it was. I
wanted the rest of the night off, but he wouldn't give it to
me."

"Oh," I said. "He must be a mean guy."

"Ah, he's okay. He just likes to go by the book, that's
all."

"What book?"

He laughed. "Never mind. It's a long story."

As we pulled out, another police car pulled in front of
us.

"Come on," he snarled impatiently at the car that blocked
him in.

A policeman got out of the car. He was tall and all dressed up in a fancy uniform with a gold badge and gold buttons.

"Who's that?"

"That's the captain."

We waited for the car in front of us to move.

"Didn't Officer Frank say to ask the captain?"

"Oh, yeah!" He slapped his hand on his forehead. "Dummy!" He was talking about himself. "Listen, Jennings! If I leave you here for a minute, will you promise to wait and not run away?"

I nodded my head.

"No," he said, "say the words."

"I promise."

He got out of the car and went back into the station house. He was gone a lot longer than a minute. It was more like half an hour. He came back smiling.

"Did you get the night off?" I asked.

"I sure did. Just as soon as I drop you, I'm off." He made believe one of his hands was a plane—it took off from his other hand.

He started the car and pulled out. As we rode along the avenue, he began to whistle. He then sang a song that didn't really have any words. He reminded me a little of Sal. I'm not sure why exactly, but he did. Maybe because he seemed kind and gentle like Sal.

After a little while and a lot of turns, we stopped in front of a small white house. My heart pounded. It was like St. Teresa's, or the Carpenters', all right. It wasn't a big building with a courtyard and a fence. I was frightened.

"This is Martin Hall?" I asked almost to myself.

He frowned. "Oh, yeah. You're gonna hate it."

I got out of the car and saw a blond-haired lady wearing a flowered apron coming down the path. She reached me and smiled.

"So you're Jennings," she said.

"Jennings," Officer Daily said, "this is Mrs. Daily, my wife."

I shot a glance at him, and then back to her. They were smiling. He hadn't taken me to jail after all.

I sat at the kitchen table while Mrs. Daily fixed hot cocoa. She set a plate of cookies down near me. I was so hungry, I wanted to eat them all right away, but I didn't. I waited. I looked down by the side of my chair to make sure I had my laundry bag and Doggie.

Officer Daily had returned to his station house to change his clothes and bring back his police car. He said he wouldn't be gone long.

"My, but you're the quietest little boy I've ever seen," she said.

I smiled.

She came over to me and brushed back my hair. I wonder why big people like to do that?

"Isn't there anything you'd like to talk about or ask me?" she said.

"Uh . . . yes, ma'am."

"Oh, good! What?"

"Is Thanksgiving over or didn't it come yet?"

Her eyes filled with tears. Gosh, I wonder what's so sad about Thanksgiving?

"Is there something wrong?" I asked.

"No," she said. She leaned down and kissed the top of my head. "There's nothing wrong." She went over to the stove and filled two cups with cocoa. She set them on the table, then sat across from me. She moved the plate of cookies.

"Thanksgiving is next week," she said. "Would you like a great big turkey with cranberry sauce?"

"Oh, yeah!" I said. Just the thought of turkey made my mouth water.

"Good! Right now, have some cookies."

"Thank you."

I heard the front door close.

"That must be Bob," she said. "Gosh, that was quick."

"Hi," he said as he stuck his head in the kitchen door.

I liked the way Mrs. Daily said "gosh." I gobbled down two cookies, one right after the other.

"My God," she said, "he's starving."

"When did you eat last?" he asked.

I looked up toward the ceiling to think.

"Well, if you have to think about it . . ." She broke off. "Didn't you guys ask him if he was hungry?" she huffed. She moved quickly about the kitchen fixing me something.

Officer Daily shrugged his shoulders.

"Men!" she snapped. She handed me a piece of bread and butter. "Never mind the cookies," she said. "Eat this! I'll fix you a hamburger."

"Thank you."

"Would you like something, dear?" she asked more calmly.

"No, thanks. I'll just have some coffee and try to get our little friend here to talk."

"Oh! He'll talk to me."

"Don't bet on it." He smiled, then pinched my cheek.

"Won't you?" she asked. She leaned down for my answer.

"What do you want to know?"

Officer Daily threw his hands in the air. "Would you look at this! The whole police department couldn't get him to say a word . . ." He paused to shake his head. "Then you come along, give him a few cookies, and he spills everything."

We all laughed. I knew he already knew everything he

needed to know from my papers and talking to the home. If he knew my name, I thought, he knew everything.

We talked a little bit while Mrs. Daily fixed me a hamburger. I told them why I ran away from the home. I told them I knew running wasn't a good thing to do, but I was too ashamed to stay.

"Listen, son," he said, "running away isn't good, but sometimes it's better to run to find help or safety than it is to stay and suffer hurt or shame. The important thing about running," he added, "is to make sure you honestly feel you have a good reason."

Mrs. Daily placed the hamburger in front of me. My eyes widened.

"Dig in," she said. "We'll talk later."

I bit into the hamburger. It was delicious.

"Aren't you going to give Doggie a bite?" Officer Daily asked.

"Doggie? Who's Doggie?" she asked.

"He's my friend."

"Well, if he's as hungry as you are . . ."

I reached down and brought Doggie out of the bag.

"Oh, he's cute," she said. "But he's filthy."

I looked at Doggie. He was a bit dusty. "He's been kind of busy," I said.

They laughed.

They asked me a million questions about my family, the homes I was in, and the people I met along the way. They asked me everything. Sometimes Mrs. Daily's eyes filled with tears. At other times they both laughed or just stared at me. I couldn't tell what they were thinking. I told them almost everything. The only parts I left out were about the times I stayed in the zoo. I figured if Mr. Daily was a policeman, he might arrest me for sneaking into the zoo.

"Tell me a little more about Sal," he asked.

"What about him?"

"Well, he sounds like a very nice person."

"Oh, he is. He's wonderful. He tickles me and makes me laugh."

"Did he ever say why he couldn't stay and take care of you?"

"Uh . . ." I tapped my upper lip, trying to think of what Sal had said.

"Let's not worry about that now," Mrs. Daily said. "I'm sure he has his reasons."

"Oh, he does," I said. "I'm trying to think of the words he used. He said he couldn't . . . uh. He couldn't . . . uh. Well, he said he didn't want to lie to me and say he was gonna come when he wasn't. He wasn't ready to . . . he wasn't ready to . . ."

"Make a commitment?" Officer Daily said.

"That's it! He wasn't ready to make a commitment. He wanted to change jobs and get things settled."

"That's why I couldn't find him."

"Did you look for him? Did you look for Sal?"

"Yes, I did," he said. "But I didn't have much luck."

"He's in a truck."

"I know," he laughed. "I'll find him, don't worry about it."

"Why do you want to find Sal?"

"Well, we thought he might be ready to take care of you."

"No." I shook my head. "He's not."

"How can you be so sure?"

"He didn't come for me. He said he wouldn't come for me till he could keep me."

"Oh," he said, "I see."

"Okay, boys, the grilling is over. Time for a bath."

"Are you going to take a bath, sir?"

They laughed.

"*You* are!" she said. She started to tickle me.

She took me to a small bedroom. It was just off the hallway, near the bathroom.

"Wait one second," she said. "Let me run your bathwater."

She ducked into the bathroom and turned on the water. "Do you like bubbles?" she asked.

"Oh, yeah."

"Me too." She smiled. She poured in the bubble-bath soap.

Mrs. Daily had the nicest smile. Her face was smooth and pretty. Her eyes were blue like Officer Daily's, and she had the same deep dimples.

Mrs. Daily showed me into the bedroom. The room was very bright and cheery. The walls were yellow, and so were the curtains and the bedspread. She switched on a lamp next to the bed.

"Now, let's see what you have," she said as she lifted my laundry bag. "May I?"

I nodded my head yes.

She pulled Doggie out first and made a face. "One dirty dog."

I laughed.

"One shirt." She took it from the bag. "One sock. Is that it?"

"Yes, ma'am."

"How do you wear only one sock?"

"On one foot."

She laughed. She started me laughing too.

"What's so funny?" Officer Daily asked from the doorway.

"We have to buy this little guy some clothes tomorrow," she said. "Right now I need a pair of your pajamas."

"Comin' right up."

She took me back into the bathroom. She started removing my clothes.

"Where do you want them?" he asked.

"On the bed, please."

She got off all my clothes down to my underpants.

"I'll close my eyes for this last part," she said. She closed her eyes and faced the ceiling.

She slipped off my underpants and I jumped into the bubbles.

"I'll wash all these things so they'll be nice and clean for tomorrow."

She scrubbed my back and my front. She scrubbed my face and my ears. She washed my hair and cleaned my nails. When she was all done, she held up a giant fluffy towel and closed her eyes.

"Jump out," she said.

I jumped out. She surrounded me with the towel. She was crouched on the floor while she dried me.

"Gosh, you were a dirty little boy," she said.

She closed her arms around me and held me. She held me very close to her for a long time. She sounded like she was crying.

"Is somethin' wrong?" I asked.

"No," she said. "I just got a lousy cold, that's all." She stood up quickly.

She took me into the bedroom and helped me on with Officer Daily's pajamas.

"They're a little big," she said, "but I'll fix 'em up."

She rolled up the sleeves and the legs. She put me in bed and laid Doggie in next to me. She made another face. I laughed.

"Is it all right to turn off the light?" she asked.

I nodded my head yes.

She brought the blanket up to my chin and kissed my forehead. "In case you have an accident, honey," she said, "there's no penalty here for wetting the bed. It can happen to anyone." She started to leave.

"Mrs. Daily."

"Yes?"

I reached my arms up to her. She came back to me and I hugged her. She hugged me back and kissed my ear.

"Thank you," I said.

I lay with Doggie cuddled close to me in the darkness of this new place.

"Aren't the Dailys nice?"

He thought they were.

"I think if I didn't want to be with Sal so much, I wouldn't mind being here."

I hugged Doggie and went to sleep.

I was jolted awake. When I turned over and felt for Doggie, he was gone. I switched on the lamp to see if he fell on the floor. He didn't, he was gone. I got out of bed and opened the door. As I stepped into the hallway, I heard voices coming from the kitchen. I started to return to the bedroom, when I heard my name. I got closer to the kitchen door.

"I don't understand that rule," Mrs. Daily said.

"What's not to understand? The rule states no member of the force shall become personally involved in any case. Period."

"But it ain't fair."

"Look, the captain went way out on a limb as it is, giving me three days."

"Poor little thing. He's been through so much."

"Don't you think I know it? After all, I'm only the guy who called you when I found him."

"I know, I know. I just wish there were something we could do."

"I can keep trying to find Sal. He left his last job. Now only God knows where he is."

The room became quiet. I started to back up in case they came into the hallway.

"Couldn't we take him?" she asked.

My eyes widened.

"I'd love to take him. The problem's in the system."

"How do you mean?"

"Unless a guardian files for him, he has to remain in an institution until they process the paperwork and make a ruling."

"How long does that take?"

"Maybe months."

"Months!" she said.

Once again the room became quiet. I heard the water run and some dishes being put in the sink.

"So even if Martha wanted him . . ." she started to say.

"Same thing," he said. "The only one who could get around all that is Sal."

"Why?" she asked. "He's no more his guardian than we are."

"Yeah, but he doesn't have a residence. If Sal wanted him," he said, "it's no problem for him to give Jennings' last address as his residence. If he claimed to be his guardian, who's gonna argue with him?"

"It sounds so complicated," she said.

I agreed with her. I leaned against the wall.

"Look," he said, "if we can't find Sal in the next three days, and it seems unlikely we will, we'll take him ourselves, okay? It'll mean he'll have to go back," he said, "at least for the time it takes to process the papers."

"The poor little thing," she said. "He won't believe we'll really come back for him."

Oh yes I will, I said to myself. I won't have any choice.

"Well," he said, "I don't know what else to do."

I slid along the wall, then backed into the bathroom. I reached in and flushed the toilet. I started down the hall.

"Is that you, honey?" Mrs. Daily called. She came to the doorway. "What's the matter?"

"I can't find Doggie," I said as I reached the kitchen door.

I looked up, and there he was. He was hanging by his ears from a clothesline. He was dripping wet, but clean.

"I gave him a bath," she said. "I was hoping you would stay asleep till he was dry."

"I turned over and missed him."

She hugged me around the neck. "I should have known you might do that. I'm sorry."

"It's okay," I said. "I guess he needed a little bath."

"Well, just as soon as he's dry, I'll give him to you. All right?"

"All right."

I went back down the hall and into the bedroom. I climbed into bed. A little while later, Mrs. Daily switched the light on. I covered my eyes with my hand until I got used to the brightness. She came over to the bed and placed Doggie down beside me. He was all wrapped up in a big thick towel.

"He's a little damp," she said, "but he'll be all right till morning."

The next two days were really wonderful. There were times when I almost forgot I had to go back. Officer Daily took off from work so we could all do some things together. We went shopping. They said whatever they bought me was mine, and mine to keep. They bought me pants and shirts, underwear and socks. Mrs. Daily said they had something new now, "two socks—one for each foot." We all laughed. They bought me pajamas and my first pair of slippers. They were blue, with pictures of Hopalong Cassidy and Topper on the sides.

Officer Daily took me and Doggie to the movies, while Mrs. Daily stayed home to cook. She said she was making something very special for dinner. I couldn't wait to see what it was. The movie we saw was *The Crimson Pirate*. I loved the way Burt Lancaster and his little friend who couldn't talk swung around like monkeys. One time when they were trying to get away from the soldiers, they hid in a barrel of fish. Doggie and I laughed and laughed.

The dinner Mrs. Daily had made for us was turkey with stuffing and cranberry sauce. She said it was a special Thanksgiving for all the ones I missed. Officer Daily sliced the turkey and gave me a drumstick. Before we ate, he said a prayer:

"Bless us, O Lord, for the gifts we are about to receive, and for letting us see through Jennings just how blessed we really are."

284

"I didn't know my name was in a prayer."

He laughed. "Well, I just sort of slipped that in."

"Oh, thank you," I said. "Can we eat now?"

The following day we went to the Museum of Natural History. They asked me if I would like to go to the zoo, but I said no.

"I thought all kids liked the zoo," he said.

"They do, but I . . . I seen the zoo."

"Well, you can see it more than once, can't you?"

"Oh, yeah, I've seen it more than once. In fact, I seen it so many times, it's almost like I lived there."

That night dinner was altogether different from the night before. The Dailys were very quiet. I was sure they were thinking about sending me back. The phone rang.

Officer Daily nearly jumped out of his skin. The phone bell reminded me of the clicker back at the Home of the Angels.

"Yes, Captain," he said into the phone. "But . . ." He stopped to listen. "Yes, sir, I understand. But . . ." He again stopped to listen.

"Do you want something else?" Mrs. Daily asked me.

"Oh, no, thank you."

"Does Doggie want a bone?"

"No." I laughed. "He has to watch his weight. He's gettin' real fat."

I knew she was trying to keep me from overhearing the phone call, and she did.

"All right, sir. Five o'clock," he said, and hung up.

He came back to the table but said nothing. It was almost like the phone call had never happened. I was sure they were going to talk after I went to bed. I decided to help that along a little.

"I'm very sleppy," I said. "Could I go to bed now?"

"Sure you can," she said. "You don't have to ask permission."

I got up from the chair.

"Do you need any help?"

"No, thank you."

"All right," she said. "Why don't you get ready, and I'll come and tuck you in."

"Okay," I said, and left the room.

I went down the hall to the bedroom and opened the door.

"I'm sorry about this, Doggie, but I just got to know what's going on."

He understood. I placed him on the bed and doubled back down the hall.

"It could mean your job," she said.

"I know. But I just can't see sending him to Martin Hall."

"And nothing from Sal?"

"Nothing. I'm sure if he knew, he would take him. Look," he said, "if it's all right with you, we'll just keep him and weather the storm."

"Oh, I love you," she said.

I backed down the hall and slipped into the bedroom.

"Whew," I breathed out. "He's gonna get in trouble if we stay, Doggie. What do you think?"

Doggie didn't know.

"This is a fine time for you to stop talking to me. Now, let me think." I tapped my upper lip. "Let's see, now. She said, 'It could mean your job.' What does that mean?"

Doggie didn't know.

"You're no help," I said. "I think it means they won't let him be a policeman anymore if he keeps me. What do you think?"

He agreed.

"Officer Daily said the important thing to think about when you run away is to be sure you have an honest good reason. I think this is an honest good reason, Doggie."

I looked through the bed chest for a piece of paper and a pencil.

"Aren't you ready for bed?" Mrs. Daily asked as she came into the bedroom.

"Not yet."

"Can I help you?"

"I was just looking for some paper and a pencil."

"Whatever for? Do you want to write to someone?"

"Uh . . . no. I wanted to draw a picture."

"Now? Aren't you tired?"

"A little, but I wanted to—"

"You don't have to explain," she said. "If you want paper and a pencil, you'll have them." She left the room.

"Gosh, Doggie," I said, "I sure wish we could stay here."

Mrs. Daily brought me the paper and pencil, then helped me change into my pajamas. When I was finished in the bathroom, I got into bed. Officer Daily said good night from the doorway.

"Sir."

"Yes?"

"Thank you for everything."

"Anytime, son. I'll see you tomorrow."

"Now, little fella," she said as she brought the blanket up to my chin, "tomorrow afternoon I'm going to find a school for you to go to. What do you think about that?"

"That would be nice."

"Now, get some sleep. If you want to draw, the paper is there. But there'll be plenty of time to do that tomorrow."

"All right."

She kissed me and started to leave.

"Please don't go."

She came back and sat down. "What's the matter?" she asked. "Are you frightened of something.

"No."

"You look upset."

"No, I just wanted to hug you, that's all."

She put her arms around me and hugged me. I tried to loosen the words in my throat, but I couldn't. She rocked and hugged me for a few minutes before she left.

I lay in the dark, thinking. There was no other way. I couldn't let Officer Daily get in trouble over me. I got out of bed and put on the lamp. I wrote:

Dear Officer and Mrs. Daily,
Thank you for wanting to keep me. I don't want to get you into bad trouble, so I have to go. Thank you for the turkey and the movies and the other stuff.

Jennings and Doggie

I lay awake for hours until I was sure they were asleep. I got up and packed my things in the laundry bag. I got dressed, slipped Doggie into the bag, then climbed out the window.

I walked in the same direction they walked when they took me shopping. I ducked in and out of doorways. I didn't want to be spotted by anyone and taken to jail. I remembered the upstairs train station near the zoo, when I saw another one just like it. I went up to the man in the change booth. I asked him how to get to Boston Road and Tremont Avenue. I knew it was better to ask him that than how to get to the zoo, especially in the middle of the night.

"Are you lost, sonny?"

Gosh, I thought, I wish big people would stop asking me if I'm lost. Don't they think kids ever know where they're going?

"No, sir. I'm not lost. I'm here."

"But it's five o'clock in the morning. What's a little kid like you doing out at this hour?"

"Uh . . . asking you how to get to Boston—"

"I know that," he said. "But ain't it kind of late for you to be out?"

"Gosh," I said, "I thought it was early."

He laughed. "You win, kid. Let me make a call. I'll get you directions."

288

I ducked down below his window and ran for the stairs. I heard him yelling as I reached the street.

"Which way?" I said out loud to myself. "Pick one." I picked one and started walking.

I walked a few blocks, staying very close to the stores and ducking in every so often. I saw a police car with its lights flashing speed down the street toward the train station.

"Now," I said, "I'll find out which way Boston Road is."

I stepped into a doorway and waited. I watched the police car stop. About two minutes later it turned around and zoomed past me. I smiled to myself. I knew the man in the change booth told the policeman what directions I had asked for. I also knew the police car would go that way.

I arrived at the zoo a few hours later. I slipped beneath the fence and carefully made my way to the pine bushes. It was still cold, but at least the snow was almost all melted.

I lay down and took Doggie from the bag. We were tired.

"We're never gonna leave here," I said. "It's too dangerous. If we go out again and get caught, it means we go to jail."

I hugged Doggie to my cheek. He knew we could never leave.

I lay back and fell asleep.

I woke up to the sound of lots of voices. For a second I didn't know where I was. I popped my head out and saw dozens of kids all dressed the same.

"That's a bunch of schoolkids," I told Doggie. "Now we'll get some food."

I jumped from the bushes and followed them. I stayed with them all afternoon. I couldn't believe how much stuff they threw away. I made several trips back and forth to my hideout. I got popcorn, pretzels, and french-fried potatoes. I even got a cheese sandwich. Someone had thrown it away without even opening it. I had enough food for a week.

"You know, Doggie," I said, "if we get a crowd of kids like that every week, we wouldn't ever have to worry about food."

He agreed.

Later that night, I was lying on some rocks near the hideout. I wasn't worried about the guard. He carried a light and I could easily see him coming. It started to rain.

"Oh, gosh," I said. I gathered up Doggie and all my stuff. I stashed all the food and my laundry bag deep in the bushes. I made my way over to the lion house. There was a back staircase with a deep doorway where I could stand. I stood there all night. In the morning the rain still continued to drizzle. I carefully made my way back to my hideout to eat. Deep under the bushes, I found it wasn't all that wet. I ate and went to sleep. The rain finally stopped toward evening. The sun was just setting, and I was cold.

"I sure am glad we got this food, Doggie."

He was too.

"I wish I had a comic book or some baseball cards to read."

I lay back against the trunk of the bush.

"I think more than anything, Doggie, I wish you could really talk."

He laughed. I hugged him and kissed his nose. I heard some voices.

"Uh-oh," I whispered. I clasped my hand over Doggie's mouth.

I sat up a little. I wanted to see out through some of the spaces in the pine needles. The voices got louder. There's a whole bunch of people coming, I said to myself. There shouldn't be—the zoo is closed. Just then someone yelled.

"Jennings!"

Chills ran all over me and my heart stopped. I clutched Doggie tightly in my arms and listened.

"Yoo-hoo, where are you?" the voice sang out. "Jennings!"

Suddenly I saw them. I ripped open the bushes and sprang onto the path.

"*Sal!*" I screamed. "Sal."

He crouched down and opened his arms. Officer Daily

and a patrol guard were standing alongside him. I ran up and into Sal's open arms. He lifted me high in the air, then swung me around. He brought me down to his chest and cradled me.

"Sal," I cried. "You came for me. You came for me."

"Yes, I did, son." He hugged me tightly.

"Well, I'll be," Officer Daily said. "How did you know he'd be here?"

Sal laughed. "I know my son," he said. He tried wiping some of the tears streaming down my face.

"Sal, I . . . Sal . . ."

"What is it, son? What are you trying to say?"

"I'm trying to say I . . . I love you."

"I love you too." He hugged and kissed me.

"I love you," I cried. "I love you. I love you. I love you."

EPILOGUE

A lot has happened since that November day back in 1952:

Sal kept his word and stayed with us. He saw Gene and me through our teenage years. He helped us with school, took us on summer truck trips, and was as close to us as any father would have been. He is retired now and lives on Long Island with a woman he married back in the seventies. He has raised her children too;

Mom recovered from her back and neck injuries some five years later. But those years took a heavy toll on her. She has never since been quite free of illness or pain. She lives in New Jersey;

George is married and lives in the East with his wife and children. Although he's had some troubled years, he is now a member of Alcoholics Anonymous;

Walter continued his education until he reached that place of safety. He lives with his family in the Midwest;

Larry ran from one place to another, from one thing to another. He's estranged from his wife and children and lives somewhere in the East;

Jerome came home for short periods of time until 1958. He then came home and stayed until his death in 1961. He was twenty-one years old.

Gene learned computer operation while he served in the Marine Corps. He now lives and works on the West Coast;

As for the others, the Dailys, the Fraziers, Martha, and Stacy, they are my memories. Clarence said it best when he said, "And now I gots room fo' mo'."

I was a police officer in the late sixties when I adopted my daughter, Carolyn. That's one less animal they'll have to cage at night;

And last, but not least, Doggie is still with me. He hasn't learned how to talk yet, but we do understand each other. Doggie, say hi.

Acknowledgment

Obie and Mary Clifford

have my undying love for their faith in me

Art Avielhe
Maureen and Harry Baron
Dan Frank
and
Barbara Veals

have my total gratitude for making this book possible

Steve Penn
John and Tony Bueti
Nancy Pratt
Dave Tiffany
Sal Lorello
Scott Zimmer
Carlos Fernandez
and
Dick Harvell

have my deepest friendship for their kindness

Tom Litwack
Frank and Edith Arco

a special thank you